Peri Urban Livelihoods

About the Author

Shahab Fazal is currently Associate Professor in the Department of Geography at Aligarh Muslim University, Aligarh. He obtained his graduation and post graduation from Rajasthan University in Ist Division. Later he joined AMU and completed his Ph.D. He has published twelve books and fifty research articles in various national and international journals such as – Land Use Policy, Environment and Urbanization, Landscape and Urban Planning, Asian Profile, Annals of the Indian Geographers and Journal of the Indian Society of Remote Sensing etc.

He was also recipient of prestigious doctoral and post doctoral fellowships such as – CSIR Fellowship, Shastri Faculty Research Fellowship (Canada), Commonwealth Academic Staff Fellowship (Great Britain), ICSSR-NWO Faculty Exchange Fellowship (The Netherlands), Fulbright Fellowship (United States of America) etc.

He has successfully completed Seven Research Projects and was also a member of Indo-German Joint Research Team working for DST - DAAD Research Project. Currently he is leading an International Research Project in collaboration with Montreal University, Canada.

Peri Urban Livelihoods
Opportunities and Challenges

Dr. Shahab Fazal
Department of Geography
Aligarh Muslim University
Aligarh

CONCEPT PUBLISHING COMPANY PVT. LTD.
NEW DELHI-110059

ISBN-13 : 978-81-8069-973-3

First Published 2014

Published and Printed by

Concept Since 1974

Concept Publishing Company Pvt. Ltd.
A/15-16, Commercial Block, Mohan Garden
New Delhi-110059 (India)
T: 25351460, 25351794, *F*: 091-11-25357109
E: publishing@conceptpub.com, W: www.conceptpub.com
Editorial Office: H-13, Bali Nagar, New Delhi-110 015, India.

Cataloging in Publication Data--*Courtesy:* D.K. Agencies (P) Ltd. <docinfo@dkagencies.com>

Fazal, Shahab, 1966-
Peri urban livelihoods : opportunities and challenges / Shahab Fazal.
p. cm.
Includes bibliographical references (p.) and index.
ISBN 9788180699733

1. Land use—India—Aligarh. 2. Land use, Rural—India—Aligarh. 3. Dairy farming—India—Aligarh. 4. Land reform—India—Aligarh. 5. Urbanization Economic aspects—India—Aligarh. 6. Rural development—India—Aligarh. I. Title.

DDC 333.771309542 23

Preface

Urbanization is a worldwide phenomenon and in recent years this phenomena has been more pronounced among developing countries. This dynamism is attributed to transformations in economic activities. India is also experiencing accelerated rate of urbanization process. This urbanization process in India is peculiar in the sense that the growth of urban population is not so high as compared to other countries but the absolute numbers in urban population is significantly large. This is characterized by dispersed urban growth, urban sprawl and rapidly transformed peripheral urban areas. The urban settlements have become centre of all the changes (social, economic, cultural, etc.) and with the spread of urbanism, its elements are spilling over to the peripheral areas. This peripheral area surrounding urban centres has many different manifestations, but the present work uses the term *Peri-urban Interface* (PUI). . The PUI is conceptualized as transitory zone between rural and urban settlements characterized by area with mixed rural and urban populations and land-uses, which begins at the point where agricultural land-uses appear near the city and extends up to the point where villages have distinct urban land-uses.

The present work focuses on livelihood in the *Peri-Urban Interface* of Aligarh city. The term livelihood refers to the various "means of maintenance", i.e., methods of acquiring food, income, property or inherited resources. The fundamental characteristic of PUI livelihood is their ability to adapt in order to survive and maximize output as the PUI livelihood is an ongoing process. Here the elements of livelihood do not remain static but varies with time and space.

Thus, the present work focuses on PUI livelihood

transformations and because of the socio-economic characteristics of Aligarh city, household was chosen as the unit of analysis. This is the lowest level unit within which individuals operate collectively and it permits a better understanding of people organizing their livelihood options. The study draws upon a comprehensive range of information using variety of resources and methods. Primary information was collected through household level purposive sample survey. This provided informations for the research questions but also allowed to generalize its effect on—and the response by—the PUI respondents. It collected not only quantifiable variables but also longitudinal elements of the respondents. The secondary data included Census data, published statistical informations, satellite images of the city and settlement forms and their expansions. The study integrated the primary and secondary data to assess the influences of urbanization process on natural, demographic and socio-economic-cultural structure of livelihood framework. The results suggest that the developments in Aligarh city and the resultant expansion of the city strongly influences the peripheral rural settlements in terms of natural resources as well as people, both physically and in socio-economic and cultural sense.

The author acknowledges the research grant from Indian Council of Social Science Research (ICSSR), New Delhi. The author also acknowledges the Aligarh Muslim University for its support. Thanks are also due to the Chairman and colleagues at the Department of Geography, Aligarh Muslim University for their cooperation and support in many ways. Finally, special thanks to my family—my parents, my wife and my adorable children—Shaad, Samra and Samya.

Aligarh **Shahab Fazal**

Contents

List of Tables

List of Figures

List of Box

List of Box

1

Introduction

Today, India remains by and large a rural agricultural country as the share of agricultural workers in the workforce is still 59 per cent or the above 70 per cent people living in rural areas in 2011. Meanwhile, the share of population living in urban areas has also increased and is about 27.8 per cent in 2011. But these figures do not tell the whole story. There are evidences that urban growth is increasingly dispersed and urban sprawl promotes the spread of urban land-use into the rural-urban fringe and draws a larger number

BOX 1.1: What does 'Cities', 'Urban', and 'Rural' mean?

'Rural' and 'urban' areas are often conceptualized in opposing terms to each other. Population density and economic activity are the predominant criteria that have been used to define 'urban' *versus* 'rural' areas. However, related criteria such as administrative functions and infrastructure development are also used. Rural areas are generally regarded as places of low population densities with predominantly agricultural economies whereas "urban" areas are regarded as places with high population densities distinguished by a service economy. Hence, small towns with even a minimum of 'urban' characteristics are regarded as urban.

The term urban is typically used as a synonym for city, however, the two are not the same, all cities are urban areas but not all urban areas are cities. "Urban" is a statistically variable concept. It is defined differently by different governments and there is significant variability between countries in the official classification of urban areas.

Source: World Resources Institute,1996-97 and Cecilia Tacoli, 1998

of people into the rural-urban interface (Fazal, S., 2008). Although, the growth rate is not increasing sharply, the absolute increase in urban population is very large, having increased up to 286 million in 2011. In the course of development, it is likely that out of the enormous number of rural people lacking opportunity in the economically lesser developed places where they usually come from, many will continue to migrate to the cities.

What is "urban" and what is "rural"?

The difference between urban centres and rural areas may seem so obvious that definitions is not an issue, however, there are major variations in the ways in which different nations classify an urban centre or a rural settlement. The criteria used include population size and density, and availability of services such as schools, hospitals and banks, etc. Mostly, combinations of criteria are used to classify them, which vary greatly in different parts of the world. In India, the Census of India uses the unit of classification in this regard as "town" for urban areas and "village" for rural areas. In the Census of India 2001, the definition of urban area adopted is as follows:

(a) All statutory places with a municipality, corporation, cantonment board or notified town area committee, etc.
(b) A place satisfying the following three criteria simultaneously:
    (i) A minimum population of 5,000;
    (ii) At least 75 per cent of male working population engaged in non-agricultural pursuits; and
    (iii) A density of population of at least 400 per sq. km. (1,000 per sq. mile).

For identification of places which would qualify to be classified as "urban" all villages, which, as per the 1991 Census had a population of 4,000 and above, a population density of 400 persons per sq. km. and having at least 75 per cent of male working Presspulation engaged in non-agricultural activity were considered.

Towns with population of 1,00,000 and above are called cities.

BOX 1.2 : Rural and Urban Living

People inhabit different parts of the world and lead different types of lives. Their lifestyles change across the various regions on Earth and so do their mentalities. The resources available in their regions have a direct impact on their way of living. People all over the world have been divided into two distinct groups by this marked line of difference between an urban and a rural life. Those inhabiting urban areas lead an urban life while inhabitants of rural parts of the world experience a rural living.

Urban Living

Urban areas are equipped with all the modern amenities. The modernday facilities are widely available in the urban areas. A majority of the households of the urban areas are blessed with this technological advancement.

Due to a greater availability of all the modern facilities along with an increase in career opportunities, people of the urban areas lead an economically more stable and a luxurious life.

The increasing attraction of the people towards the urban parts of the world has resulted in crowding of urban areas. The increasing population, majority of which prefers settling in urban cities, has led to an imbalance in the density of human population. Excessive industrialization has invited environmental problems like pollution.

However, the rise in economic growth that has resulted in self-sufficiency in the common masses has resulted in a self-centred nature of society. While technological advancement has brought the world closer, human beings have gone far apart from each other.

Rural Living

Rural areas are not crowded with concrete constructions all over. Houses are rather widely spaced with ample room for farms and open spaces. Rural areas are some of the only areas fortunate enough to house the greens. People in rural areas live in close proximity of nature. Apart from people, there is room for pets and grazing animals that help maintain equilibrium in nature.

The rural parts are not overcrowded by people. These areas are blessed to have least amounts of pollution.

The life may not be as lavishly led as that in the urban areas, but the people there are generous and their hearts have room for emotions. Rural are the ones where humanity is still alive.

Every coin has two sides to it. While the rural living is deprived of luxury and technology, it is rich in terms of its relationship with 'nature'. The urban life is update in terms of technology and career prospects. However, the falling humane qualities and a disrupted environmental balance shadow the bright future of urban living.

Outside the City Boundaries: The Areas surrounding Urban Centres

The areas surrounding urban centres have many different manifestations in the literature in terms of the way it is conceptualized and delimited. Wehrwein (1942), in his work on cities in the United States used the term rural-urban fringe. His example was followed by many others, including Ramachandran (1989), Thakur (1991), Lin (1994), Nangia (1976), Yadav (1987), Fazal (2000) and Lucas and Van Oort (1993). Many other terms are also found in the literature for the areas surrounding urban centres, implying different delimitations and levels of analysis. There has been great diversity in the terminology used: *rurban fringe* (Schenk 1997), *urban fringe* (Kumar, 1998; Kabra, 1980, Hill, 1986), *edge lands* (Gant *et al.*, 2011), *rural hinterland of the city* (Kundu, 1991), the *city's countryside* (Bryant *et al.*, 1982), *periurban fringe* (Swindell, 1988), *rural fringe of the city* (Leeming and Soussan 1979), *periurban areas* (Dupont, 1997 McGee, 1991), *desakota regions* (McGee 1991), *metropolitan fringe* (Browder *et al.* 1995, Rao 1991, Saini 1989) and *edgelands* (Gant *et al.*, 2011). Research in languages other than English includes descriptions such as the Dutch *ruraal-urbane overgangszone tussen stad en platteland* (Druijven 1996) and the French *Periurbanization* (Dupont, 1997), *le périurbain* (Banzo, 1998), *espace periurbains* (Vennetier, 1989). *This research uses to the term periurban interface, which is defined as an area of mixed rural and urban populations and land-uses, which begins at the point where agricultural land-uses appear near the city and extends up to the point where villages have distinct urban land-uses or where some persons, at least, from the village community commute to the city daily for work or other purposes.*

Importantly, the areas surrounding urban centres (PUI) in general is frequently ignored as a specific area within the study of urbanization. "It is symptomatic that 'urban studies' and 'rural and regional studies' prevail over 'fringe studies'" (Ansari and von Einsiedel, 1998). Moreover, in India most of the studies are for metropolitan or large urban centres and smaller cities lying in the shadow of these large cities are mostly untouched. The *periurban interface* of Aligarh city, therefore, promises to be an interesting area in which to explore important aspects of the development in modern India.

Although Aligarh is a relatively small city, compared to other cities of which literature is available (most of them are for metropolitan cities) but it is also a fast growing city in India, the issues examined here are certainly not limited to Aligarh city and many of the features can be traced with other cities as well. Like many other cities in north India, Aligarh is expanding fast, moreover, it too is surrounded by a populous rural area with productive and rich agricultural hinterland. Such conditions give rise to many conflicts between rural and urban economies, values, and people. However, they can also generate mutually beneficial complementarities in the rural and urban spheres. The net outcome is highly selective for different groups and different locations.

The expansion of the city strongly influences the villages in terms of land-use and population, both physically and in a socio-economic sense. Its influence stretches far beyond the immediately adjacent area. This study concentrates on the livelihood of the villagers who have lived there for generations as well on that of the migrants residing in the villages. Livelihood according to the *Oxford English Dictionary* refers to a "manner of life" but also to "the various means of maintenance', it suggests that it is a method to acquire food, income, property or inherit resources. Thus, this study considers livelihood as all the activities forming the means of generating a living, the notion of livelihood is narrowed down here to reflect social and economic household variables (during the course of sample survey one respondent used the term *grahasthi*); of these, especially the occupational characteristics are studied thoroughly.

A fundamental characteristic of PUI livelihood in contemporary developing economies like India is their ability to adapt in order to survive. Thus, the definition of livelihood also includes change over time and adaptation to evolving circumstances. The livelihood, therefore, is an ongoing process in which the elements do not remain static but varies from one season or from one year to the next. The assets can be built up, eroded or instantaneously destroyed as available activities and access to resource and opportunities may fluctuate seasonally and across the year.

With modernization and transformation of economic activities, the traditionally dominant agricultural activities are under increasing pressure, although new possibilities are emerging for market-oriented agriculture. There are great differences in access to resources and opportunities among villagers, leading to interesting new patterns of livelihood. For non-agricultural occupations, the villagers' options are enhanced by their proximity to the expanding city. Land-use and occupational trends are highly interrelated. For example, Brookfield *et al.* (1991) found that in Kuala Lumpur's fringe there was migration of working population and the land acquires an aspect of neglect. Other sources emphasize the stimulating effects on agriculture (e.g. Mulay and Ray 1973 or Hill 1986). This inspired us to investigate to what extent the transformation of agriculture in urban fringe has taken place. A number of other consequences of urbanization, namely, the pace and direction of city expansion, land markets, the actors and environmental concerns are also treated in this study.

BOX 1.3: Activities, Livelihood and Income

The terms activities, livelihood and income are not synonymous. They are nevertheless inextricably related because the composition and level of individual or household income at a given point in time is the most direct and measurable outcome of the livelihood process.

Economic activities are all those acts, of man, which is performed in order to earn living and to satisfy needs. It can be primary (exploitation of natural resources), secondary (processing of primary resources), tertiary (services) or quaternary and quinary (specialized and personalized services).

Livelihoods are the ways in which people satisfy their needs or gain a living (Chambers and Conway, 1992). A livelihood comprises the assets (natural, physical, human, financial and social capital), the activities and the access to these (mediated by institutions and social relations) that together determine the living gained by the individual or household (Frank Ellis, 2000).

Income comprises both cash and in kind contributions to the material welfare of the individual or household deriving from the set of livelihood activities in which household members are engaged. The cash earnings component of income includes items like crop or livestock sales, wages, rents and remittances. The in kind component of income refers to consumption of own-farm produce, payments in kind (e.g., in food), and transfers or exchanges of consumption items that occur between households within rural communities or between urban and rural households.

In order to study the socio-economic impact, this research has used a more concrete operationalization in view of the manifestation of urbanization on the micro level. Some indications of its scope were derived from the various descriptions in the literature (e.g. Ramachandran, 1989; McGee, 1991; Nangia, 1976; Thakur, 1991). But exploratory fieldwork was needed to find leads to relevant aspects of urbanization at the village level in the study area. For the villages near Aligarh city, it was necessary to translate terms with a profoundly "Western" bias into their Hindi equivalent. Nagari *karan* (literally means urban development) proved to be the most appropriate term to explain the purpose of the study during the interviews, as it evoked references to changes in the lives of households and their villages as a result of urbanization.

The following aspects are supposed to be directly or indirectly caused by urbanization: land-use changes in favour of urban types of land-use, value addition to the products, diversification in their economic activities, location of urban-related activities in or near the village; better access from the village to urban areas and *vice versa*; and expansion of urban types of amenities and infrastructure. All these processes have far reaching consequences for the livelihood of the PUI population, as they lead to a diversification of sources of income among the villagers, to different uses of the agricultural land, and to change in living conditions. A period of about 30 years, approximately one generation, was chosen as the time frame for two reasons.

- First, there are some relevant secondary sources that provide insight into local history and the situation in the 1980s; and
- Second, this time span corresponds with the period of reliable 'recall' by most respondents and is manageable for the researcher.

The selected research area encompasses a wide range of villages: from places that have remained relatively rural, deriving an income mainly from agriculture, to villages that have been entirely enveloped by urbanization. The distance from city, land-use pattern and the transformation of the occupational structure are the most important criteria for clustering and selecting villages for further study. A basic household survey has been conducted to describe the situation in 21 villages.

The primary data collection was collected from stratified random sampling method; where on the basis of distance (3 buffer zones at 10 km distance were drawn from the city municipal boundary). They were named as immediate PUI zone (villages located in 0 – 10 km from city municipal boundary), intermediate PUI zone (villages located between 10 – 20 km from city municipal boundary) and distant PUI zone (villages located in 20 km and beyond the city municipal boundary). The selection was further made considering the following indicators – accessibility, Population size, dominant caste, economic activity and existing infrastructure facilities. A total of 21 villages sampled for in-depth analysis, 9 villages from immediate PUI zone, 7 villages from intermediate PUI zone and 5 villages from distant PUI zone. Of these 21 villages about 10 per cent households were sampled, where again the selection of household was made giving representation to all sections of the population. A total of 769 households were sampled, 372 households from villages of immediate PUI zone, 213 from villages of intermediate PUI zone and 184 from villages of distant PUI zone.

***Table 1.1** : Aligarh PUI — Sampled villages in different PUI zones*

Immediate PUI (Up to 5 km)	Intermediate PUI (5 – 10 km)	Distant PUI (10 km and above)
1. *Mukundpur*	1. *Digsi*	1. *Jalalpur*
2. *Lodha*	2. *Suhawali*	2. *Datawali*
3. *Bhankri Khas*	3. *Barautha*	3. *Badri*
4. *Ramgarh Punjupur*	4. *Palar*	4. *Haibat Pur*
5. *Baraula Jafrabad*	5. *Lalpur*	5. *Naval Pur*
6. *Cherrat Sudhal*	6. *Haivatpur*	
7. *Kwarsi*	7. *Pipli*	
8. *Manjurgarhi*		
9. *Talaspur Khurd*		
9 Villages	***7 Villages***	***5 Villages***

In the literature, various approaches are taken to obtain a grip on the complex and multidimensional process of urbanization, particularly in the case of developing country like India. Methodologically, a mix of techniques was chosen as the best way to gather comprehensive and reliable information for the purposes of this study. Most of the research effort is invested in interviews with the local population (household in-depth survey), emphasizing the empirical orientation of the study.

Table 1.2: Aligarh PUI — Population Size of Sampled Villages in different PUI Zones.

Size of Population	*Immediate (Up to 5 km)*	*Intermediate (5 – 10 km)*	*Distant (10 km and above)*
Up to 3000 Persons	Mukundpur (325) Bhankri Khas (291) Talaspur Khurd (386)	Digsi (193) Barautha (422) Palar (130) Lalpur (214) Haivatpur (135) Pipli (281)	Jalalpur (255) Haibat Pur (228) Badri (79) Naval Pur (130)
3000 to 6000 Persons	Lodha (543) Baraula Jafrabad (591) Cherrat Sudhal (851) Manjurgarhi (735)	Suhawali (545)	Datawali (857)
More than 6000 Persons	Ramgarh Punjupur (1388) Kwarsi (1401)		
Total Sampled Villages	**9 Villages**	**7 Villages**	**5 Villages**

Note: Figures in brackets are population density of the village.

The household, rather than the individual, was adopted as the basic unit of analysis, considering the socio-economic characteristics of the society. It is the "lowest level unit within which individuals are collectively organized", and "a household focus and permits a better understanding of how and why people organize their activities" (Preston, 1994, p. 203). A central feature of the household is that there is a common practice of pooling of income and expenditure. This makes the assessment at the level of the household more meaningful in representing the potential command over goods and services than would be in the case if the incomes of the individual members were treated separately. Schmink (1984) puts it in a broader sense: "the household is regarded as a production as well as a consumption unit in which individuals take joint decisions regarding the allocation of production factors such as labour and capital in order to satisfy common household needs". Druijven *et al.* (1992) also advocating for the household level study stated it as a relevant entity in micro-level livelihood research, especially in rural areas of developing countries where family and household coherence is strong. However, some research also point out some shortcomings of household level research. As it ignores the process of decision-making by the individual, identifying the "common" goal of a household and intra-household relations and strategies are difficult to measure (Druijven, 1990).

Despite of its drawbacks, the household approach is the most workable level to measure livelihood issues in traditional north Indian PUI society. The "head" of the household was considered as decision maker, although other members also exert influence, despite this individual dimension, decisions about the management of agricultural land, employment, and other economic activities are usually made according to the possibilities, needs, and availability of labour, etc., within the household and the last word is of head of the household (in most cases it is the elder male member of the household).

A household is defined here as "*A small group of persons who share the same living accommodation, who pool some, or all, of their income and wealth and who consume certain types of goods and services collectively, mainly housing and food. (The criteria of the existence of family or emotional ties also added).*

Table 1.3 : Aligarh PUI — Distribution of Sampled Household in different PUI Zones.

	Immediate PUI (Up to 5 km)	*Intermediate PUI (5 – 10 km)*	*Distant PUI (10 km and above)*	*Total*
Total Household Sampled (769)	372	213	184	769
Total Population (5323)	2046	1691	1586	5323

Table 1.4 : Aligarh PUI — Economic Sector-wise Workers in different PUI Zones.

Sampled Villages	*Primary Sector*	*Secondary Sector*	*Tertiary Sector*
Immediate PUI (Up to 5 km)			
Mukundpur	50.2 %	7.6 %	42.1 %
Lodha	45.9 %	4.5 %	49.5 %
Bhankri Khas	45.4 %	3.8 %	50.8 %
Ramgarh Punjupur	17.9 %	4.5 %	77.6 %
Baraula Jafrabad	18.9 %	13.8 %	67.2 %
Cherrat Sudhal	30.5 %	2.7 %	66.7 %
Kwarsi	9.9 %	2.4 %	87.7 %
Manjurgarhi	24.6 %	4.9 %	70.5 %
Talaspur Khurd	17.1%	1.9 %	80.9 %
Intermediate PUI (5 – 10 km)			
Digsi	61.4 %	21.0 %	17.7%
Suhawali	67.1 %	2.8 %	30.1 %
Barautha	39.1 %	1.4 %	59.4 %
Palar	57.0 %	31.9 %	11.1 %
Lalpur	52.8 %	9.9 %	37.3 %
Haivatpur	68.1 %	3.8 %	28.1 %
Pipli	81.2 %	1.6 %	17.2 %
Distant PUI (10 km and above)			
Jalalpur	69.4 %	5.9 %	24.8 %
Datawali	46.8 %	5.2 %	22.1 %
Badri	100.0 %	—	—
Haibatpur	85.3 %	0.2 %	14.5 %
Navalpur	97.5 %	0.5 %	2.1 %
Total Sampled Villages	**9 Villages**	**7 Villages**	**5 Villages**

Source: Census of India 2001 and Aligarh Municipal Board 2004.

LOCATION OF ALIGARH CITY

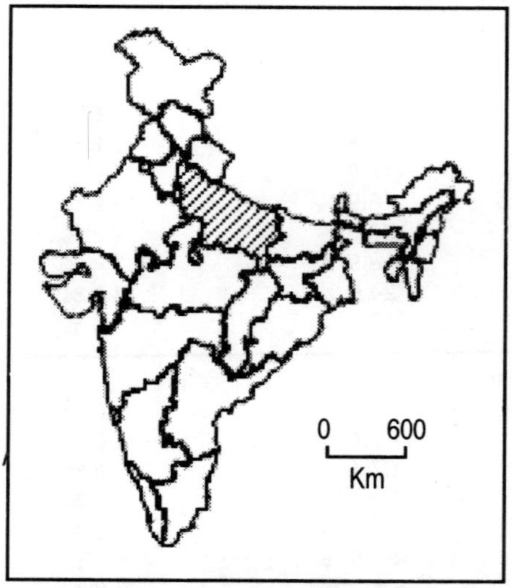

Fig. 1.1(a) : Location of Uttar Pradesh in India

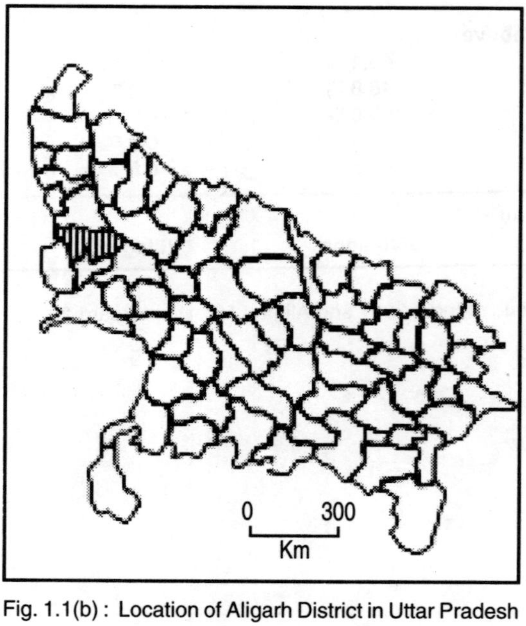

Fig. 1.1(b) : Location of Aligarh District in Uttar Pradesh

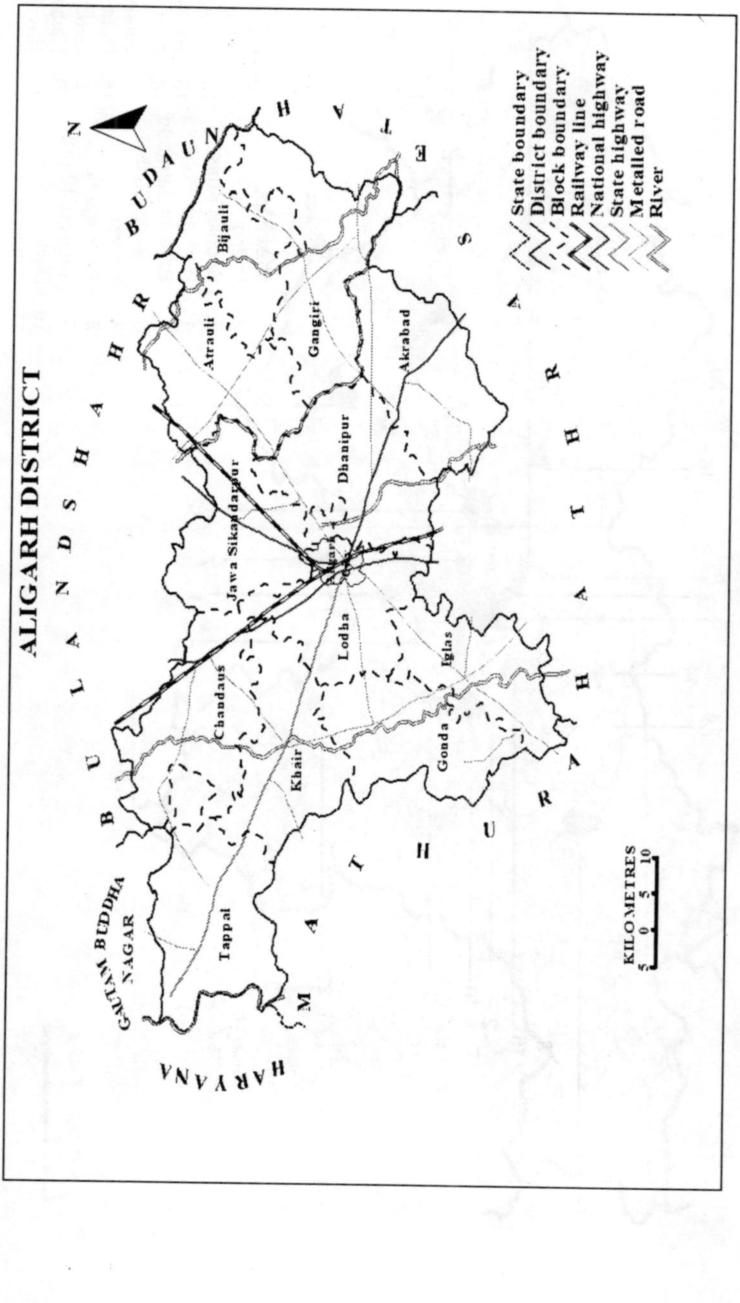

Fig. 1.1(c) : Location of Aligarh District.

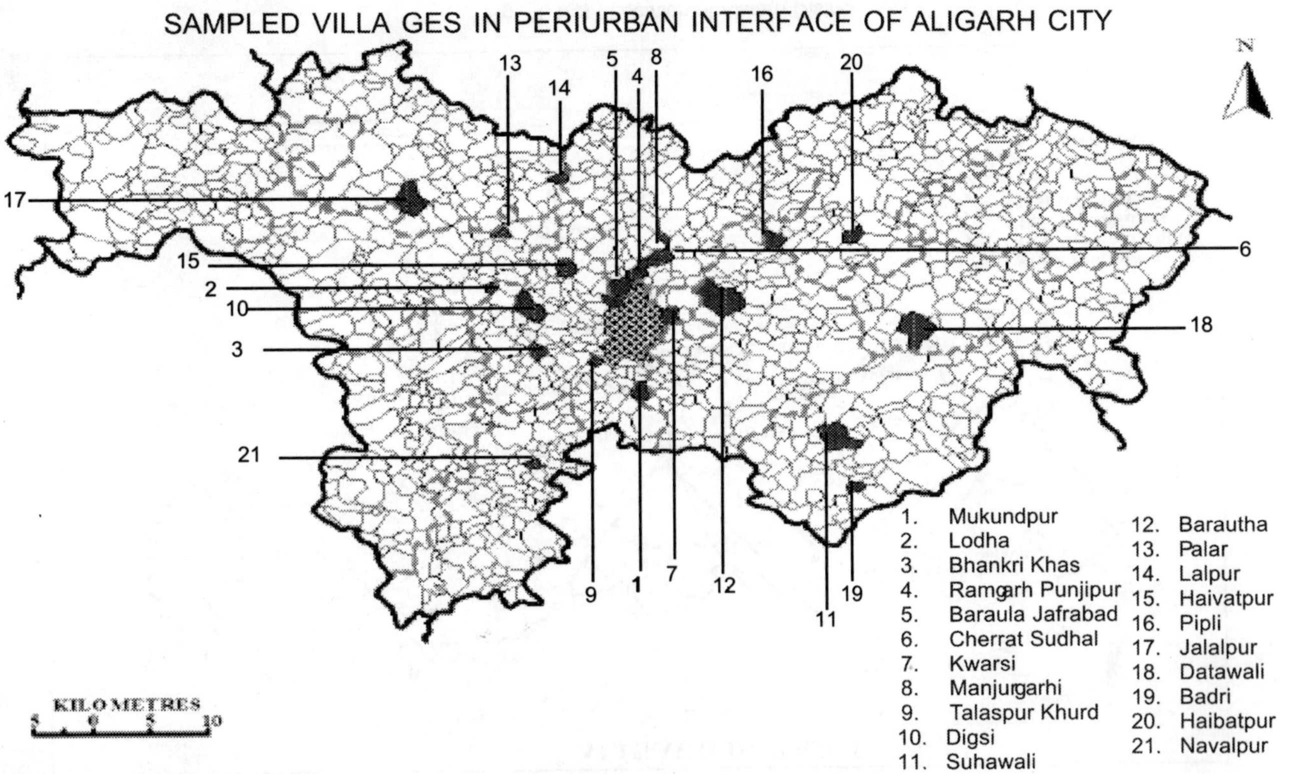

Fig. 1.2 : Sampled villages in Periurban Interface of Aligarh City.

BOX 1.4: Joint v/s Nuclear household

There is a basic distinction between 'joint' (sometimes called 'extended') and 'nuclear' households. "Nuclear households consist of a married or cohabiting couple and their children", while joint households "consist of a core nuclear or one-parent family residing with other relatives who share in daily consumption and financial arrangements" (Brydon and Chant 1989, pp. 135-136). In rural areas of India, there is a traditional predominance of joint households as compared to nuclear households. This tradition is often partly explained by the socio-economic strategy that the household pursues in the light of continuity *vis-á-vis* social and economic uncertainty. With respect to agricultural work, for example, an extended household offers the advantage of flexible labour and prevents the fragmentation of agricultural land. Cultural factors play an important role as well. In the research area, extended households proved to be less prevalent than could be expected in an area with a rural background, although this might just be one of the effects of urbanization. The most common type of extended household is limited to one nuclear family with parents of male in the house. Cohabitation of all married brothers with their families, their elder male (father or uncle and in their absence mother) as head of the family is now less common, which was earlier the norm of the rural society. This practice disappeared largely because of emergence of urban oriented activities and decline in the dependence of land resource based farming activity. The basic objective which was to restrict fragmentation of landholdings is no longer an issue for households. On the contrary, the younger generation wants ownership of land even if it results in smaller un-economic land- holding, so that he can make decision according to his own requirement and preference.

Table 1.5 : Aligarh PUI — Family type of the Sampled Households in different PUI zones.

Family Type	Immediate PUI (Up to 5 km)	Intermediate PUI (5 – 10 km)	Distant PUI (10 km and above)	Total
Joint	**35** (17.8) (9.4)	**58** (29.6) (27.2)	**103** (52.6) (55.9)	**196** (100) (25.5)
Nuclear	**319** (57.5) (85.7)	**155** (27.9) (72.8)	**81** (14.6) (44.02)	**555** (100) (72.2
Single	**18** (100) (4.8)	—	—	**18** (100) (2.3)
Total	**372** (48.3) (100)	**213** (23.7) (100)	**184** (23.9) (100)	**769** (100) (100)

Notes : (i) Figures in bold are absolute number of sampled respondents in the particular distance zones. (ii) Figures in brackets (beside the bold figures) are percentages to the total from that particular variable. (iii) Figures in brackets (beside the bold figures) are percentages to the total from that particular distance zone.

Source : Based on field survey (2009-10).

In the present study, the basic issues which have been investigated are, first to examine and refine the concepts relating to periurban interface and rural transformation due to urbanization, second, the study investigates land-use issues and the pressing problem of how land degradation should be interpreted in a rural-urban fringe. Third, the study explores how different "actors" interact to influence land transformation. The present research also investigated issues related to livelihood and modifications therein, for which the village and household are important levels of observation. The final part discusses the socio-economic environmental implications of the urbanization process in PUI villages.

Methodology and Data Sources

In order to draw upon a comprehensive range of information, the study makes use of a variety of resources and methods. The study is based on both primary and secondary source of data.

Primary Data

Primary information was collected through field survey with sampled farmers and other local actors in the study area. The quantitative data regarding social, economic and livelihood structure were collected from primary sources using a well structured questionnaire. This household based purposive sample survey was conducted on 769 households from 21 villages representing 5,323 people in the Aligarh city's PUI.

The sample survey provides grounds for answering most of the research questions about livelihood transformation in Aligarh city PUI. Specifically, it allows us to generalize its effects on — and the response by — the village population. The sample survey not only collected quantifiable variables but also acquired longitudinal elements of the respondents. The focus was on livelihood structure and changes in the households. The questions elicit information on circumstances that influence reactions, choices, and strategies. Furthermore, the sample survey covered household histories over the last 30 years. This period more or less coincides with the secondary data analysis. Moreover, it seems to reflect what an average middle-aged respondent can reasonably recall.

The researcher also took help of local informants which included village headmen, property dealers, elderly people who know the village history, and local teachers and other well-informed local people. Persons in relevant positions at government departments, planning agencies, academic institutions, and in the local administration have also been consulted. They were particularly helpful when starting the research. Later they provided a means to double-check informations, and they gave feedback on research results. Various people in such positions were interviewed to find out about policy and practice and to appreciate the discrepancy between the two.

Secondary Data

These include statistical information on the city and the various settlement forms and their expansion in the regions and field areas concerned. The proposed study of secondary data, which aims to set the overall context of land-use change as well as to measure it, will cover a 30-year time-span (1980-2000-2010).

Census data provided useful information at the village level and more generally, about the land and population in the area. Census data were used to categorize the sample villages within the PUI on the basis of land-use and occupational characteristics (Table 1.4). The village level secondary data were collected through village revenue officer (*Patwari*) who keeps records on village land, including its use and ownership. The aggregated data on crop patterns at the village level was used to supplement the village description. Disaggregated data at the household level were used to analyze land ownership and transactions. Some additional background information about the villages was derived from various statistical bulletins and governmental publications, as they provided a historical perspective.

Satellite images were crucial to this study because they represented the physical aspects of the urbanizing environment of the PUI villages. IRS 1d pan images for Aligarh city and its environs for 2000 and 2010 were used. The base map was prepared taking help from the topo sheet maps and Aligarh city guide map prepared by Survey of India (1978) at the scales 1 : 50,000 and 1:20,000. Cadastral maps were also obtained from the local land administrator providing details about the ownership of individual plots.

Data Analysis

The study basically integrated the primary and secondary data to assess the primary influences of urbanization processes on land-use, demographic and changes in the structure of livelihood framework in the Aligarh's periurban interface. The spatial analysis was done mainly using GIS techniques (simple overlaying, cross operations, buffer operations, etc.), and basic statistical techniques (simple percentage distribution and cross tabulation) was also used for the analysis of data.

Structure of the Book

The structure of this book more or less reflects the sequence of the research questions. The introductory chapter outlines the academic context and the methodology used for the study. Chapter 2 examines the concepts of the periurban Interface and identifies the most important literature and the academic context. Chapter 3 describes the concepts of the periurban interactions and the linkages. Chapter 4 evaluates the regional and local setting of the study area and its evolution and development. Chapter 5 presents the livelihood options in the Aligarh's PUI, the cash and non-cash based, farm and off-farm based livelihoods and their important features. Chapter 6 evaluates the recent development of livelihood option in periurban interface, the emergence of livestock based livelihood especially the dairy farming. Chapter 7, highlights the concerns and the extent of the land-use changes in the research area. The types of land-use are classified to reveal the impact of urbanization on the land-use pattern. In addition, remote sensing images are used here for two purposes: to localise and quantify the land-uses; and to compare the types of land-use change with the land classification according to the physical criteria distinguished by remote sensing. Chapter 8 identifies the actors who have a stake in the expansion of urban land and the degree of economic strength of each actor. Chapter 9, deals with the effects of urbanization process on livelihood as well as economic, social, infrastructural and environmental phenomena. Finally, Chapter 10 presents the conclusions of this research.

2

Periurban Interface : The Concepts

Cities are dynamic human artifacts, they constantly undergo structural change, redevelopment, and growth. Such processes also involve changes in urban relationships with the surrounding territory, most conspicuously on their outskirts. The spatial and environment-development issues in the transitional zones between distinctly urban and clearly rural areas, which have historically been labelled, studied, and understood in different ways. Nevertheless, their importance everywhere lies in their dynamic mix of functions and land-uses; increasing population densities; growing significance as sources of urban food, construction materials, and other resources; as urban waste disposal or treatment sites; and as recreational zones.

Traditionally, social scientists concerned with urbanization, the relationships between urban areas and their hinterlands, or human activities and behaviour within such areas have relied on a simple urban-rural dichotomy. Implicit in this construct was the idea that urban and rural areas were characterized by very different land-use patterns and human behaviours and that the boundaries between these spaces and places were easily discernible and clear-cut. The widespread perception that the urban fringe represented a short-term transitional area that had little enduring interest or importance. Rural and urban areas, and the differences between them, therefore, dominated research agendas until quite recently.

On account of these characteristics, and the interactions between such areas and the cities, they came to be known as periurban zones or interfaces (PUIs) and have become major research foci in their own right. In other European or Europeanized languages, the PUI concept is expressed somewhat differently, e.g., *halfstedig* (half or semi-urban) in Dutch; *urban-l¨andlichen Zonen* (urban-rural zones) in German; and *buitestedelik* (outer city or beyond the city) in Afrikaans (12, 13, p. 5). There is a tendency, not least in Germany and the United States, to equate the rural-urban fringe or PUI with suburbanization, but these are not identical or equivalent processes. Although there is clearly an overlap in both concepts and actual usage of the terms, suburbs would more helpfully be distinguished as principally residential areas already forming part of the built-up urban area, the outermost edge of which constitutes the start of the urban fringe. PUIs would then comprise distinctive zones of mixed character beyond the suburbs.

Traditional Conceptions of the Periurban Interface

The literature on the *periurban interface* is included in different groups of works dealing with topics such as urban and rural relationships and their links, the extension of metropolitan growth on its surroundings, or changes and transformations in the economic, social, cultural and environmental realms etc. The PUI is conceptualized as transitory zone between rural and urban settlements.

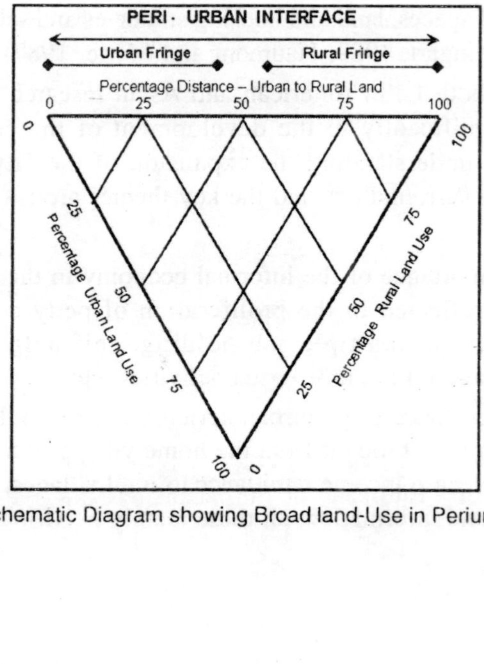

Fig. 2.1: Schematic Diagram showing Broad land-Use in Periurban interface.

One of the literature reviews on the PUI, Nottingham and Liverpool Universities (1998) recognize "the complexities of building a spatial framework around what is essentially an amorphous and mobile site for the interaction of various social, economic and cultural processes and inter-linkages between the rural and the urban". Rakodi stressed the relationship between urban and the immediate rural areas being the result of a process over time, The periurban interface is a dynamic zone both spatially and structurally (Rakodi 1998). Here the idea of "shifts" or evolution of the edge of the cities moving "outwards" is clear. The periurban interface seems thus to be considered as the result of urban driven processes more than of territorial processes where rural and urban forces interact. Browder *et al.* (1995), has underlined it by stating "traditional conceptions of the metropolitan fringe", the term that are preferred to *periurban areas*, considering it as somewhat specific to the French research literature.

The French literature on African cities is seen as constituting "the most robust and thematically unified conception of fringe development" (Browder *et al.* 1995). This trend of research saw the poor or "informal" fringes of the city as spaces that are the product of the interaction of state intervention and policies and the action and practices of the inhabitants seen as everyday use and appropriation of spaces, land and housing strategies and self-building practices (Schteingart, 1989; Haumont and Marie, 1987).

Similarly, both Latin American and Asian research have also contributed significantly to the development of the conceptual framework for understanding the expansion of the city into the peripheral rural surroundings and the key themes are :

(i) The importance of the informal economy in the periurban areas, reflected in the proliferation of petty commodity production, multiple job-holding, self-help housing, informal lending, unlicensed activities, etc.

(ii) the importance of periurban agriculture and rural linkages, such as food brought from the home village of a periurban resident, cash income remittance to rural villages, consumer goods and information, all these mainly in African context, while in Latin America rural-urban linkages on the metropolitan fringe are not typically strong, and in Asia the increased mobility between sectors is blurring the economic distinctions;

(iii) conflictive land property ownership issues are typical on the fringe, because of pressures from squatters, private developers or speculators, large tenants, etc. Different land market conditions feature dual systems (informal and formal) and various property and tenancy arrangements such as rental or customary right systems; and

(iv) the demographic processes that underpin fringe development, where they can range from organized land invasion to planned expansion of the fringe subsuming existing rural villages, including the speculative subdivision of farmland near the city, the resettlement of eradicated down-town slum inhabitants into public housing projects, or even temporary (daily, seasonal or circular) migration "especially in the Asian metro-fringe sites" (Browder *et al.*, 1995).

Periurban Linkages : The Growth Pole Theory

The *growth pole* theory is based on the belief that governments of developing countries can induce positive interaction, growth and welfare by investing heavily in capital-intensive industries in large urban centres or regional capitals. This growth is supposed to spread to the rural areas in a process of regional development (Rondinelli, 1985; Unwin, 1989). The growth pole theory is underpinned by the belief that "free market forces" provide conditions for positive interaction through the existence of the so-called "trickle-down effect" that is meant to put together various economic forces, creating a virtuous cycle (linkages) that spreads economic growth from urban to rural areas. The *growth pole* theory has been related to "top-down planning" where a centralized planning system, in response to external demand and innovation impulses, heavily invests in "high technology" urban industrial development (Stöhr and Taylor, 1981).

The centralized and "monolithic" planning system that makes

possible this kind of strategy has not only allowed experiences in capitalist countries, but tempted socialist planners as well. But experiences from Latin America and Africa have proved difficult to achieve success, specially because of the failure of the expected "trickle down effects". These have been replaced instead by adverse "backwash effects" that have maintained or even increased inequality between urban and rural areas (Unwin, 1989).

Douglass summarizes the rural-urban divide acting as the backdrop of *growth pole theories* in development planning and his work is mainly based in the South-East Asian context argued that economic growth and modernization required a surplus transfer from the agricultural sector to industry, thus justifying the appropriation of rural resources, capital and labour by cities.

Firman, 1996 in his research for Indonesia has also confirmed the failure of *growth pole* oriented policy models like the "counter magnet strategy" applied to the Bandung *extended metropolitan region*. This set of policies has been aimed at slowing down the physical development of Bandung City, the core of the region considered too congested by planners, in favour of the small towns surrounding it.

Periurban Linkages : The Urban Bias Critique

Perhaps the most influential and strong critique of uneven development generated or maintained by urban-oriented policies in poor countries comes from Michael Lipton (1977). Lipton states that the most important class conflict in the poor countries of the world today is not between labour and capital, nor between foreign and national interests, but it is between the rural classes and the urban classes. The rural sector contains most of the poverty, and most of the low-cost sources of potential advance; but the urban sector contains most of the articulateness, organization, and power (Lipton, 1977).

In specifically relating the explanation of "why poor people stay poor" on the rural-urban divide, Lipton's basic argument of "urban bias" is that the urban dwellers, having far more power than the rural ones, are able to divert a disproportionate share of resources towards their own interests and against the rural sector. The government being urban based, external credits are received, funds are allocated and development policies are generated by the urban elites that hold class alliances with the rural elite, thus maintaining privileged situations in both sides: the city obtaining cheap food and savings surpluses, while the rural better-off get subsidies and all of the rural investment (Unwin, 1989). In this process, the more efficient and labour-intensive small and poor farmers are forced either to sell their produce to the bigger farmers in disadvantageous conditions, to turn out to subsistence production or to finish joining the ranges of ruralurban migrants.

Several critiques have been raised against Lipton's formulation. The most important one concerns the problem of class definition being at the same time too simplistic to be realistic, and too deterministic to be explanatory enough of much more complex social situations. But what Lipton managed to do is to draw attention to the power relationships currently acting in these societies, especially the ones concerning elites with an intermediate distributive role of external aid as they held the government.

By stressing the importance of *urban bias* in policies, Lipton acknowledges a radical difference between rural and urban, but this is explained under socially reductionist assumptions like the one that would state that urban people are rich powerful and have greater access while rural people are poor and powerless. In assuming that the main difference between rural and urban consists in their social "classes". People, not places, are responsible for creating the flows between rural and urban areas (Unwin, 1989). The *urban bias* critique has the merit of highlighting the problem of a power divide (more than a physical one) between the rural and urban worlds, where a domination relationship is established and has in most cases taken the form of an alliance between urban and rural elites. Even though the direction and determinism of the influence of these groups have been strongly criticized and suggested erroneous.

Periurban Linkages : The Secondary Cities and Urban Diffusion

The work of Rondinelli (1983, 1985), although not explicitly, could be seen as trying to conceal two approaches, one based on the central place theory (and thus close to the *growth centre* approach) and one more rural oriented, that could be paralleled with the *agropolitan* approach proposed by Friedmann and Douglass (1975, 1978). Rondinelli states that the inequitable development is not related to the *urban population*, but with the *city size system and hierarchy* of the country. A geographically dispersed pattern of investment, based in a network of secondary cities and market towns or rural villages, is seen as important to achieve widespread development (Unwin, 1989). Rondinelli considers that increasing poverty in rural areas have played a determinant role in a certain "neglect of cities". This effect has been reinforced by the evidence of the disparities in living conditions and conditions of development between urban and rural areas in the developing world.

Rondinelli stated that lack of a system of secondary cities that supports economic activities and decentralized administrative functions which are necessary for the development of both urban and rural sectors. At the same time, rural-urban linkages are the promoters of this widespread development. He mentioned these linkages are crucial because the major markets for agricultural surpluses are in urban centres, most agricultural inputs come from organizations in cities, workers seek employment in towns as technological developments free rural labour, and many of the social, health, educational, and other services that satisfy basic human needs in rural areas are distributed from urban centres (Rondinelli, 1983). At the same time, he argued that no matter how carefully development goals are conceived it only matter as to how these linkages worked, as well as how they are conceived and by whom. They cannot be achieved in isolation from the cities or entirely through "bottom-up" stimuli. Economic growth with social equity requires both accelerated agricultural development and expansion of urban industry and commerce. (Rondinelli, 1983).

Unwin (1989) stresses the importance of Rondinelli's contribution to the consideration of the urban-rural interaction in that it relies heavily on "linkages both between rural areas and small cities, and on those between smaller and larger cities". He also argues that Rondinelli's approach to development planning can be summarized in two main points: "it is essentially concerned with the implementation of change through the manipulation of the urban settlement hierarchy, and it is implicitly based on a 'free market', capitalist framework of change" (Unwin, 1989).

Tacoli has identified the "underlying conceptual problem" of the Urban Functions in Rural Development approach as being the assumption that the constrictions to development come from the lack of central places, instead of considering rural-urban interaction issues like ecological capacity, land-owning structures, crop types and price control, and access to markets (Tacoli, 1998b).

Periurban Linkages : The Changing Periurban Linkages and Flows

Unwin and Potter (1989) analyzed the urban-rural relationships in developing countries under the general framework of the theory of dependence. Potter's article was marked by an ideological choice that proved an abstract socialist framework to analyze rural-urban linkages. It is posited that the nature of the settlement pattern of a given country, is merely the reflection of deeper socio-economic difficulties and inequalities. Thus, rather than trying to solve them through specific urban solutions as growth poles, new towns and the like, one has to turn to "more fundamental socio-political issues that are of crucial significance, not least, the mode of production and the development path that have been adopted in particular countries. (Potter, 1989).

Unwin's (1989) article is focused from the point of view of the interactions, linkages and flows between rural and urban areas. These three terms being generally used in the literature interchangeably, Unwin proposed a framework which are to be seen as separate but closely linked concepts. At the broad theoretical level it suggests that there are economic, social, political and ideological *linkages* between urban and rural places. These find their physical expression in measurable *flows* of, for example, people, money and budgetary allocation. These flows are associated with *interactions* between people, places and objects, but do not in themselves actually embody those interactions (Unwin, 1989). This system proposes four kinds of linkages (i.e., economic, social, political and ideological) and many more flows that are derived from them.

Lerner and Eakin (2010) using the word hybrid landscape for PUI elaborated changing livelihood and their linkages with urban settlement. They stressed on PUI social changes which also incorporate significant changes in lifestyle, land-uses and livelihood. The fusion of livelihoods in PUI is seen along streets, where livestock and gardens occupy back patios, and the younger generations commute to the locations of their professional careers. They want to show the potentiality of PUI to address the challenges of sustaining food security, environmental integrity and economic growth.

Periurban Linkages : The City Expansion and Dispersal

The general move towards dispersal and location of growth on the peripheries or fringes of cities is becoming a worldwide phenomenon. Evidence of strong empirical regularities in the patterns of metropolitan development in market-oriented economies of both industrialized and developing countries (Ingram, 1998). These movements towards the fringes are as follows :

- A dispersal process from the centre to the periphery of both population and employment, with the largest metropolitan areas converging to decentralized and multiple sub-centred areas, (cities in developing countries tend to have higher population densities, but the difference is narrowing);
- Highly decentralized manufacturing employment and emerging specialization of the central business district in service employment;
- Land-markets are strong determinants of this outward movement, land rents being closely related to development densities;
- Urban housing demand patterns are similar across cities in industrial and developing countries, but the supply side varies, as does the efficiency of the public infrastructures provision; and
- Increased reliance on road-based transport for both

passengers and freight (industrial countries have experienced decreases in transit level as automobile ownership rises; developing countries have higher transit-ridership levels and a mix of options in terms of vehicle sizes and levels of services) (Ingram, 1998).

Ingram states that population growth in large cities usually promotes densification of less developed areas and expansion at the urban fringe, largely following either price constraints or preferences of households acting within the housing market. This kind of process has been analyzed in different countries. Indeed, the formation of vast and ever-expanding metropolitan regions seems to be "an inevitable feature of very large populous countries" in the developing world. The potential of growth of such agglomerations has been constantly enhanced by technological development, especially by major improvements in transports and telecommunications (Jones and Visaria, 1997).

Adedayo in his study for developing countries also found that the urban frontier of housing estates and factories encroaches into formerly rural landscapes; these households in developing countries had become occupationally diversified, incorporating work patterns and networks tied into the metropolitan economy (Adedayo Adesina, 2007).

In South-East Asia, while suggesting the formation of an extended metropolitan region, Firman (1997) has described the fast process of land conversion in the Northern Region of West Java, Indonesia, mainly from agricultural to industrial and residential uses. This process has been led by domestic and foreign investment in the manufacturing, finance and service sectors, and has also been encouraged by a series of financial deregulation policies from the 1980s, aiming to stimulate economic growth.

The development of investment in housing and industrial estates has thus transformed mainly peripheral agricultural areas to large town and industrial estates. An influx of population into these peripheral areas, mainly middle-income groups, has boosted land speculation and a strong and dynamic activity of developers, not always under the regulation of the state (Fazal, 2001). This process must also be interpreted in the light of a general economic and physical restructuring of the region, where Jakarta City, the core, is shifting its former industrial function to a business, finance and services centre. Meanwhile, population growth in peripheral areas is far exceeding the one in the core (Firman, 1997).

Puntip also stated that the metropolitan region of Bangkok as a whole was in the stage of suburbanization indicating by the high rate of population growth in periurban areas, by transforming economic base to non-farming economy, and by rapid expansion of built-up areas (Puntip Jongkroy, 2009).

The *mega-urban regions* resulting from processes like those mentioned above are often composed of one or more large urban cores linked by major transportation axes plus the periurban zones and an extensive zone of mixed rural-urban land-use alongside the main routes (McGee, 1991). Common features of these rural-urban areas include :

- Rapid commercialization of agriculture;
- Expansion of transport systems; and
- An employment shift from farming to other activities, accompanied by migration or commutation to cities. Factories and other non-agricultural activities are also developing within the zone but outside the city proper.

Another characteristic feature of these mega-urban regions is that the distinctions between urban and rural are tending to become increasingly blurred as a result of technological changes and globalization processes that make available to rural dwellers, goods and services that were the preserve of urban residents only a very short time ago (Jones and Visaria, 1997).

Periurban Linkages : The Metropolitan Regions in a Globalizing World

The evolution of extended metropolitan regions can be subsumed into two main features that are "changing the face of the world geography":

- Globalization, "which assumes the increasing integration of national economies into global systems of production, distribution and consumption"; and
- Space-time collapse which is the consequence of the technological improvements in transport, communication and computer technology (McGee and Watters, 1997).

When analyzing the complex interactions between the global and the local, it is argued, there is a need to escape from "the idea of the global steamroller" constructing new regions, which is the common ideology underpinning globalization discourses. A local global dialectic where local forces in a variety of forms and levels negotiate with the global would thus be a more adequate framework to analyze the territorial changes that are produced by this dialectic interaction. The second way proposed to escape from the idea of globalization as a steamroller is "to attack it on empirical grounds". A confrontation against the different degrees by which countries are affected by globalization processes can cast light on the extent of these processes:

Almost 80 per cent of the world's inhabitants, particularly in Asia, Africa and Latin America, still exist in localities where networks remain primarily interpersonal and local; indeed, such local networks may be the crucial elements in their battle for survival (McGee and Watters, 1997). McGee further argues that the globalization process is followed by an inevitable increase in urbanization and the emergence of global and sub-global systems of highly linked cities. If current patterns of urban concentration persist, the developing world is expected to experience the emergence of mega-urban regions as major components of their urban systems. Although it has been argued that the current phase of globalization in developing countries is the second after the one represented by their incorporation into the colonial system, the urban consequences are at least of the same importance. Delik *et. al.* (2007) explained the uniqueness of periurbanisation in East Asian countries in relation to its dependence on the metropolitan centres, capital accumulation and dynamic coexistence of urban and rural livelihoods.

One of the consequences of the first wave of "globalisation" had been the creation of large primate cities dominating the urban hierarchies of their countries, like New Delhi, Kolkata, Mumbai, Rio de Janeiro, Jakarta or Nairobi which were administrative centres and conduits for the flows of raw materials for the developing world. At the same time, dualistic societies were created, with much of the rural population living in poverty (as the informal sectors of the cities), dominated by a small elite of colonialists, foreign entrepreneurs and indigenous oligarchy (McGee, 1997). Even if differences in the time and processes of decolonization (earlier in Latin America) have produced different patterns of urbanization — where Latin America has attained the levels of urbanization of developed countries, and Asia and Africa have just entered the "accelerated" phase of urban transition from rural to urban population — in each of these continents population from migration and endogenous growth of those large primate cities and industrial location on their fringes are actually expanding the urban areas to form what has been labelled extended metropolitan regions. McGee's major conclusion from this analysis is that macro-trends do not necessarily indicate a deconcentration of urban settlement or counter-urbanisation. In fact, while changing the scale and the definition of the urban agglomeration, these processes are actually occurring in a *larger zone*, where one can find at the same time residential outward movement, changing land-use of the inner cores, industrial decentralization into new industrial states and the creation and amelioration of transportation networks. This larger zone is the Extended Metropolitan Region.

Following Rigg and McGee (Rigg, 1997 from McGee, 1991), the features of South-East Asian EMRs are :

- Large and dense population engaged in wet rice cultivation;
- Good transport networks;
- Highly mobile population;
- An increase in non-farm (non-agricultural) activities;
- A mosaic of interlocking land-uses;
- Increased female participation in the labour force; and
- Lack of planning controls.

Rigg has pointed out that the features cited above for many city-regions of the Asian countries being the same that one could find at the national level: "it could be said that in functional terms there is no "edge" to the EMR" (Rigg, 1997). Rigg further maintains that: the formerly distinctive attributes of "rural" and "urban" are becoming increasingly blurred. In terms of physical fabric this can be seen in the expansion of South-East Asia's metropolitan regions; at a functional level it can be seen in the spatial intrusion of industry into rural areas; and in human and household terms in the diversification of livelihoods and the increasing movement of people between regions and jobs. It is interpreting these changes that the real challenge lies: what is driving the process and what are its implications, particularly for the people who are caught up in the maelstrom of change (Rigg, 1997).

McGee (1991) having argued that these EMR are mainly shaped by the dynamic linkages between agriculture and non-agriculture, from the macro-regional point of view, an evolving system of urban linkages between these mega-urban regions is emerging as a phenomenon of growing economic interaction. A further consequence is the emergence of sub-global regions: regional blocs of states (such as the Asia-Pacific region) within the global system (McGee, 1997).

Periurban Linkages : Review of Selected Case Studies

Leeming and Soussan (1979) described the fringe area as the zone of land on the periphery of city which is experiencing a process of transformation from rural modes of production, social interaction and land-use to characteristically urban ones, or which has experienced this process in the recent past. At one time this fringe acts as the interface between the city and the surrounding rural areas. Thus, the fringe is a transitional zone into which the city is expanding. This is a different phenomena from the zone of urban influence, which is much more extensive, usually called its hinterland.

Ramachandran (1989), while reviewing urbanization and urban systems in India has attempted to trace the origins and definition of the phenomenon of the rural-urban fringe in India. Since post independence in India when the urban scene has changed, the rapid growth of cities could not be accommodated within the limits of the existing cities and the character of the peripheral villages underwent significant change. He sticks to the term rural-urban fringe and also stated "the rural-urban fringe is an area of mixed rural and urban populations and land-uses, which begins at the point where agricultural land-uses appear near the city and extends up to the point where villages have distinct urban land-uses or where some persons, at least, from the village community commute to the city daily for work or other purposes (Ramachandran, 1989).

According to Ramachandran (based on the above definition) the fringe in Delhi extends well beyond the city limits. It is an area outside the municipal limits and is an important area of new residential, industrial and commercial development, representing the outward expansion of the city. Urban corridors and suburbs fall within the rural-urban fringe zone, while satellites, green belts, new towns and counter magnets lie outside the zone of rural-urban fringe. This area lacks civic services such as water supply, sewage, drainage and garbage disposal.

McGee (1991) in his book *The Extended Metropolis-Settlement Transition in Asia* reviews the conventional definition, i.e., the concept of "urban transition" positioned within a broader paradigm of transition in the space-economy of countries, which is quite significant in the Asian context. McGee in his model of spatial configuration for Asian country, identifies five main regions of the spatial economy as follows:

- Major cities of the urban hierarchy and in case of Asia dominated by one or two extremely big cities;
- Periurban regions are those areas surrounding the cities within a daily commuting reach of the city core;
- *Desakotasi* (derived from Bahasa Indonesia—*desa* for village and *kota* for town or city, *si* for process)—are regions of an intense mixture of agriculture and non-agricultural activities that often stretch along corridors between large city cores, characterized by dense populations engaged in agriculture;

- Densely populated rural regions; and
- the sparsely populated frontier.

McGee defines Periurban as "those areas surrounding the cities within a daily commuting reach of the city core. In some parts of Asia, these regions can stretch for up to thirty kilometres away from city core" (1991, p. 6-7). According to McGee there are at least three types of spatial economy transition occurring in Asia with the historical evolution of high density and mostly rice growing areas:

- *Desakota* Type 1 — These are regions that have seen a decline in rural settlement, land-use and where agricultural population has moved to urban centres. For example, a country like South Korea and Japan with rural landscapes in which most of the economically active work is based on non-agricultural activities.
- *Desakota* Type 2 — These are regions where over a varying period of time with productivity gains in agriculture and industry and shifts from agricultural to non-agricultural population concentrated on core city and adjacent regions. These are also areas of rapid economic growth compared to other regions of the country.
- *Desakota* Type 3 — These are regions with high density but slow economic growth and marked with involuntary economic activities. Such regions are generally located along secondary urban centres.

Later Robinson (1995) described the growth of mega-cities and emerging spatial patterns, i.e., decentralization and dispersal in ASEAN mega urban regions. Decentralization and dispersal is seen as one of the effective ways of relieving or reducing the extreme negative effects of these rapidly growing metropolises. *Decentralization* happens where people and/or economic activities are moved from the urban cores into the peripheral areas and along major transportation corridors radiating from urban cores with metropolitan region. *Dispersal* happens when people and activities are located outside secondary or provincial cities or other growth centres. It is observed that most of the decentralization has occurred mainly as a result of natural market forces rather than government policy. Though in recognition of the advantages of poly-centricity, most Asian mega-cities have adopted spatial planning strategies aimed at developing a decentralized form in their metropolitan regions. These are usually incorporated in their master plans. Robinson (1995) reviewed his experiences of a number of Asian mega-cities Calcutta, Delhi, Bombay, Dhaka, Seoul, Manila, Jakarta and Bangkok. According to significant decentralization has been achieved in Asian mega cities. The urban area/built-up expanded manifold and also the bulk of decentralization have been occurring in the form of 'ribbon development' along major transport corridors leading out of the core city.

Overseas Development Agency's Renewable Natural Resources Research Strategy, defined the periurban and stated that 'the periurban interface is characterized by strong urban influences, easy access to markets, services and other inputs, ready supplies of labour, but relative shortages of land and risks from pollution and urban growth' (ODA, 1999) and deliberately defined the periurban interface into two broad zones:

- The Zone of direct impact; and
- A wider, market-related zone of influence.

Simon (2008) addresses the complexities of changing periurban production and livelihood systems in the context of rapid urbanization in poorer countries, distinctive periurban challenges of appropriate and flexible planning and development, and the future prospects for enhanced sustainability in the most challenging category of development-environment interfaces.

Bentinck (2000) focused on the rural-urban fringe and referred to it as the ultimate 'battlefield' of the environmental and socio-economic change brought about by urbanization. He finds that "urban studies" and "rural/regional studies" prevail over "fringe" studies and rural-urban fringe is ignored as a specific area within the study of urbanization. In his research work on urban land-use in fringe of Delhi, he stated his area of focus based on "The same criteria—urban land-use on the urban side of the fringe and occupation on the rural side of the fringe are used here to formulate a working definition of rural fringe:

The rural-urban fringe extends from the contiguous built-up area of the city (no rural land-use) to the area where most villages show a majority of workers engaged in non-agricultural occupations (many of whom commute). Bentinck's work focuses on urbanization at the micro level and within a twenty-five years time period. The researched area is the Alipur Development Block (administrative division), comprising 59 villages and situated on the north of the National Capital Territory (NCT) of Delhi. Using the land-use pattern and the transformation in occupational structure of six villages were selected to study the "stages of metropolitanization" were studied. The study described three selected villages that are subject to the strong impact of urbanization. In addition, the study evaluates a completely urbanized village that shows the ultimate impact urbanization is having on the living conditions of villagers as well as migrants.

Similarly Lintelo *et al.* (2001) examined the nature and significance of urban and periurban agriculture in general and with particular reference to Delhi. They observed that demographic and economic extension of cities, through processes such as migration and industrialization tend to be accompanied by spatial expansion, resulting in encroachments by cities upon adjacent urban areas. In a detailed study of "urban" as well as "rural" Delhi using satellite images for 1998 Lintelo observed that the actual conurbation is noted to have stretched beyond the administrative boundaries in southern (Gurgaon), south-eastern (Faridabad) and eastern (NOIDA and Ghaziabad) directions.

The area beyond these above-mentioned towns is predominantly agricultural and within the NCT Delhi referred to as wider Delhi in north, north-west and west between the urban city centre and the towns situated on the peripheries lie important but diminishing agricultural areas. Around the city in NCT Delhi, large areas still follow crop production, fallow land cycle and plantation or grassland. In fact, 17 per cent consists of built-up areas clearly indicating that agriculture was still a major land-use in and around Delhi.

The research study focuses on 30 select revenue villages concentrated in three clusters in south-western, north-western and north directions in the fringe areas of Delhi. The authors have taken six villages for detailed case study of occupational pattern. It has been observed that urban and periurban agriculture is a dominant and dynamic land-use in Delhi although geographic locations of the fringe may shift over time with waves of urbanization. According to their need the study on periurban agriculture concentrates on area/ villages between Delhi and the towns situated on its peripheries "areas distant from city and rural in character will subsequently start falling within the cities reach or "band of influence".

Dupont (2004) has analyzed the developments in urban forms and population redistribution in the Delhi Metropolitan Area as part of the development of the mega-city of Delhi in terms of:

- Focusing on the processes of periurbanization and rurbanization; and
- Population redistribution within the metropolitan area.

The emphasis is on the major role migration has played in the demographic evolution of the capital city. The urban development of Delhi has been seen to be shaped by planned as well as informal urbanization in the periphery thereby resulting in the interweaving of urbanized zones, as well as to a blurring of the distinction between rural and urban population categories.

Dupont stated in the conclusion that "the urban development in the metropolitan area of Delhi results from the combined effects of spontaneous dynamics of new migrants and city dwellers, market forces and attempts of town planning at the level of National Capital Region, the distinction made between three planning zones (the territory of Delhi, the first urban ring, i.e., the peripheral towns of the Metropolitan Area, and the zone beyond the Metropolitan), runs the risk of becoming an obsolete theoretical distinction, overtaken by the rate at which the actual dynamics at work is evolving. The ring towns have thus become an integral part of gigantic conurbation extending from the capital outwards. In the framework of growing globalization of economies and the growing influence of the liberalization and disengagement policies of the states, the control of the development of megalopolis appears more and more problematic in the face of contradictory interests and forces' (Dupont, 2004).

Laquinta and Drescher (2001) attempted to introduce new typologies of periurban and applied the typology to issues of natural resources planning and management. Their work is based on seven premises and different from others:

- *Rural, Periurban and Urban form a linked system (R/PU/U) — an uneven or lumpy multidimensional continuum;*
- *In terms of migration and urbanization periurban environments play a mediating role between rural and urban;*
- *Periurban environments are places of social compression and dynamic social change;*
- *Understanding the nature and operation of the system requires a focus on the underlying dynamic processes rather than the 'fixed states';*
- *The potential for food production and its relationship to food security must be evaluated across the entire R/PU/U system;*
- *Effective policy intervention rests on interdisciplinary understanding, which incorporates physical, biological and socio-cultural paradigms; and*
- *The "social footprints" of urbanization manifest differently in the urban, periurban and rural context but is understandable when addressed in view of a linked system (R/PU/U).*

They argued that it is not an essential element of the definition that periurban has to have "proximity to the city". It is just incidental to an elemental understanding of periurban. Concentration on simple geographic location as the basis for defining periurban misses the point of a clear understanding of rural-urban spectrum as dynamic, interactive and transformative. Thus, periurban is clearly more than just an urban fringe. According to Iaquinta and Drescher (2001), *urbanisation* is a process of concentration and intensification of human life and activity. It is an uneven process as a result of three fundamental population processes — fertility, mortality, and migration that takes place in a physical environment. Such processes occur due to individual and household decisions undertaken in a socio-cultural, economic, political and environmental context.

The typology of periurban by Iaquinta and Drescher is composed of five ideal types: Village Periurban, Diffuse Periurban, Chain Periurban, In-place Periurban, Absorbed Periurban and the five elements embedded within the broader rural-urban dynamic. The typology derives from underlying socio-demographic processes, especially migration in which the transformative linkages are organized along the dimensions of migration and time. The typology remains connected in the form of organic two-way exchange networks, which can be summarized as follows:

- *Village Periurban:* Rural villages with an urban consciousness, these areas are geographically non-proximate to an urban area. Its designation as periurban rests on its social psychological transformation rather than geography and size.
- *Diffuse Periurban :* A separate category of periurban comprising areas proximate to the city and which are settled depending on migration. The immigrants come from a variety of geographic source points.
- *Chain Periurban :* Geographically close to the city; this is an urban fringe that undergoes settlement *vis-à-vis* a process of chain migration. Areas identified as "squatter settlements" around the cities of developing countries mostly relate to this type.

- *In-Place Periurban :* Geographically close to the city and result from in-place (*in situ*) urbanization, natural increase and some migration. These are areas in the process of being wholly absorbed by actual expansion of the urban fringe or simple reclassification.
- *Absorbed Periurban :* These are areas proximate to or within the city that have been absorbed for a considerable period of time. These areas derive from either in-place periurban areas or from chain periurban areas.

Based on the above typology, Iaquinta and Drescher have argued that rural migrants move first to villages or small towns then successively to more urban environments. There are two kinds of links that persist across *space* in face of geographic displacement and links that persist across *time.* Together, Diffuse Periurban and Chain Periurban most closely approximate the 'urban fringe' definition used by geographers. In-place periurban has some similarities of the fringe but would more closely fit into *Desakota* type. Village Periurban on the other hand is completely unrelated to the urban fringe concept.

Stephenson (2001) examines various problems of the developing countries with reference to urban water management and periurban structure. He observed 'periurban areas' to be different from both the high income suburban sprawl which is distinct from the rapidly growing unstructured settlements springing up around developing areas such as Rio de Janeiro/Sao Paulo, Buenos Aires (villa's miseries) Kampung in Jakarta, squatter settlements around Johannesburg, the urban sprawl in India among other such settlements across the South.

Kumar (2002) looks at the process of metropolization in urban agglomeration across India and defines periurban in regional context as outgrowths. He observed that "the question of periurban development cannot be addressed outside the framework of balanced development of both rural and urban areas. He stated "urban is not a homogeneous category and bias in the differential scale needs to be acknowledged" (2002, p. 13).

Brook *et al.* (2003) working under a DFID sponsored project working in the Hubli-Dharwad region (India) have emphasized that the periurban interface is not primarily a location, although it has a place where it exists and it has a process. This includes people, flows and interactions—flows of people, goods, finance, and pollution, among other similar issues that are part of the process. According to them "there is no single satisfactory definition of the periurban interface, and moreover, different definitions will probably apply in different circumstances, and may even change in the same location over time; for example, as a medium-size city becomes large one" (2003, p. 2). Thus, the *definition will differ* for different situations.

Rohilla (2004) observes urban growth as an evolutionary process. His research focus is on groundwater and urban development in the process of metropolization of Delhi over a period of time. He defines the "periurban" areas of Delhi in his case as "an area/villages in the evolutionary process of urban development, including villages engulfed in the process of urbanization (referred as 'urban villages') already part of the city and the suburban areas/villages including outgrowths on the fringe of an existing city, which are in the transitional phase of urban development (planned/unplanned) which in a period of one or two decades will become part of the city limits".

The DFID 1999 Report outlined periurban area as an interface, a transitory zone of mixed rural and urban economic, social, cultural and natural resource uses at the periphery of cities in developing nations. The principle findings of the report are as follows:

- The periurban may be best examined in terms of the development processes;
- No single theory or model adequately explains activities in the rural-urban fringes;
- The periurban areas locate new populations, which in turn is the cause of natural resource depletion as well as pollution; and
- Most periurban developments have biophysical impacts extending beyond their immediate boundaries.

According to the DFID report, periurban development can be considered as part of this wider urbanization process. With the growth of cities in developing countries, the periurban area moves in waves. The report concludes that "definitions of what constitutes 'periurban' are thin and inconsistent and literature directly relating to periurban areas is not substantial". Further it stated that statistics related to urbanization is varied and definition of "urban" settlement and quality of data differs country to country which makes international comparisons difficult and local factors more important than generalized assumptions characterizing the nature of periurban.

To conclude, it can be said that the literature on periurban interface is in large volume but because of its dynamic nature the definition and delimitation are rather inconsistent. This is largely due to differences in site and situation which results in different kinds of urbanization process and the resultant impacts on PUI. There is general acceptance for PUI as transitory zone, where combination of rural and urban activities meet. PUI is dynamic and generalization and comparisons are difficult as local factors act differently at different locations. The PUI is to be considered as a region of change and not a distinct boundary, where the process of change is crucial.

3

Periurban Interface : The Linkages

Concept of Periurban Interaction

The PUI (periurban interface) is a social, economic and environmental space where three systems (agricultural, urban and the natural) are in constant interaction. The peripheral areas of the urban settlement have been defined, conceptualized and delimited in various ways. It began in 1940's, when changes on the surrounding areas of the city came under increasing attention from spatial disciplines, (urban geography) in western world. The urban geographers focused on investigating the processes which were shaping the urban peripheries, the place where urban and rural activities met. The term urban fringe was used firstly by American geographers and by 1940's and 1950's, it was widely adopted in the academic literature for the transition zone between city and countryside (Johnson, 1974). Soon the complex functional relations and heterogeneity of dynamic social structure of the urban fringe set to originate debate on its physical and conceptual boundaries.

A morphological and functional approach of the urban fringe used for analysis of morphology, land-use change in an irradiating pattern from the urban side. This was argued by human and rural geographers as the transitional landscapes between urban and rural were not necessarily the result of urban driven processes and they coined the term rural–urban or rurban fringe. Thereafter, some terminological and conceptual work was initiated like Kurtz and Richer (1958) tried to differentiate the urban fringe from suburbs,

Wissink (1962) identified pseudo–suburbs, satellites and pseudo-satellite towns and inner and outer urban fringe. Andrews (1952) distinguished between urban fringe and rural-urban fringe. Some other terms were also used like Duncan and Reiss (1956) called as rural non-farm areas and rural farm areas. Pryor (1968) in his study define the changes in the periurban interface with a new categorization based on the analysis of different phases according to land-use to differentiate periurban areas from rurban periphery. Pahl (1965) moving away from physical definition of the fringe and defined it as being the result of particular social processes. Carter (1981) proposed a definition of rural-urban fringe as the space on which the town extends as the process of dispersion operates, an area with distinctive characteristics which is only partly assimilated into the growing urban complex, that is partly rural and where many of the residents live in the country but are not socially and economically of it.

The city in western world since 1960s become less and less a discrete local place as the urban experience becomes more "universal". The basic urban expansions from central city, first to suburbs and then to the larger decentralized 'urban field'. Thus, urban-rural dichotomy vanished against the emergence of the rural-urban continuum, where pattern of activities developing not on a place but on a region. In this context, Melvin Webber (1964) introduced the concept of "non place urban realm".

More recently within the framework of current discussions, new terminologies were used, either making reference to a new kind of urban development (a new landscape of employment and other activity concentrations away and independent from older urban centres), or stressing the processes underpinning the new developments (in particular the impact of flexibility in production systems and technology) (Oatley, 1997).

Thereafter, the discussion was around the argument that the central transition in urban form, involves a shift from the compact / suburban dualistic pattern to the spread metropolitan and from mono-centric cities to multi-centred urban areas (Garreau, 1991; Harvey, 1995; Hall, 1996; Dick and Rimmed, 1998, etc.).

During 1990"s, a new lexicon has emerged that attempts to

capture contemporary forms of urbanization like edge city, technourbs, technopolis, flex space, super urbia, outer cities, perimeter cities or even peri-metropolitan bow waves, etc. (Oatley, 1997). The transition to the conceptualization of these new landscapes is challenging perceptions and knowledge raising questions about the necessary adaptations of the urban and regional planning set of conceptual and practical tools to cope with the new territorial reality across the continents (Adell, 1999).

PUI : A Changing Conceptual Landscape

The perceived link between the city and the countryside evolved, shifting to new conceptual landscapes where rural-urban links were redefined. In this conceptual field, the PUI is considered as a transitional zone between city and countryside described as not a discrete area but rather a diffuse territory identified by combinations of features and phenomena, generated largely by activities within the urban zone (Nottingham and Liverpool Universities, 1998). These areas are difficult to define as it is associated with problems inherent to the conceptualization of both rural and urban worlds.

A sharp distinction between urban and rural settlements generally assumes that the livelihood is based on two broad categories — agriculture based in rural areas and manufacture and service based in urban centre. Despite the activities are spatially separated, there is always a continued and varied exchange of resources between urban and rural areas. This sectoral interaction consists of primary activities in urban areas (like urban agriculture or dairying) or secondary and tertiary activities in rural areas (Tacoli, 1998). This results in the boundaries between urban and rural areas increasingly blurred (Jones and Visaria, 1997).

Amy M Lerner, Hallie Eakin (2010) used the word hybrid landscape for PUI which also incorporate significant changes in lifestyle, land-use and livelihood .The fusion of livelihoods is seen all around the PUI and the younger generations commute to the urban locations to take advantage in their professional careers. The PUI demonstrate the potentiality to address the challenges of sustaining food security, environmental integrity and economic growth.

The conceptual background on PUI case studies by many such as McGee, 1991; Robinson, 1995; Marshall *et. al*., 2001; Lintelo *et. al*., 2001; Kundu, 2001; Dupont, 2004; Taquinta and Drescher, 2002, etc. indicates that all studies have defined PUI according to their needs, scope of work and data availability.

BOX 3.1 : Livelihoods and the Rural-Urban Continuum

RURAL >>		<< URBAN
Livelihoods drawn from crop cultivation, livestock, forestry or fishing (i.e., key for livelihood is access to natural capital). Access to natural capital as the key asset and basis for livelihood. Access to land for housing and building materials not generally a problem. More distant from government as regulator and provider of services Access to infrastructure and services limited (largely because of distance, low density and limited capacity to pay?) Fewer opportunities for earning cash; more for self-provisioning. Greater reliance on favourable weather conditions.	**Rural-urban interface**	Livelihoods drawn from labour markets within non-agricultural production or making/selling goods or services Greater reliance on house as an economic resource (space for production, access to income-earning opportunities; asset and income-earner for owners – including *de facto* owners) Access to land for housing very difficult; housing and land markets highly commercialized More vulnerable to 'bad' governance Access to infrastructure and services difficult for low-income groups because of high prices, illegal nature of their homes (for many) and poor governance Greater reliance on cash for access to food, water, sanitation, employment, garbage disposal....
Urban characteristics in rural locations (e.g., prosperous tourist areas, mining areas, areas with high value crops and many local multiplier links, rural areas with diverse non-agricultural production and strong links to cities....)		Rural characteristics in urban location (urban agriculture, "village" enclaves, access to land for housing through non-monetary traditional forms.......)

BOX 3.2 : Approaches to Rural-Urban Linkages

There are several studies highlighting different approaches for rural-urban linkages and there is a need to adopt flexible approach, as the flows may wax and wane over time. Some of the important approaches by leading agencies and the framework adopted for evaluation are given below:

The World Bank have identified the following themes for measuring rural-urban linkages (World Bank, 2000):

- *The need for a broad analytical framework that can integrate the processes and approaches that span the realms at various scales;*
- *The need to consider the role that spatial dimensions play, along with the dynamics, vulnerabilities and movements in and out of poverty;*
- *The importance of a long-term perspective in relation to shifts in settlement and economic patterns;*
- *Recognition that local economies advance and decline and that different approaches may, therefore, be required, and the need to understand the linkages and their role in the changes;*
- *The need to recognize the importance of the trend towards decentralization;*
- *The need for approaches that facilitate working across sectors; and*
- *The need to recognize the heterogeneity of constructs of town and country and the divisions between them, including agriculture in towns and non-farm activities in the country.*

The Overseas Development Institute, U.K. (ODI, 2002) in its summary sheet outlined the major challenges for rural-urban linkages as:

- *The poorest areas may have little more than consumption linkages.*
- *Production linkages emerge in more diversified settings, such as where rural-based workshops start to supply urban-based factories.*
- *Financial linkages appear in all settings, but with different outcomes for rural economies.*
- *The rise of network societies may contribute to bypass effects, when financial flows link rural areas directly with distant, larger cities at the expense of local towns.*

In another report Mutizwa-Mangiza (1999), for UNCHS, highlights past views on the rural-urban divide as either pro-urban or anti-urban. The report highlights the importance of balanced approach, referring to its place in the Habitat Agenda agreed at the Habitat II Conference organised by UNCHS in Istanbul in 1996.

(Contd...)

BOX 3.2 :*(Contd...)*

- *"To promote the sustainable development of rural settlements and to reduce rural-to-urban migration".*
- *"To promote the utilization of new and improved technologies and appropriate traditional practices in rural settlements development".*
- *"To establish... policies for sustainable regional development and management".*
- *"To strengthen sustainable development and employment opportunities in impoverished rural areas"*
- *"To adopt an integrated approach to promote balanced and mutually supportive urban-rural development".*

The PUI Linkages

The physical boundary of urban built-up often extends beyond their administrative boundaries, so is its influence area. This influence area depends on the social-economic characteristics and its linkages with its surrounding areas. The area surrounding urban centres generally have a major role in providing agricultural and other primary products for urban residents because of its location. It is rather difficult to make generalizations on the nature of this region — the periurban interface, which is depended on various interrelated as well as complexed natural, social, economic and infrastructural factors existing within and even outside PUI.

The PUI linkages reflect the regional development that:

- Encompasses both rural and urban populations and the interconnections between them.
- Recognizes that there are typical "urban" and "rural" characteristics which influence their residents livelihood despite diversity between urban and rural locations.
- Acknowledges that where people live and work influences the scale and nature of deprivation or advantages.

Fig. 3.1 shows the most general linkages within the periurban interface. Despite of the limitation of a basic two dimensional representation of a rather complex system, the important feature is the possibility of each link to move in either direction. These linkages may observe one way flow or the intensity of flow may change over time and space or from one context to another. The flows of people, commodity and natural resources are represented above surface because their flows can be witnessed and measured in absolute terms. Whereas capital and ideas are less tangible and represented below surface as these flows can be felt but difficult to measure in absolute terms. Here, the flows are between two separate entities — urban and rural. This obviously ignores the periurban interface, where a distinction between rural and urban becomes blurred.

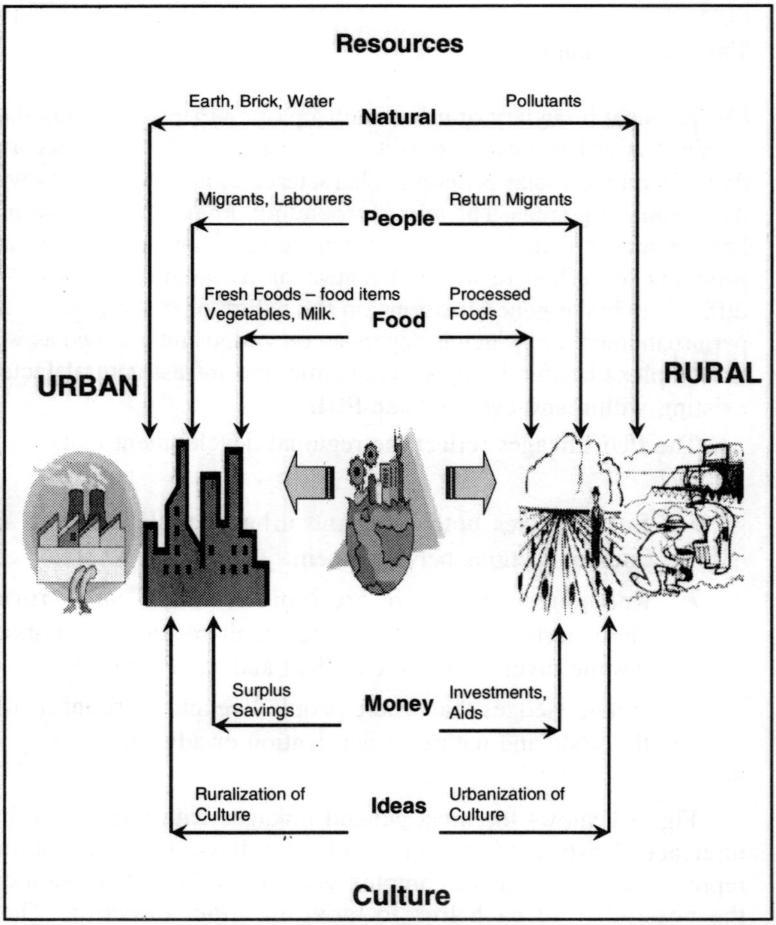

Fig. 3.1: Rural-Urban Interaction

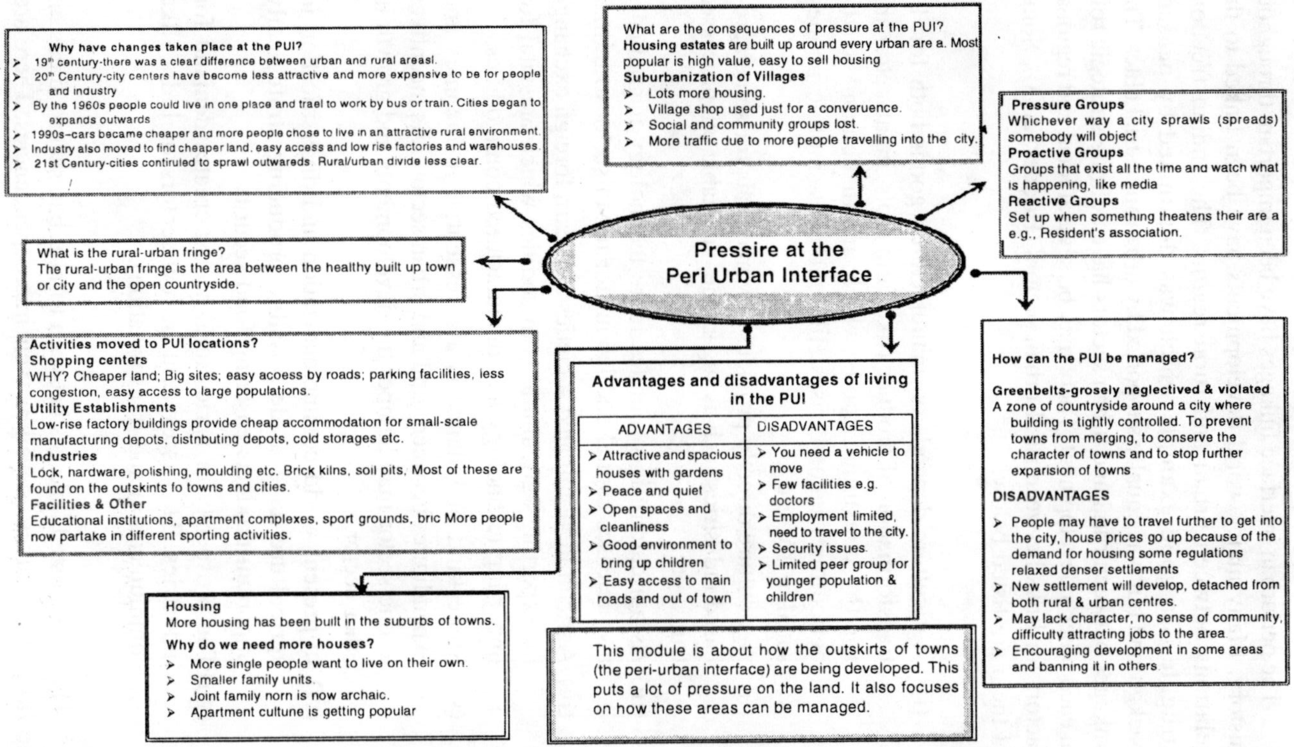

Fig. 3.2 : Pressure at the periurban interface

The periurban interface linkages have been important throughout history. Many major world developments have been linked to the relations between urban and rural realms. The Indian freedom struggle is a good example which was dominated by peasant background but was equally supported by urban-industrial elites. The linkages between rural and urban sectors have definite strategic role in each other's development. There may be several local and regional factors for links between rural-urban sectors (Hodder, 2000). Some of them are listed below:

(i) Agriculture depends on manufactured goods both for the transformation of produce (like farm tools, inputs, etc.) and for the consumer goods which are in demand as the agricultural income rises (like mobikes, mobile phones, satellite TV, etc.).

(ii) Agriculture directly provides raw materials for some agro–based industries such as sugarcane, vegetable oil, processed fruits, etc.

(iii) As agriculture incorporates more technology it gradually also releases capital and labour for urban sector to utilize.

(iv) Agriculture dominated societies also earn foreign exchange by exporting agricultural commodities which are vital for importing technology and manufactured commodities.

(v) Some kind of balance is also essential in incomes and expenditures between rural and urban sectors. As incentives to one sector may hamper the developments and growth in other sector.

(vi) In present world commercialization and diversification in agriculture have made possible producing strategically important products ensuring food security.

(vii) The prosperity in agricultural sector creates demand for industries. This is evident in few sectors of India (like communication and transportation).

The above listed linkages between rural-urban sectors focus on the flow of resources as well as their interdependencies. There are many studies on rural-urban sectors, the basic objective here is to highlight the linkages between rural and urban areas rather than boundaries between them—the periurban interface. This allows assessing relations that may favour one or the other sector emphasizing interdependence of city and country (Lynch, 2005; Pugh, 1996).

In India and other developing countries this linkage is more tilted towards rural hinterland than cities as in the developed world. Particularly, because of the large population is still rural but increases in urban population lately have made their relationship even more important. One aspect of these linkages which is very important between urban and rural areas has their very different ways of life which also makes comparative analysis rather difficult. Urban dwellers tend to have a more monetary based existence in which consumption practices are limited by income and decisions are defined more comprehensively by income in relation to the cost of living. In rural areas by contrast, income is important but their livelihood is influenced by their cultural and natural assets.

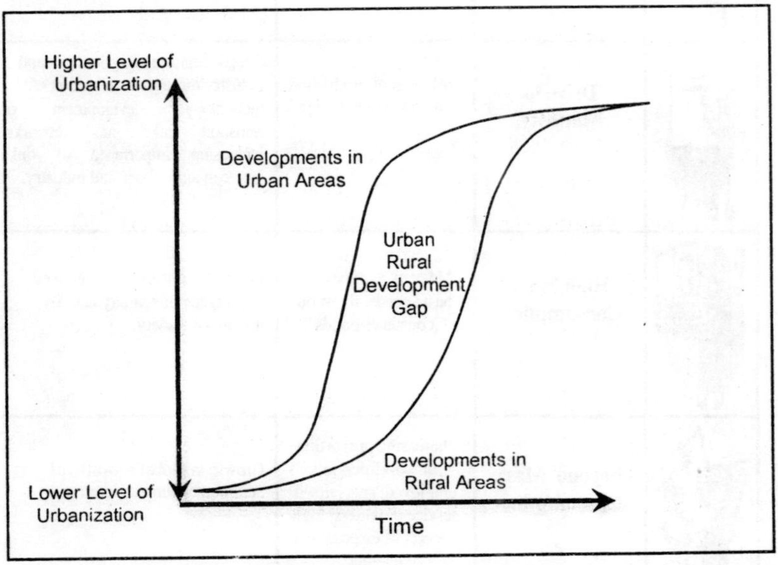

Fig. 3.3 : Process of Urbanization

	STAGES	ECONOMIC FEATURES	IMPLICATIONS FOR RURAL URBAN INTERACTION
	**Traditional Society**	Primary activity dependent	Most production subsistence or feudal
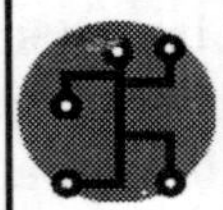	**Preconditions for Take-off**	Loss of power for landed elites	Growing settlements offer opportunities for commercial agriculture and some migration; generation of investment through growth in agriculture and extractive industries.
	**Take-off**	Increasing focus on industry and commercial agriculture	Growing cities lead to increased demand for food and raw materials; improving communications and transport; rapid rural urban migration.
	**Drive to Maturity**	Diffusion of production and trade technology	Transformation of agriculture and industry through introduction of technology; development of transport links into networks; increasing importance of links between agriculture and industry.
	**High Mass Consumption**	Majority earn beyond basic needs; focus on consumer goods	Focus on consumption; reduced importance of primary activity; urbanized society.
	**Beyond Mass Consumption**	Increasing proportion of workforce self employed; specialized service providers; high levels of disposable income	Growth in global networks of communication and interaction

Fig. 3.4 : Stages of Socio-Economic Development (adapted from Rostow)

The periurban interface linkages have a bearing on the livelihood and well-being over space and can create resilient regional economies. There can be various types of linkages, here an attempt has been made to give an explanatory description of existing linkages within the periurban interface. The key interest in describing linkages in PUI is to understand the nature and direction of these flows and to identify driving forces to promote mutually supportive rural-urban development.

Demographic Flows

Rural to urban migration is a central characteristic of urbanization in India as in many developing countries. Migration is one of the few avenues open to poor households to increase income and combat increasing improvishment. The dominant trend is for members of a rural household to migrate to urban areas to sell their labour and remit their income to their respective families back in rural areas. With the opening up of economies, diversifying activities have created opportunities leading to rural-urban migration in the recent past (McGurn. 1997; Sjoberg, 1994; Liu, 1991; Wong, 1994; Fazal, 2001). Migration also has observable gender biases depending upon the type of jobs available in rural and urban areas and social environment of the rural place in terms of facilitating or hindering male/female migration. In India, men have traditionally dominated migrant streams but some newly industrialized countries with labour intensive trans-national assembly line operations have also observed women as dominant migrants to urban areas (Lynch, 2005). In either situation, migration is a highly selective process within households and among rural as well as urban places of origin and destination.

In India, migration has several dimensions. It is not a one time, one way movement of people, but rather, it is part of a dynamically adaptive strategy that allows poor households to tap into resources available in both sending and receiving urban and rural areas in order to cope with conditions of poverty and to try to enhance their well-being. Especially, north Indian migrants as a survival strategy return back to their rural native place during harvesting period to augment their earnings from the urban employment. An estimated 20 million people migrate temporarily each year in India, of which almost two-third migration is rural to urban.

The pattern of migration may vary in different regions according to their socio-economic-cultural set-up but migration is certainly pervasive and dynamic process of poverty alleviation. In India, remittances account for about one-third of annual incomes of poor households in rural areas (Deshingbar, 2006). Migrant remittance to rural households plays an important role in well-being of their rural based families. Remittances at household level make a significant contribution in raising education, health and living standard in rural areas. It also make a difference in rural society as a whole as investments also flow into the development of rural farming enterprises promoting rural economic development. These investments from migrants in social welfare, education, housing, etc., in their native rural areas fetch them social respect and recognition.

Driving Forces for Migration

Empirical studies and historical trends indicate that rural-urban migration has been primarily driven by differences in expected income over space, which in the extreme is manifested in the inability of households to earn-incomes to sustain their existence. Several factors contribute to both income inequalities over space and the fall below levels of subsistence in particular regions. Traditional approaches to migration have relied on the notion of "push-pull" factors are the main explanatory elements. Individuals rationally decide to migrate because they are attracted by the bright lights of the city which promise, in long term to offer better economic opportunities than the countryside.

Structural Changes in Economies and Migration

Economic policies and government intervention in the economy greatly influence what will be produced and consumed and in turn profoundly affect rural-urban migration. They affect the structure of rural production and the availability of jobs to both the urban and rural workers. Migrants are rational decision makers that respond to income opportunities and resource availability (Tacoli, 1998). India is undergoing structural adjustments and the effects of these policies have bearing on rural-urban migration also. For instance, small farmers in the absence of government subsidies and support, found it difficult to overcome high input costs. They also cannot afford to hold on to their produce and sell at higher prices. They are also vulnerable to price squeeze as the cost of inputs and consumer goods rose much steeper than the prices they fetch from primary commodities. This pushes small farmers to urban areas for sustenance. Empirical evidences suggest that movements are not necessarily permanent but many times circular and seasonal as migrants try to capture the economic benefits of both rural and urban areas.

Environmental Considerations for Rural Resources and Migration

It is increasingly being recognized that a significant driving force behind rural to urban migration is the lack of access by poor households to natural resources. Empirical studies shows that there is a strong economic relationship between direct access to natural resources and the sustainability of livelihood in rural areas. Poor households depend greatly on environmental natural resources to meet their minimum needs. Like harvesting forest materials, fishing or collecting fuelwood, etc., which supplements their farming or off farming employment. Therefore, to the rural household income, this is part of a "portfolio" of earnings contributing to total household earnings, which is both subsistence and income as well. But in recent past governmental policies have greatly restricted access and exploitation of these resources. The conservation policies which protect rural environmental natural resources by restricting local communities from accessing subsistence resources and changes in land tenure associated with certain types of rural development and conservation investments prevent access to environmental resources and inadvertently create poverty which stimulates migration.

Conflict, Instability and Migration

The increasing globalization of the development process also affects natural socio-economic and political changes even in the remote rural settlement. This instability makes the marginalized rural population difficult to guarantee the conditions for survival. This also leads to migration for protecting themselves as well as sustaining their living. Famine, riots, land acquisition are some examples for migration instigated by regional or even local instability and conflicts.

Migration and Gender

The causes, nature and outcomes of urbanization are found to be highly gendered. Gender selective migration reflects a range of social and economic imperatives and constraints surrounding men's and women's activities, power and status in rural communities. It also induces new patterns of behaviour, access to resources and social organization (UNDP, 1996). Migration tends to be male dominated in India because women's chances of getting job is lower than livelihood possibilities in rural areas. With income being the important motive for migration, it is recognized that women may not move to urban areas under their own volition, but at the behest or through pressure from their rural families (UNDP,1996). Traditionally, women are responsible to take care of the general well-being of other household members than their male counterparts. In some cases their migration is resisted so that remittances continue to flow for the benefit of her extended family.

Flow of Materials and Goods

Raw materials derived from the extraction of natural resources in rural areas tend to flow towards urban centres where most of the industrial transformation and manufacturing are based. Rapid urbanization draws enormous amounts of resources into urban centres from its hinterland. Theoretically, rural links to urban markets supposed to promote the purchase of key inputs for rural agriculture from adjacent urban areas, which would spur the productivity and income in rural areas. This may lead to increases in purchasing power of rural population creating demand for manufactured urban commodities. However, the flow of goods from urban to rural areas have not been up to the expectations. On the contrary, rural resources are often depleted in the urban expansion and development process. This in many ways depletes the resource base for rural production and fails to generate local economic linkages beyond the extractive process. In such a situation, rural and urban regions are unable to build on the synergies that have been expected of them. There is an urgent need to link towns and cities with rural production in a more positive way. This would gradually offer opportunities to improve living conditions in rural areas, the very reason for which migration occurs.

Majority of rural producers are unable to participate in ever increasing urban demands due to poor collection, storage, marketing and transportation services. The institutional support is also found to be far deficient than required. Lack of credit to consistently produce at sufficient scales needed to supply urban markets or the role of middleman that discriminate against or ignore the potential of smaller, more distant producers. Generally, the access to urban markets is controlled by a few buyers, spatial monopolies and dominance over rural producers dampen economic returns to farmers and inhibit further processing of resources with the region.

The Flow of Capital

Financial flows are an important component of rural-urban interaction. There is a diverse range of ways in which capital flows between rural and urban areas occurs which can go in either direction. While there are diverse capital flows such as remittances to rural areas and urban based investments in rural areas. The dominant pattern in such flow is generally concentrated and attracted to few prosperous urban centres. An integral part of this rural to urban transfer is the concentration of resources in hands of wealthy and powerful individuals of the society. This phenomenon signified by the growing inequality and income gap between rich and poor as well as rural and urban dwellers.

The Flow of Waste

The flow of wastes between urban and rural areas is closely related to both the flows of raw materials derived from natural resources and extracting the benefits from the processing of these materials. Rural areas are the source of raw materials for almost all manufacturing and processing industries and are in advertently the base for the generation of capital. The dominant rural-urban pattern of natural resource use and waste is such that natural resources in rural areas are developed and channelled to urban centres where they are consumed and the wastes are returned back to rural areas, commonly termed as "ecological footprints of the cities".

The pattern and magnitude of flows in resources and wastes is at the core of several problems that are identified by the international community as global environmental problems, as shrinking biodiversity and forest loss, etc., urban production and consumption is a significant driving force for rural resource degradation. Both production and consumption are fed by the exploitation of resources and with the rapid acceleration of production and consumption patterns, it is widely accepted we are catapulting towards environmental breakdown.

The links between rural-urban flows of waste is circular and mostly have regional consequences. The cyclic nature of rural-urban environmental linkages is illustrated by the relationship between unsustainable livelihoods in rural and urban areas. Unsustainable levels of demand that tends to be concentrated in urban centres encourage inappropriate development and the degradation of rural environments.

The Flow of Information and Ideas

The flows of information between rural and urban places have a core function in effective development planning. Decision about the flow of materials, resources and capital flow to the rural areas with pronounced urban bias, while the ability for rural voices are somewhat limited. The poor human development of rural areas is largely attributed to poor communication linkages. The decisions about their economies and welfare from higher levels of administration are firstly made ignoring the local ground condition, secondly these decisions are filtered in such a way that benefits of these decisions are further reduced.

BOX 3.3 : Rural-Urban Linkages and Environment

It is apparent that traditional 'urban–rural' problems of resource management are not just linked, but are shared. They are shared in 'space' in terms of the ability of particular rural areas being able to sustain themselves and urban demand at a particular time, and in 'time' as the fairly environmental integrity of rural areas may not be able to sustain future generations of both rural and urban settlements.

The flow of pollutants between rural and urban places within a region illustrates how linkages between rural-urban environmental problems, though often contextual, are bidirectional. The problems of pollution are often shared in both consequences and cause by urban, periurban and rural areas. For example, municipal waste that is improperly disposed into waterways, inappropriately designed landfills and open dumps, polluting air, land and water in the vicinity. On the other hand, inappropriate agricultural practices in rural and periurban areas can result in soil erosion, siltation, lowering of underground watertable and more directly chemically contaminated food products.

The developments of information and communication technologies have helped significantly in connecting rural and urban areas more effectively and at low costs. While flows of goods and people are tangible and observable, the flows of information and ideas that usually accompany them are far more complex and difficult to research. This is partly because it is less tangible as well as the relations that structure the flows of other elements also influence the flows of ideas.

The movement of people to and from cities and the numerical growth of city dwellers have had profound effects on societies more generally. In particular, increased movement of people has resulted in increase of information.

The information flow between rural and urban areas falls in four categories:

- The information flow on resources from rural areas.
- The information flow about markets, price of agricultural and other rural commodities.

- ❖ The information flow manifested through political decision making.
- ❖ The information flow on opportunities and technologies.

The spread of mass media has helped considerably in blurring the differences in periurban interface. The people have greater access to newspaper, radio, television, phones, etc., which is facilitated by improvements in technology. Despite traditionally authoritarian state control, these mediums have showed in breaking the state control, increasing free and increased exchange of information and ideas.

4

Aligarh City's PUI : The Study Area

Aligarh City : Geographic Location

Aligarh city is a Class I city of the State of Uttar Pradesh, situated in its western part between Ganga and Yamuna rivers at 27º53´ north latitude and 78 º 35´ east longitudes. It is the headquarters of Aligarh district, spread over an area of about 44.82 square kilometres.

The district of Aligarh extends from 27 º 29´ to 28 º 11´ north latitude and 77 º 29´ to78 º 38´ east longitude. River Ganga and Yamuna makes its east and west boundary respectively while in north Bulandshahar district and in south Hathras district are situated. Aligarh district has been divided into 6 tehsils, namely Koil, Autrauli, Sikandrarao, Iglas and Khair. Aligarh city is located in Koil tehsil of Lodha block and the city lies almost in the centre of Aligarh district. Presently, Aligarh city has been divided into 70 wards. This city has gained importance because of its proximity to the national capital (New Delhi) and also known for the Aligarh Muslim University.

Aligarh City : Historical Evolution

In early history the settlement was associated with the kingdom of *Surasena*. The settlement in this region begun around 1500 B.C. An ancient town existed here which was known as *Koil* or *Kol,* named after an *Asura* king. Atkinson regards origin of Aligarh as a Buddhist settlement following 400 B.C. Around 2nd century A.D. the area came under the possessions of *Mauryas, Sakas, Kushans* and *Naga* rulers. Archaeological remains of 5th to 9th century A.D. belonging to *Gupta* period and *Harsha* empire have also recorded from Aligarh. In 10th century A.D. one of the old settlement identified in Aligarh city as *Achal Tal* (tank) area located in south-east. 12th century A.D. marks the arrival of Muslims in this region. In 1194, *Qutubuddin Aibek* took the fortress of *Kol and Balbon* and constructed *minar* tower in 1253 just close to present *Jama Masjid* on the great mound. Four dynasties namely the *Slave's* from 1194-1240, *Khilji's* from 1290-1320, *Tughlaq's* from 1320-1414 and *Lodha's* from 1451-1526 contributed to the control and construction of Aligarh. During the reign of *Ibrahim Lodhi* (1526 A.D.), a permanent fortress known as *Ramgarh* was constructed, which is still existing. *Umar Khan* built the fort of *Mohammadgarh* in 1526, which was later known as Aligarh. During the medieval period *Balai Qila* area acted as the socio-economic and political hub. Throughout this period, there were walls and gates around the city, i.e. *Madar, Delhi, Turkman, Sasni* and *Aligarh Darwaza*. In 18th century *Sabit Khan* was appointed as governor of *Kol* and he constructed the *Jama Masjid*. Marathas took over the Aligarh Fort in 1785. Thereafter the Britishers rule the city, during their rule the city spread northwards and economically progressed. After the British occupation in 1804, the present district of Aligarh was formed and the term Kol ruined. With the increase of population industries were developed. Initially cotton industry (1802) was established, beside this, other industries like crude glass, glass bangles and later lock industry were established and flourished.

The most remarkable during the evolution and development of the city was the establishment of *Mohammedan Anglo Oriental (MAO) College* in 1875 which is now known as Aligarh Muslim University. This was founded by *Sir Sayed Ahmed Khan* to educate Muslim people. Now, it is one of central university of India and is situated in Civil Line area.

Aligarh city because of its historical background and evolution consist of three different socio-cultural areas.

- The ancient area, dominated by Hindu Population.
- The medieval area, dominated by Muslim Population.
- The modern area, dominated by mixed Population of both Hindus and Muslims.

These areas instead of losing their identity with time have retained it. Incidences of communal riots have strengthened the segregation on communal lines.

Aligarh City : Physical Setting

Physiographically, the study region contains vast alluvial plains, having a gentle slope from north to south and south-east. Topographically, the district represents a shallow trough (sauce-pan shape) and it can be divided into :

- The khadar plain found mainly along the river Ganga in the east and along the Yamuna River in the west.
- Eastern and western uplands.
- The central low-lying tract.

Aligarh city is located almost in the centre of this central low lying tract. The average elevation of the city from the mean sea level is 178 metres. The flat monotonous plain of the city is dotted by several waterbodies like *Gursikharan, Sheka,* etc. The Ganga and Yamuna flowing along the boundary of Aligarh district are the source of bringing alluvial soil, which is spread over the whole of the district. The major types of soil found in the district are *domat* (clay), *baloi-domat* (sandy clay), *bhur* (sandy), *reh* (alkaline) and loam soil. Large part of Aligarh city and its environs falls under saline and alkaline type of soil (*reh*). This is mainly due to bad drainage resulting in high concentration of salts and PH value.

Aligarh city is drained by river *Kali.* It is a seasonal river and becomes very significant during rainy season. The upper *Ganga* canal and the *Hathras* branch canal and other distributaries like the *Machua* distributary, *Harduagunj* distributary, *Kohiri* distributary, *Maheshpur* minor, etc., also flow in this area. The small seasonal streams and *nalas* (drains) which have no permanent source of water like *Aligarh* drain, *Somna* drain, *Chandhana* drain and *Ahraula* drain also flow in this area.

Aligarh City : Climate

The climate of Aligarh city falls under the sub-tropical climate zone and is characterized by hot summer and chilly winter. Extreme climatic conditions can be found here because in summer the temperature reaches up to 47° C and in winter it may fall to 2° C. The summer season confined to the months of April to June, records an average temperature between 30° C to 37° C. which occasionally rises up to 47° C. Most of the rainfall occurs under the influence of South-West monsoon, in the months of July, August and September. During this period, temperature is much lower but humidity accentuates the heat .The rainfall is scanty in this area and ranges from 60-75 centimetres per annum. In winter heavy fog in the morning, lasting till afternoon and frost during nights are hallmarks of the severe winter spells especially in the month of January which is the coldest month.

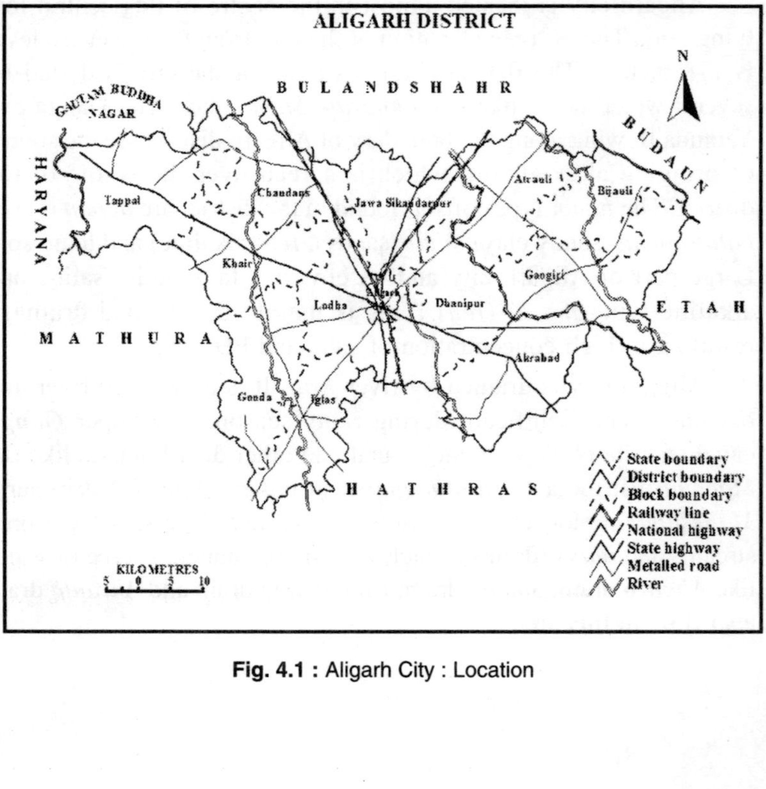

Fig. 4.1 : Aligarh City : Location

Aligarh City : Flora and Fauna

Aligarh city lies in the sub-tropical division of deciduous type of vegetation. Aligarh district was largely covered with heavy *dhak* jungles once which gradually are turned into agricultural lands. In the *khadar* of Ganga river, there is a considerable extent of *jhau* or tamarisk. Aligarh city cannot be described as wooded. The most common trees found around the city are mango, *babul, neem, pipal, ber, sheesham, gular and jamun,* etc.

Aligarh City: Administrative Set-up

Aligarh city is the main urban and administrative centre of Aligarh district. Aligarh came into existence as a district in 1804. The district is further divided into six sub-districts (tehsils), each with its own divisional headquarters. These six tehsils have been further sub-divided into 17 blocks. These blocks again sub-divided into total 1,210 villages.

Aligarh city is located at the Lodha block of Koil tehsil. Municipal Corporation was formed for Aligarh city in 1975, while the formation of Aligarh Development Authority was taken place in 1981. The First Master Plan and Second Master Plan were drafted in 1981 and 2001 respectively for the city. The city which initially had 19 wards (1971), but now it is divided into 70 wards (2008) and a mayor is elected to administer the city.

Aligarh City: Marketing Centres

Aligarh city has a good number of markets to meet the requirements of the people. The CBD of Aligarh encompasses Railway road, *Phaphala, Barahdwari and Chauraha Abdul Karim.* There is an agglomeration of both wholesale and retail trade in this area. Certain areas of the city are famous for wholesale and retail goods. The important ones are *Mamu-Bhanja* area for hardware items and electronics goods, *Phaphala* for pharmaceuticals items, *Dhanipur* for vegetables and cereals and *Banski Mandi* for timber and house building materials. There are about 90 marketing centres in Aligarh city. Every locality in the city has a market centre and some of them have grown up in recent years to become new commercial hubs such as *Jamalpur, Dodhpur, Amir Nishan, Kelanagar, Kuwarsi, Soot Mill, Sasni Gate,* etc.

Aligarh City: Transport and Communication

There are ten major roads which all converge at Gandhi Park, almost at the centre of the city. These roads include national highway (N.H.-91) or G.T. Road which connects the city with *Delhi and Kanpur*, N.H.-93, which connects with *Anupshahar*. Apart from these roads there are several State highways which radiate out of the city to connect other important towns of the State. Among them important are *Ramghat* road, *Khair* road, *Gonda* road, *Agra* road and *Mathura* road, etc. These roads have acted as the important agent helping in the development of the city. Recently big factories and other industrial establishment have sprung up along these roads providing the city a radial dimension. Besides these roads there is well developed internal road network connecting important locations within the city. However, the roads of older city are narrow and congested while the newer part has wider roads.

There are two main bus terminals — *Masoodabad* bus terminal along G.T. Road and *Gandhi* park bus Terminal from where U.P. State Road Transport Corporation buses serve cities all over the State of Uttar Pradesh and many other cities in Uttarakhand, Rajasthan, Madhya Pradesh, Delhi, Punjab and Haryana. There are 5 other private bus terminals in Aligarh city, which connects the city with nearby rural settlements.

Aligarh is also connected with rail network, the Aligarh railway station is a railway Junction. It is on the main railway route connecting national capital Delhi with States of West Bengal, Orissa, Bihar, Jharkhand, North-Eastern States of Assam and most of the parts of U.P.

Aligarh City: Employment Opportunities

The city offers different type of occupational opportunities, which fit in to different sectors and draw different incomes. The city has well developed secondary activities where a large number of skilled

Table 4.1: Aligarh City — Passengers Movements by Bus from Different Terminals (2010)

Serial No.	*Name of the Bus Terminals*	*No. of Buses*	*Average No of Passengers*	*Name of the Route*
1.	Gandhi Park Terminal	176	8800	Lucknow, Agra, Moradabad, Mathura
2.	Masoodabad Bus Terminal	75	3375	Delhi,
3.	Khair	40	1600	Zebar, Tappal, Khair
4.	Gonda	24	760	Gonda
5.	Chharra	25	1025	Chharra, Sankar
6.	Gangiri	20	800	Gangiri
7.	Jalai	35	1400	Jalali
8.	Autaruli	33	1485	Autrauli, Ramghat, Bijauli
9.	Qasimpur Ramghat	20	800	Sadhuasram
10.	Anupshahar	90	3150	Aniupshahar, Nonora
11.	Sambhal	22	550	Sambhal
12.	Pahasu	12	370	Pahasu
13.	Barauli	12	510	Barauli
14.	Amrauli, Barauli,Pahasu	24	960	Amrauli,Barauli, Pahasu
15.	Qasimpur	20	600	Qasimpur

Source : ADA, 2001.

and semi-skilled workers (37 per cent of total workers) are engaged. The most famous is lock industry besides it other industries like engineering industries, building fitting, electrical goods industries, chemical industries have also helped the city for its development. A good number of small scale units of brass work, edible oil, sugar, cotton textile, cotton ginning, dairy, glassware, readymade garments, handloom and weaving provide jobs to the city population. The city also has a large number of people engaged in tertiary sector (61 per cent of total workers), associated with Aligarh Muslim University, other educational institutions, banks, postoffices, health, communication, trade and commerce, etc.

Aligarh City : The Population

The total population of Aligarh city is 6,69,087 according to 2001 census. With the increase of population, the city requires developments in housing, amenities and facilities and employment opportunities, etc. which as in other cities of India do not match with the city population. This leads to stress on existing facilities creating problems such as mushrooming of slums, environmental pollution, unemployment, congestion, water and electricity crisis, etc.

Table 4.2: Aligarh City — Decadal Growth of Population

Census Year	*Population*	*Difference of Population between two decade*	*Difference in per cent*
1901	72084	–	–
1911	66344	-5740	–8
1921	66963	619	0.93
1931	83878	16915	25.26
1941	112655	2877	34.31
1951	141618	28963	25.71
1961	185020	43402	30.65
1971	252314	67294	36.36
1981	320861	68547	27.17
1991	480520	159659	49.76
2001	669087	188567	39.24

Source: Census of India.

Table 4.3: Aligarh City — Working Population engaged in Different Economic Activities.

	1981		*1991*		*2011*	
Economic Activities	*No. of Workers*	*% age*	*No. of Workers*	*%age*	*No. of Workers*	*%age*
Primary	–	–	–	–	–	–
workers and	–	–	–	–	–	–
agricultural labourers	3320	5.21	4234	3.40	5648	2.43
Households workers	4253	6.68	6883	5.51	12416	5.34
Other than households industries	17615	27.65	40449	32.38	78976	33.98
Construction	1790	2.81	4206	3.37	7919	3.41
Trade and commerce	13200	20.72	29304	23.46	55412	23.85
Transportation and commu-nication	7270	11.41	7400	5.92	11510	4.95
Other activities	16250	25.52	32432	25.96	60496	26.03
Total	257065	100	490202	100	232377	100

Source: Census of India.

Aligarh City: Transformations in Agriculture based Activities

The study area receives scanty and erratic rainfall, where 80 per cent of total rainfall happens in the month of south-west monsoon from mid-June to September. Rest of the year it is mostly dry. On the other hand soil is generally sandy-loam having high rate of permeability. Thus, the agriculture is heavily depended on the irrigation especially through tubewell and canal irrigation which are expensive. The urban shadow effect is greatly affecting the agriculture activity in the surrounding rural areas of Aligarh city. The land value is increasing and the high cost of farming inputs have made small and marginal farmers vulnerable in modern monetized urban economy. This has seen as one of the reason for the trend of transformation from farming activities to non-farming activities in the study area. Another cause of livelihood transformation is high growth of population which is resulting fragmented and smaller landholdings. All this is making agriculture, which was preferred livelihood option as lesser favoured occupation.

Aligarh City: Evolvement of Periurban Interface

Rural areas surrounding the Aligarh city lack the amenities and facilities like employment in secondary and tertiary sectors, education, transportation-communication system, water supply, etc., which are available in the city. These availabilities are the pull factor to attract migrants from the surrounding villages. The influx of migration into the city caused the residential population to grow and the city expanded physically to accommodate it, first through the development of vacant land within the city itself, and later by the slow encroachment on land in areas lying outside the city limits. The net result has been the intrusion of urban land-uses within the rural areas surrounding the rapidly growing Aligarh city.

There is a particular pattern of stages through which village community (surrounding Aligarh city) passes as the villages get transformed from a rural entity to an urban one. The increase in population by natural growth and migration in Aligarh city, it expanded from city centre towards surrounding villages to accommodate these people. The village economy gets tied up with the growing city. There is phenomenal increase in linkages with daily movement from the village to the city in order to supply the different commodities such as perishables, like vegetables, milk, and flowers or low valued natural resources such as bricks, earth, fuel wood, etc., to the city. There are metalled roads connecting the peripheral rural settlements with Aligarh city and even the city transport system also extends its services to these settlements. Daily visits to the city for job, domestic requirements, recreation and medical facilities have become increasingly important. With time and improvements in the communication and transport facilities, the linkage with the city has improved significantly. The village in the fringe area is no longer inhabited by traditional village population only. It also becomes a living place for industrial workers, etc., who like to take advantage of comparatively low rents. Thus the rural settlements around the Aligarh city have evolved into rural-urban fringe. The city spreads in Lodha, Akrabad, Sasni, Dhanipur, Jawan, Atrauli, Iglas, Gonda and Khair blocks. Many of these areas were, till recent past were predominantly rural settlements but now absorbed the urban character also. Many villages have come into the direct influence of urban expansion and now lie in the urban limit. Kishanpur, Dodhpur, Begpur, Jamalpur, Bhamola and Nagla Baraula are all examples of urban absorption as these settlement witnessed in mute silence their transformation from rural to urban.

5

Aligarh City's PUI : Features of Livelihoods

The PUI is described as a complex zone spatially located between urban and rural areas where livelihoods of the population are under constant pressure from urban forces. The nature of the PUI varies considerably according to the level of urbanization, the economy and the geographical location from urban centre. It is a common understanding that urban growth has not only impacts over natural and built environment but also livelihoods of people living in the PUI. Urbanization offers livelihood choices for people in the PUI and also enables them of better access to urban services and infrastructure. This provides opportunities for them to exploit benefits from both urban and rural activities. In this sense PUI is symbiotically interlinked with urban and rural areas. Yet, urbanization is also accompanied by intense competition for land, tenure insecurity, population pressure, stressed infrastructure and polluted environment. The urbanization processes in many cases have posed threat to traditional livelihood practices. These situations and the monetized economy in PUI have significantly affected the natural resource based primary economic activity and also result in the poverty and vulnerability to the livelihoods of poor people.

Livelihood

Livelihoods are the ways in which people satisfy their needs or gain a living (Chambers and Conway, 1992). A livelihood is a set of flows of income, which comes from a variety of sources and activities; however, it happens to be variable over time. Scones (1998) defines, livelihood as all the activities forming the means of generating a living, also that they are dynamic in that they respond to external pressure and opportunity.

A livelihood comprises the assets (natural, physical, human, financial and social capital), the activities and the access to these (mediated by institutions and social relations) that together determine the living gained by the individual or household (Frank Ellis, 2000). Every individual or household avails the opportunity differently, it is a continuous evolving process which changes with time (season to season and year to year). The activity may change depending upon the opportunity and access to resources. Similarly, the assets can also be increased or decreased depending upon the individual's ability to adopt and his performance in his activity.

Livelihood in PUI

The livelihood in Aligarh's PUI can be categorized into two broad categories — cash based livelihood and non-cash based livelihood.

The Non-Cash based Livelihood

The households engaged in non-cash based livelihood in PUI, are engaged with food production, fuel or fodder collection from common land. But this form of livelihood has been almost wiped out in Aligarh's PUI. In Aligarh's PUI, the urban elements linked to the growing importance of inclusion within a monetized economy while the rural element was linked to depleting natural resources. Poor people lacked control over these changes in PUI which adversely affecting their non-cash based livelihood in particular.

This was most glaring around the natural resources, destruction of natural and common resources (common land, forest and water-bodies) to urban space demands, loss of soil fertility (due to extraction of construction materials, dumping of garbage) insecurity of tenure (due to opportunistic farming practices) and soil and water pollution (due to urban wastes). The pressure of growing populations made natural common resources as the most contested asset in the PUI. Political empowerment at grass root level has also led to encroach upon the common natural resources. At some places the common resources are used for the benefit of community while at other places using it for the benefit of their own clan or caste. But in most cases and places, general deterioration and disappearance of common land is observed. All this led to reduction in the availability of the natural resource based products needed to support traditional non-cash based livelihood elements. The households which were dependent on these common lands for their livelihood have now either earn livelihood from labouring in rural areas or they have migrated to city where they sell labour for cash returns. Here, the sample survey found that women (old, widow, abandoned by family) are the main sufferers, who now cannot labour to earn with disappearing common land and they are at the mercy of government aid (*vridhavastha pension*).

The Cash Based Livelihoods

Cash based periurban livelihoods can be categorized in four broad categories. These are livelihoods based on casual employment, livelihoods based on business and trade, livelihoods based on farming activity and livelihoods based on dairy farming.

Cash Based Casual Employment

The casual employment in Aligarh's PUI has many dimensions. Most of the lesser educated and lesser skilled workers belong to this category. There is ever increasing demands for this low level, mostly labour oriented jobs in PUI. The employment opportunity of this kind is typically casual, short term and seasonal in nature fetching low and varying wages.

This kind of labour work can be divided into two categories:

- *Labouring in Agricultural Sector:* In this type of employment the wages are comparatively lesser. This is despite of competition for labour apparently driving agricultural wage levels higher. This kind of labouring in the Aligarh's PUI has a peculiar feature, there is considerable shortage of labour in the agricultural sector but its remuneration does not increases to the levels of labour in non-agricultural sector of urban areas.

Another feature of this kind of labouring is that it is highly seasonal and is not gender biased. In fact women are found to have almost equal opportunity for work. However, the wages for women are little lesser than their male counterparts. Another feature of this kind of livelihood is that male members during peak demand (farming seasons — especially sowing or harvesting) come back from urban centres and join this sector for limited period, till they are required and afterwards they return back to the urban centre. This seasonal migration to them is like "*Paid holiday*". As they take leave from work in urban areas, join their families and also earn. They also take advantage of this period for managing social events during their stay with the family.

This type of labour in the agricultural sector is highly seasonal which is the main reason for the male members of the households to work outside agricultural sector for sustaining their livelihoods.

- *Labouring Outside Agricultural Sector:* This is a cash based livelihood opportunity mostly in unorganized sector, a common feature of PUI. It is adopted by households belonging to rural poor, uneducated, unskilled landless or small-uneconomic landholdings, week and downtrodden section of the society. Traditionally, these labourers worked in the rural agricultural sector, many of them were exploited with poor wages. The PUI offered them opportunities to sell their labour for remittance in cash.

  This provided an opening for rural labourers to move away from primary sector and earn relatively higher wages, but these kinds of employment also have some inherent drawbacks. These are typically casual, seasonal, short term 'by day' employment. The urban proximity is an important requirement for this kind of employment. Another feature of this employment is that it is highly gender biased with male dominance.

> A great variety of activities draw labourers to work for secondary and tertiary sector in PUI. Importantly, although they get associated with higher level of economic activity (secondary and tertiary) but they do not possess any skill or expertise and only sell their labour. They work in factories as labourers or porters, construction workers, quarrying, brick making, rickshaw pulling, rag picking, watchman, domestic helpers, scavengers, cleaners, etc. Among all these activities, factory worker is most preferred because of regularity of work while construction works fetch best wages.

These activities also have specific spatial existence. The PUI of Aligarh has dominance of different pockets of activity in different locations. Like, industrial area, where industrial labourers are required, university and civil lines area require domestic workers, rickshaw pullers, watchmen, etc., while Ramghat, Agra and Mathura Road, etc. (mostly newer part of the city), have demand for construction workers.

Another feature which was observed in this cash based employment outside agricultural activity was that labourers were found to make frequent changes to their work. Interestingly these changes were not mainly for better wages (as there was no big difference) but for easier less labour oriented work.

The common theme for this cash based employment outside agricultural sector is that it is more pronounced for males. There were cultural limitations on what women can do in Indian rural society. It was considered socially degrading for women to have work outside family enterprise. Interestingly, this tradition was applied for only off farm activity. There was no such attitude for in-farm activities. The domestic duties of women also restrict them to work outside their homes. Women only from immediate PUI villages were found to work outside agricultural sector. This indicates towards evolvement of a different social class, with modified values in PUI.

BOX 5.1 : Differences in the Characteristics of the Poor in Urban, Periurban and Rural Areas

Livelihoods	*Poor in urban*	*Poor in PUI*	*Poor in rural*
	Poor are concentrated in the informal economy, trades and as domestic labourers.	Poor are involved in both agricultural and in the urban informal sector. The very poor in the PUI are typically agricultural labourers.	Poor are involved mainly in agricultural work.
Nature of and reasons for migration	The urban poor do not tend to migrate back to villages. When they migrate it is permanent and often to other cities in search of urban jobs such as the construction industry.	The periurban poor are involved in circular migration commuting back and forth from cities to villages for shorter period from daily to weekly commuting.	The rural poor migrate due to distress factors, sometimes seasonally, sometimes permanently.
Types of wage	Wages are paid in cash.	Wages are paid in cash for labour.	Wages are paid in cash and/ or in kind.
Opportunities	There are more opportunities to find work throughout the year.	Some of the poor have the opportunity to work both in agriculture or take advantage of urban and periurban opportunities. Others cannot avail of urban opportunities due to lack of skills, health, alcoholism, lesser mobility, particularly the females. This group also suffers the negative consequences of urbanization in the form of insufficient well paid work in the PUI.	Work is agriculturally related and completely season bound. The majority do not work in the off-season periods, but a small minority engage in small enterprises.
Human capital	The poor have varied skills relevant to petty business and jobs in the informal sector.	The poor who seek urban opportunities may not be as skilled as their urban counterparts. The periurban youth try to pick up urban skills or skills related to agriculture which they can encash in the cities (gardening).	The poor have skilled relevant to agriculture.
Government programmes	Government programmes are designed to target the urban poor. However, the access is limited and depends on local influential people.	Villages in the PUI have a mixed scenario. Those under the Municipal Corporation have no access to rural government programmes or subsidized credit, but some urban facilities are provided. They enjoy only partial benefits compared to the truly urban population but also have to pay higher taxes than rural villages. Villages under the Panchayati Raj System have access to all the rural development programmes.	Government programmes cater to the needs of rural poor. whereas in the recent past developments have taken place. The governmental efforts as well as local population awareness have contributed for this change.

Table 5.1: Aligarh PUI — Sampled Households Association with Different Types of Tertiary Activities (2009-10).

Engagement in Tertiary Sector	*Immediate PUI (Upto 5 km)*	*Intermediate PUI (5 – 10 km)*	*Distant PUI(10 km and above)*	*Total*
Teachers	14	4	2	20
Traders	19	6	—	25
Semi-skilled workers (Carpenter, Plumber, Electrician)	27	8	1	36
Un-skilled workers (Rickshaw pullers, Construction/ Brick/Quarry workers)	22	9	1	32
Others	10	3	—	13
Total Tertiary Sector	92	30	4	126

Note: Figures are in absolute number of sampled respondents in the particular distance zones.
Source: Based on Field Survey (2009-10).

Cash Based Off Farm Livelihood in Tertiary Sector

One striking feature observed in Aligarh's PUI was declining preference to agricultural activity as livelihood option among younger generation. This change had a clear periurban character, becoming particularly strong with proximity to the city, where people also have a greater choice of livelihood options. The people were also found to make more and frequent changes to their livelihoods in immediate PUI than distant PUI.

The immediate PUI had reported a wide and diverse range of income generating activities, mostly requiring some skills (most of them are craft based, artisanal activities or providing lower level services) and found to be employed by some organized group or self employed. The people belonging to this section were relatively younger, have attained some level of education but were distancing themselves from labour oriented agricultural activities. This younger PUI population prefer to work and stay in urban area, enjoy the advantages of urban infrastructure and perform a wide range of activities which require some skills such as, mason, carpenter, driver, tailor, welder, plumber, electrician, hair dresser, auto mechanic, etc. If they do not qualify for any of these activities then they opt for small time trading which is also one of the livelihood options for this section. The urban proximity is essential for these activities because they are required only in urban areas.

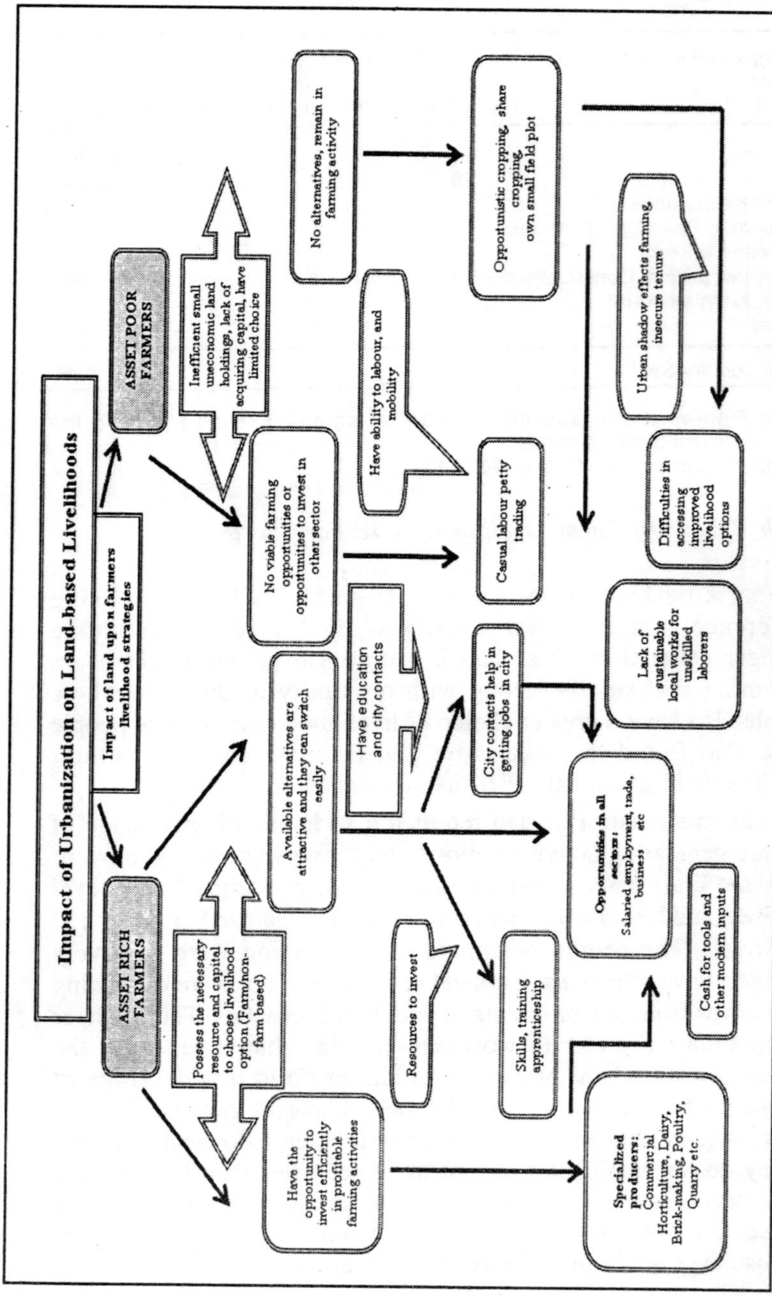

Fig. 5.1 : Impact of Urbanization on Land-based Livelihoods

BOX 5.2 : PUI Youth and Education

The youth in PUI had some exposure to education. This is an important phenomenon of PUI, where education certainly has made inroads in the society and every section of the society has some level of education. But this education does not guarantee employment opportunities in urban area (especially white collar job, for which they aspire). This is a very critical situation among the PUI youth, leading to frustration, desperation and depression. They have education (academic degrees) and they now do not want to associate themselves with traditional agricultural activity and working on farms. So the easiest option is to open a shop with small capital. In most cases their sustenance is difficult but they pursue with it to have a better social status, which is higher in trading than of soil cultivation.

Table 5.2: Aligarh PUI — Sampled Households Association with Different Types of Economic Activities (2009-10).

Type of Economic Activity Associated	*Immediate PUI (Up to 5 km)*	*Intermediate PUI (5 – 10 km)*	*Distant PUI (10 km and above)*	*Total*
Only Crop Cultivation	**34** *(16)* (9.1)	**70** *(33)* (32.9)	**108** *(51)* (58.7)	**212**
Crop Cultivation + Dairy Farming	**138** *(45.1)* (37.1)	**96** *(31.3)* (45.1)	**72** *(23.5)* (39.1)	**306**
Primary Activity	**172** *(33.2)* (46.2)	**166** *(32)* (77.9)	**180** *(34.7)* (97.8)	**518**
Secondary Activity	**108** *(86.4)* (29.03)	**17** *(13.6)* (7.9)	—	**125**
Tertiary Activity	**92** *(73)* (24.7)	**30** *(23.8)* (14.1)	**4** *(3.2)* (2.2)	**126**

Note : (i) Figures in bold are absolute number of sampled respondents in the particular distance zones.

(ii) Figures in brackets (besides the bold figures) are percentages to the total of that particular variable.

(iii) Figures in brackets (below the bold figures) are percentages to the total from that particular distance zone.

Source: Based on field survey (2009-10).

Livelihood as Crop Cultivation

The PUI, surrounding urban areas is one of the most critical areas of human acumen. It is not the extent of the resource base contained in the PUI that makes it critical to society, but rather the fact that the land and resources therein are subject to competing, often conflicting, demands. The PUI has been placed under pressure increasingly with increased demand due to rapidly changing social, cultural and economic values associated with land and its resources. The rapid sprawl of cities, outside its political boundaries and beyond its real physical-cultural domain possesses several attendant conflicts and stresses and has also stimulated various adaptations of human activities. These are reflected through diverse facets, especially changing periurban and adjacent or interstitial rural land-uses.

Table 5.3 : Aligarh PUI — Sampled Household Way of Execution of Primary Activities (2009-10).

Execution of Primary Activity	*Immediate PUI (Up to 5 km)*	*Intermediate PUI (5 – 10 km)*	*Distant PUI (10 km and above)*	*Total*
Purely Subsistence	—	**51** *(34.9)* (30.7)	**95** *(65.1)* (52.7)	**146** (28.2)
Purely Commercial	**54** *(45.4)* (31.4)	**40** *(33.6)* (24.1)	**25** *(21)* (13.9)	**119** (22.9)
Mixed	**118** *(46.6)* (68.6)	**75** *(29.6)* (45.2)	**60** *(23.7)* (33.3)	**253** (48.8)
Total Primary	**172** *(33.2)* (46.2)	**166** *(32)* (77.9)	**180** *(34.7)* (97.8)	**518**

Note: (i) Figures in bold are absolute number of sampled respondents in the particular distance zones.
(ii) Figures in brackets (besides the bold figures) are percentages to the total of that particular variable.
(iii) Figures in brackets (below the bold figures) are percentages to the total from that particular distance zone.

Source: Based on field survey (2009-10).

The sample survey in Aligarh's PUI was spread over a total of 21 villages. A total of 769 households were sampled out of which 518 (67.3%) households were indulged in primary activities. This suggests that primary activity in Aligarh's PUI is still the main livelihood component among sampled households. Significantly, only 212 (27.5%) households were depended on crop cultivation alone, while remaining 306 (39.8%) were supplementing with dairying activity along with crop cultivation. This shows that households in Aligarh's PUI were diversifying their livelihoods to enhance their earnings. This argument is also strengthen by the fact that this trend was found to be more dominant among households in villages closer to the city. The survey shows that 138 (45.1%) households in *immediate* PUI were engaged in both dairying and crop cultivation activity while only 34 (16%) of households in this zone were depended only on crop cultivation. However, the crop cultivation becomes more prominent with the distance from the city as *intermediate* PUI had 70 (33%) and *distant* PUI reported 108 (51%) households.

Table 5.4: Aligarh PUI – Size of Landholdings among Sampled Households (2009-10).

Size of Land-holding	*Immediate PUI (Upto 5 km)*	*Intermediate PUI (5 – 10 km)*	*Distant PUI (10 km and above)*	*Total*
Large (more than 10 hectares)	**4** *(6.3)* (2.3)	**23** *(36.5)* (13.8)	**36** *(57.1)* (20)	**63** (12.2)
Medium(4 – 10 hectares)	**41** *(25.8)* (23.8)	**60** *(37.7)* (36.1)	**58** *(36.5)* (32.2)	**159** (30.7)
Small (Less than 4 hectares)	**127** *(42.9)* (73.8)	**83** *(28)* (50)	**86** *(29.1)* (47.8)	**296** (57.1)
Total Primary	**172** *(33.2)* (46.2)	**166** *(32)* (77.9)	**180** *(34.8)* (97.8)	**518**

Note : (i) Figures in bold are absolute number of sampled respondents in the particular distance zones.

(ii) Figures in brackets (besides the bold figures) are percentages to the total of that particular variable.

(iii) Figures in brackets (below the bold figures) are percentages to the total from that particular distance zone.

Source: Based on field survey (2009-10).

BOX 5.3 : Conditions for Diversification of Livelihoods of the Poor

Research shows that agriculture continues to be the most important source of livelihoods for the poor. But this is not necessarily from choice. Often, it is because they are trapped in low return employment and rainfed cultivation, due to a lack of other remunerative options and the inability to break away from impoverishing agrarian arrangements. The poor are trying to diversify both within agriculture and away from it. The factors that have enabled the poor to pursue these options include access to informal credit and political patronage, social networks, entrepreneurial skills, education and access to information. The factors that limit them are their caste status, gender and location.

Deshingkar *et al.* (2002)

In this section we are focusing only on crop cultivation and try to analyze the cropping pattern, factors associated with this activity and emerging trends and patterns of farming activity in Aligarh's PUI.

Landholding in Aligarh's PUI

A total of 518 households out of 769 sampled households have reported associated with farming activity. Out of these 518 households, 63 were categorized as large farmers (farm size of more than 10 hectares), 159 were categorized as medium farmers (farm size of 4 – 10 hectares) and remaining 296 were categorized as small farmers (farm size of less than 4 hectares). Spatially, the sample survey finds that in the *immediate* PUI (closer to the city) the landholdings are smaller and with increases in distance from the city, the size of landholdings are bigger. This suggests that closer to the city, there is intense pressure on land by urban forces to accommodate expanding urban population, resulting in fragmentation of land.

Nature of Farming Activity in Aligarh's PUI

The sample survey of 518 households associated with farming activity reveals that there was fair degree of commercialization in their economic activities. It was found that almost half of these 518 households were first fulfilling their own requirements and surplus primary productions are disposed of in the market to get cash returns. Another 23 per cent were producing commodities only for markets. These producers were selling their entire productions to market for cash returns. The remaining 28 per cent were subsistence producers, they have reported to consume most of their productions themselves and very rarely they are left with surplus productions for market disposal. These subsistence producers are mostly small land owners, where they are unable to produce enough to meet with their requirements. Their economic activity has subsistence orientation largely due to small (uneconomic) landholdings which restrict them in commercializing. Significantly, distance from city has crucial bearing on nature of farming activity. The sample survey suggests that closer to the city have higher degree of commercialization and it decreases as we move away from city. There were no subsistence producers in the *immediate* PUI, on the contrary 65 per cent of the subsistence producers were in *distant* PUI. This suggests that closer to the city, there is intense urban forces resulting in higher degree of commercialization.

Modifications in Farming Activity in Aligarh's PUI

Another important information which was collected from the Aligarh's PUI was about modifications in farming activity. It was obvious that proximity to city would have greater urban and market forces as well as higher level of commercialization. The farmers would also try to maximize their returns and explore newer options for drawing maximum returns. The sample survey suggests that 27.6 per cent respondents were concern for better marketing and management for their farm products. Especially, producers from *immediate* PUI acting in urban system were found to be exploring most for possibilities of better marketing and management for their products. The PUI producers also showed interests in extension services offered by governmental agencies for upgrading their traditional skills. This modification was helping them in judiciously utilizing their stressed resources in PUI. There is intense pressure of urban and market forces on farming activity, which over the period of time has become stressed livelihood option especially among younger respondents. The PUI offers better and relatively easier opportunities in secondary and tertiary sector, attracting people from farming sector. This lure of off farm employment has led to land leasing and share cropping as one of the changes in farming system of Aligarh's PUI.

Table 5.5: Aligarh PUI — Provisions of Agricultural Inputs among Sampled Households (2009-10).

Provision of Agricultural Inputs	*Immediate PUI (Up to 5 km)*	*Intermediate PUI (5 – 10 km)*	*Distant PUI (10 km and above)*	*Total*
Irrigation	**172** *(35.2)* (100)	**156** *(31.9)* (93.9)	**160** *(32.8)* (88.9)	**488** (94.2)
High Yielding Variety Seeds	**157** *(34.9)* (91.3)	**144** *(32.1)* (86.7)	**148** *(32.9)* (82.2)	**449** (86.7)
Chemical Fertilizers	**149** *(35)* (86.6)	**139** *(32.7)* (83.7)	**137** *(32.2)* (76.1)	**425** (82)
Pesticides	**39** *(44.3)* (22.7)	**27** *(30.7)* (16.2)	**22** *(25)* (12.2)	**88** (16.9)
Mechanical Tools & Equipments	**110** *(30.2)* (63.9)	**126** *(34.6)* (75.9)	**128** *(35.2)* (71.1)	**364** (70.3)

Note : (i) Figures in bold are absolute number of sampled respondents in the particular distance zones.
(ii) Figures in brackets (besides the bold figures) are percentages to the total of that particular variable.
(iii) Figures in brackets (below the bold figures) are percentages to the total from that particular distance zone.

Source: Based on field survey (2009-10).

Provision of Agricultural Inputs

The study area lies in a relatively prosperous region of the country, where inputs of green revolution were adopted successfully. That is why the farms of Aligarh's PUI have reported higher level of application for agricultural inputs. The basic inputs of green revolution like irrigation (94.2%), high yielding varieties of seeds (86.7%), chemical fertilizers (82%), etc., were widely used by the sampled cultivators. But again the application of these inputs were found to be more in farms closer to the city, while its application declines with distance. Especially, the use of insecticides and pesticides were found to be used more in *immediate* PUI. This mainly because of production of vegetables and flowers in this zone, similarly, the use of mechanical equipments (tractors, harvesters, threshers, etc.) have been reported a little more in *distant* PUI, mainly because of relatively larger landholdings.

Table 5.6: Aligarh PUI – Area under Major Crops in the Farms of Sampled Households (2009-10).

Crop Share	*Immediate PUI (Upto 5 km)*	*Intermediate PUI (5 – 10 km)*	*Distant PUI (10 km and above)*	*Total*
Cereals	**224** *(14.3)* (33.9)	**463** *(29.6)* (52)	**875** *(56)* (67.9)	**1562** (55)
Pulses	**67** *(16.8)* (10.1)	**124** *(31.2)* (13.9)	**206** *(51.9)* (16)	**397** (13.9)
Oil Seeds	**99** *(26)* (14.9)	**128** *(33.6)* (14.4)	**154** *(40.4)* (11.9)	**381** (13.4)
Vegetables	**185** *(53)* (27.9)	**139** *(39.8)* (15.6)	**25** *(7.1)* (1.9)	**349** (12.3)
Others	**86** *(57.7)* (13)	**36** *(24.2)* (4)	**27** *(18.1)* (2.1)	**149** (5.2)

Note : (i) Figures in bold are absolute number of sampled respondents in the particular distance zones.
(ii) Figures in brackets (besides the bold figures) are percentages to the total of that particular variable.
(iii) Figures in brackets (below the bold figures) are percentages to the total from that particular distance zone.

Source: Based on field survey (2009-10).

Cropping Pattern adopted by Farmers in Aligarh's PUI

The sample survey of 518 households involved in farming activity reported to own a total of 2,838 hectares of land. The entire land is used for agriculture in *rabi* season while in *kharif* season 94 per cent (2,668 hectares) of total land was under agriculture, leaving the remaining land as fallow. There are two main agricultural seasons namely, *rabi* and *kharif.* Rabi season pertains to the winter period, it is the main dry crop season, while *kharif* season pertains to the rainy period. The main crops in *rabi* season are wheat, mustard, peas and gram, while in *kharif* season the important crops are rice, maize and *arhar*. Different varieties of vegetables, flower, fruits and *chara* are reported to be grown all round the year.

The cropping pattern is found to be greatly influenced by urban proximity and some crops like vegetables, peas, *arhar,* flowers (roses and marigold) and *chara,* etc., have substantial acreage, these commodities are basically grown to meet the urban demands. Whereas, farms at *distant* PUI have shown subsistence orientation in their cropping pattern, as the cropping pattern was dominated by foodgrains.

Farmers in Immediate *PUI*

Among the farms in *immediate* PUI, about 33 per cent was under cereals, oilseeds 15 per cent, pulses 10 per cent but significantly vegetables were devoted to 27.9 per cent and other cash crops 13 per cent (flowers, fruits and *chara*) of total land. It was noticed that farmers in *immediate* PUI grow largely cereals for their subsistence requirements. Here they are growing cereals which require lesser inputs, labour and investments (wheat and maize needs lesser inputs than rice). Farmers in *immediate* PUI faces the urban shadow effect the most, which in all sense restrict agricultural activity in *immediate* PUI. But despite of urban forces, most of them adverse for farming activity, the farmers in *immediate* PUI were also benefited from urban proximity. The cropping intensity, efficiency and provision of inputs were relatively higher in Aligarh's PUI. The farmers in *immediate* PUI were found to be most responsive to factors such as agricultural commodity price, yield and crop prospects. These factors reflect the high degree of commercialization in *immediate* PUI farms. The main problem for farming activity in *immediate* PUI was reported to be non-availability of timely and adequate labourers. The farmers in *immediate* PUI manage to get funds relatively easily and that is why availability of inputs is not a big problem for them. They also take risks and grow crops like vegetables, flowers, mustard, gram, etc., which they grow for the urban market. These crops are very important for farmers in *immediate* PUI, their survival is greatly dependent on these crops, which also fetch them good income on daily basis. The striking feature of vegetable growers in *immediate* PUI is that it is depended on urban sewage or waste water for irrigating these farms (there are five drains around the city, which carries city sewage and waste water).

Farmers in Intermediate *PUI*

Farmers in *intermediate* PUI were reported to devote 52 per cent of their land to the cultivation of cereals followed by vegetables

(15.6%), and oilseeds (14.4%). The farmers in *intermediate* PUI also have good share of their lands under cash crops because of their remunerative nature and assured urban market. The share of urban market oriented crops among farmers in *intermediate* PUI is also high, although these crops need high inputs and the chances of crop failure is always there but these farmers take risks and in return they get comparatively high profits. Vegetables have substantial share in their cropping pattern in both *rabi* and *kharif* season, even other crops such as peas, gram and *arhar* can also be put into vegetable category as they have same demand and use in the city. Another crop — *chara* grown in *kharif* season, its acreage is also influenced by urban proximity. *Chara* is basically a fodder crop, which has significant demand as the region have well developed household dairy activity and farmers supplement their income by domesticating some cattle (buffaloes and cows). Almost 80 per cent of the *chara* grown by the sampled farmers are grown on large farms. Farmers in *intermediate* PUI are the most progressive farmers of the Aligarh's PUI. These farmers take agriculture activity seriously and consider it as a business and their livelihood is largely based on agriculture. They take advantage of relative proximity to the city as all the adverse impact of urbanization process on agriculture is absorbed by the farmers in *immediate* PUI. Thus, the farmers in this PUI zone are at advantage both in terms of site and situation. They provide all the necessary inputs, that is why the yield in their farms are higher than others. The farmers of *intermediate* PUI were found to be most responsive to factors such as agricultural commodity price, yield and crop prospects. These factors reflect the high degree of commercialization in *intermediate* PUI farms. The main problem for farming activity in *intermediate* PUI was reported to be non-availability of timely and adequate provisions of irrigation, HYV seeds and labourers. These farmers were also concern of government policies and plans and make their farming decisions keeping an eye on governmental policies.

Farmers in **Distant** *PUI*

The farmers in *distant PUI* were found to be allocating little over half of their total land to cereals (52.7%), which is used as the staple food for the family but these cereal crops are also remunerative to grow because they have assured market and government and semi-government agencies procure cereals from their farms. Rest of the crops grown by farmers in *distant* PUI clearly indicates towards lesser influence of urban markets. As apart from cereals (wheat, rice and maize), the other crops are gram, *arhar* and mustard which are although commercial crops but they are not grown for direct disposal for city requirements. Vegetables are also grown but for self-consumption only and not for urban market. It was observed that farmers from *distant* PUI were affected by the cost, adequate and timely availability of irrigation water and HYV seeds. It was observed that due to farness from city the easy availability and distribution of agricultural inputs were relatively poor in *distant* PUI. But despite of farness from the city farmers of *distant* PUI were growing crops which were remunerative and commercial in nature. But these crops were not directly meant for city demands and being disposed of to either wholesalers at village site itself or at agricultural *mandi's*.

Factors influencing Agricultural Practices in the Sample Farms

Several factors influence the decision making process of the farmers regarding their farm practices. But some factors may be more dominating than others among particular category of farms. It varies from farm to farm. We tried to investigate the important factors influencing the farm practices and cropping pattern of the sample farmers in the study region. The 518 sampled households were asked questions, relating to the various factors influencing them in the selection of crops. We tried to persuade them to point out only one factor, which influenced them most. But most of the farmers insisted that only one factor was not responsible but there were more than one factor. We have taken all those factors, which were pointed out by the sample farmers. These were then arranged in descending order and the top ten factors were taken into consideration [Table 5.7(a) and 5.7(b).]

The factors which were effecting the decision making process of the sample farmers are discussed below:

Table 5.7 (a): Aligarh PUI—Factors influencing Agricultural Practices in the Sampled Households (2009-10)

Immediate PUI Households			*Intermediate PUI Households*		
Rank	*Factors*	*No. of Farmers*	*Rank*	*Factors*	*No. of Farmers*
1.	Price	**59** (34.3)	1.	Price	**84** (50.6)
2.	Yield	**53** (30.8)	2.	Yield	**55**(33.1)
3.	Crop Prospect	**42** (24.4)	3.	Crop Prospect	**47** (28.3)
4.	Labour	**27** (15.7)	4.	Irrigation Facilities	**29** (17.5)
5.	Irrigation Facilities	**17** (9.9)	5.	Availability of HYV.	**16** (9.6)
6.	Govt. Policies	**15** (8.8)	6.	Labour	**16** (9.6)
7.	Physical Factors	**12** (6.9)	7.	Govt. Policies	**16** (9.6)
8.	Traditions	**8** (4.6)	8.	Financial Problems	**9** (5.4)
9.	Financial Problems	**3** (1.7)	9.	Physical Factors	**7** (4.2)
10.	Availability of HYV.	**1** (0.6)	10.	Traditions	**5** (3)
	Total	**166**		**Total**	**172**

Note : 1. Figures in bold are absolute number of sampled respondents in the particular distance zones.
2. Figures in brackets are percentages to the total respondents.
3. Total number of respondents is more than the sampled households because all the factors pointed by farmers were taken into consideration.

Source: Based on Field Survey (2009-10).

Table 5.7 (b): Aligarh PUI — Factors influencing Agricultural Practices in the Sampled Households (2009-10)

Distant PUI Households			*Total Sampled Households*		
Rank	*Factors*	No. of *Farmers*	*Rank*	*Factors*	No. of *Farmers*
1.	Irrigation Facilities	**82** (45.6)	1.	Price	**196** (37.8)
2.	Availability of HYV	**62** (34.4)	2.	Yield	**159** (30.7)
3.	Prices	**53** (29.4)	3.	Crop Prospects	**137** (26.4)
4.	Yield	**51** (28.3)	4.	Irrigation Facilities	**128** (24.7)
5.	Crop Prospects	**48** (26.7)	5.	Availability of HYV	**79** (15.2)
6.	Financial Problems	**41** (22.8)	6.	Labour	**56** (10.8)
7.	Traditions	**31** (17.2)	7.	Financial Problems	**53** (10.2)
8.	Physical Factors	**20** (11.1)	8.	Govt. Policies	**48** (9.3)
9.	Govt. Policies	**17** (9.4)	9.	Traditions	**44** (8.5)
10.	Labour	**13** (7.2)	10.	Physical Factors	**39** (7.5)
	Total	**180**		**Total**	**518**

Notes: 1. Figures in bold are absolute number of sampled respondents in the particular distance zones.
2. Figures in brackets are percentages to the total respondents.
3. Total number of respondents is more than the sampled households because all the factors pointed by farmers were taken into consideration.

Source: Based on Field Survey (2009-10).

Market Prices of the Crop Grown

Generally, the sample farmers consider farm harvest prices, before making any decision regarding the selection of crops. These prices are the average wholesale prices at which the commodity is disposed of by the producer to the trader at the village site. However, vegetables and *chara* have highly variable prices largely determined by its demand and supply channels. Prices of crops were found to be the most influencing factor in determining the choice of crop grown by the farmers. This shows the commercialization of agriculture in Aligarh's PUI, whereas the region as a whole still has subsistence orientation in farming activity (Fazal, S. 1994). Sampled farmers (37.8%) were influenced most by the prices. The farmers prefer to grow those crops, which are profitable to them, which fetch them higher market prices and higher monetary benefits. Prices of crops were influencing the cropping pattern of mostly those farmers who are economically strong because these farmers can invest on costly inputs and they can also take risk of changing their cropping pattern. Farmers from *intermediate* PUI (50.6%) and *immediate* PUI (34.8%) farmers were found to be influenced maximum by prices.

Yield

Yield of the crops, emerged to be the second most important factor (30.7%), which influenced the cropping pattern of the sample farmers. Farmers from all the categories of farm sizes and zone were equally concerned, they prefer to grow those crops, which gave them better yield. Because higher the yield more will be the production and more will be the income. This again shows that farmers in PUI try to maximize their income from their lands. *Intermediate* PUI (33.1%) and *immediate* PUI (33.7%) and the *distant* PUI (28.3%) farmers were all found to be influenced equally by yield of the crop.

Crop Prospects

The farmers generally expect that they will get a certain quantity of produce from the crops they grow. But, some crops are more susceptible to pests, diseases and climatic changes and the risk of crop failure in these crops are high. So the farmers prefer growing those crops in which the risk of crop failure is low. In the selection of crops farmers kept an eye on the prospects of that particular crop. Farmers from *distant* and *intermediate* PUI consider this factor significantly before selecting any crop for cultivation. On the other farmers from *immediate* PUI despite being concern for this factor, grow crops which have higher risks because they need to produce for urban market. The prospect of crop is influencing more *intermediate* (28.3%) and *distant* PUI (26.6%) farmers. These farmers try to draw maximum income from their agricultural land and that is why their cropping pattern is influenced by price, yield and prospect of the crops they grow. A good balance of these three factors determines greater profit margins from their farming activity.

Irrigation Facilities

Availability of irrigation facilities, mode of irrigation, cost of irrigation, timeliness and adequacy of supply of irrigation water, etc., were taken into consideration. Irrigation is one of the important and crucial inputs in agriculture because the modern technology and inputs works only with higher watering to the plants. This factor was influencing 24.7 per cent of the sampled farmers. The cropping pattern of *distant* PUI farmers (45.5%) were the worst effected because irrigation facility is not easily available. They have to hire water, which is quite expensive and these farmers do not have easy access to capital also.

Availability of High Yielding Variety of Seeds and Chemical Fertilizers

Timely availability of high yielding variety of seeds and chemical fertilizers was also one of the most important considerations for the sample farmers. The *distant* PUI farmers (34.4%) were much influenced by this factor. Due to their unability to generate capital and non-availability of these inputs they cannot purchase these inputs from the market. The government gives subsidies on these inputs but it was observed that these facilities were available easier to *immediate* PUI but *distant* PUI farmers had difficulty in accessing these facilities. Moreover, the investments for these inputs have to be made at the beginning of the season and farmers from *distant* PUI find difficult to arrange capital for investing in agriculture. So many of the small farmers in this zone rely on local seeds and manures, which results in poor yield and low returns from their lands.

Financial Problems

These days with the introduction of new technology the cost of production has increased considerably. Inputs are quite expensive and apart from economically well off farmers, it is very difficult for most of the farmers to invest heavily for their *crops*. The farmers from *distant* PUI (22.7%) were the worst affected by it. These farmers suffer mainly because lack of access to financial institutions, whereas farmers from immediate PUI are advantageous with easy access due to proximity to city. That is why farmers of *distant* PUI unable to provide the necessary inputs in their farms and this results in relatively lesser commercialization of agriculture as compared to *immediate* PUI.

Labour

Availability of labour at peak season was a major problem and *immediate* PUI farmers (15.7%) were the worst affected. These farmers require hired labour because they themselves are not full time associated with farming activities and their family members also do not work in the field, so to manage their landholdings, they have to depend on hired labour. The labour wages are higher as well as they are not easily available. Moreover, the crops grown in this zone also require more and skilled labourers. On the other hand, *distant* PUI farmers are not at all affected by this factor. Every working person is engaged in agricultural activities including women and children in their farms.

Traditions

The farmers are bound with the age-old traditions of farming and they hesitate to make changes in their cropping pattern. Farmers cultivate crops according to their taste and preference. They like to cultivate those crops, which they have been eating traditionally, till some drastic changes come. Their customs and cultural background also plays crucial role in the selection of crops. Most of the farmers, which were referred to this factor, are illiterate. They are bound with the age-old traditional pattern of farming and hesitate to make changes in their cropping pattern.

Physical Factors

Physical factors were also seen affecting the cropping pattern of the surveyed farmers. This region is best suited to agriculture. It has good climatic conditions, flat alluvial plains and fertile soils. That is why the farmers of this region have not given much importance to this factor. However, in some surveyed areas the problem of salinity-alkalinity and waterlogging was observed.

Governmental Policies

Governmental policies regarding the distribution of loans, giving of subsidies on fertilizers and high yielding variety crops, improvement in irrigation systems, land development policies, land reforms, agricultural schemes for the benefit of small farmers, price control and establishment of credit societies are some of the government policies which influences the farmers decision in selection of crops. These days with improved communication linkages and easy access has led to greater awareness for various governmental policies. The sampled farmers were also found to be influenced by it and the author found that the farmers were voicing their concern for improvements, urban proximity is one important reason for it.

6

Aligarh City's PUI : Dairying an Emerging Livelihood Option

Periurban areas are characterized by change, often rapid, resulting from urban development and expansion. PUI is a transitional zone where urban and rural landscapes merge together and it offers lots of new avenues and a lot more opportunities which needs to be exploited judiciously for an improved livelihood in this urbanizing commercial world. This means appropriate strategies and efforts are required to utilize the opportunities for new livelihoods and also to thwart threats to existing livelihoods. Well planned and targeted interventions are required to enable people to make the best of new opportunities and overcome the threats. This requires understanding of the interactions between urban and rural areas characterizing the periurban interface. One emerging livelihood option, which needs thorough understanding, is the livestock farming in the periurban area. This activity appears to have great potential, but in India it is found to be poorly managed.

The previous chapter, focused on traditional methods of livelihood among sampled households in Aligarh PUI. In this chapter the focus is on modifications and changes to traditional livelihood practices because of rapidly transforming PUI's economic environment characterized by monetized urban economy.

Livestock in PUI has great potential because of the demand for milk and dairy products which increases with growing urban population. Since most urban populations consist of "non-productive consumers", the increase in demand has to be met by increased production from PUI. The bigger cities have large organized dairies procuring and supplying milk from PUI. But smaller cities have predominantly unorganized individual dairy producers in the PUI.

In India, urban populations, being diverse, also have diverse tastes as well as diverse demands for dairy products. One such demand is for fresh milk supplied directly by the producers and vendors at consumers doorsteps. The other is the preference of Indian taste buds for buffalo milk. The urban milk consumers also have diverse preferences for the milk price that they would like to pay. On the basis of price paid, water is added to milk, which is an indigenous way of maintaining low or high fat content in milk as well as overall milk quality. These demands though small but are the forces that offer opportunities for dairying activity in PUI.

The study assumes that the livestock based livelihoods are greatly influenced by urban growth. The study makes an attempt to understand the status of the livestock farming system in the PUI driven by urban development by analyzing sampled households in Aligarh's PUI.

BOX 6.1 : Critique of India's Livestock Policy

India's livestock legacy has *four* dimensions:

1. Cows and bulls are treated as sacred and hence are protected.
2. The conservation of farm animals is essential for the sustainability of agriculture and the survival of small farmers.
3. The conservation and utilisation of farm animals is based on diversity — both diversity of breeds as well as diversity of function of farm animals.
4. The sustenance of cattle comes from diverse sources of fodder and feed — agricultural byproducts such as straw and oilcake, fodder trees planted on farms and common property resources such a village pastures and forests.

The indigenous approach to livestock is based on diversity, decentralisation, sustainability and equity. Our cattle are not just milk machines or meat machines. They are sentient beings who serve human communities through their multidimensional role in agriculture.

This policy proposal recognises that the livestock economy is the economy of the poorest households in India. More than 850 million people reside in rural areas of which 40 per cent have incomes which place them below the poverty line. Some 70 million households keep and own livestock of one kind or another and derive

(Contd...)

BOX 6.1 : *(Contd...)*

on average 20 per cent of their income from this source. Small and marginal farmers and landless labourers constitute almost two-thirds of these livestock keeping households. The importance of the livestock sector can, therefore, not be measured purely in terms of its contribution to Gross Domestic Product (GDP) but it plays a very crucial role in generating income and employment for the weaker sections of the economy.

However, all the analysis in the policy is totally insensitive to the systems which allow cattle to serve the needs of the poorest. As a result the recommendations are a direct assault on this survival base of the poor. For the livestock policy to be ecologically sound and socially just the following elements must be urgently addressed.

1. Protection of native breeds and conservation of animal biodiversity.
2. Strengthening the role of farm animals in sustainable agriculture.
3. Stopping the slaughter of cattle for exports.
4. Stopping the export of oilcake and cattle feed
5. Taking urgent steps to improve the fodder situation through planting appropriate crop species and trees and by rejuvenating the commons.
6. Preventing the import of environmentally unsound methods of intensive factory farming of animals which degrade and pollute the environment and cause health hazards to consumers. *Shiva* (1996)

Status of Livestock Farming in PUI

In periurban systems, households also engage in livestock production to supplement their incomes. Very little attention was given to these systems, but they appear to be a growing phenomenon. At least in PUI, this is substantiated by several studies in developing countries which reported of emerging periurban livestock sector. This livelihood option has inherent PUI characteristics as households afford multiple options where the men can work in the farm as well as off-farm (in some urban activity or as middlemen), similarly, women can perform the men's as well as their own tasks of raising animals. So, dairying can be a full time job or can be done in parts (Box 6.2).

BOX 6.2: Urban Dairies in Aligarh City

In and around the city there are many large and small dairies. About thirty commercial enterprises deal in milk trade and distribution. They are not the direct producers but involved in collecting, packaging and distributing of milk and its byproducts. While a number (more than 100) of smaller dairies, which are producer as well as at local level distributor of milk. These smaller dairies keep between ten and twenty buffaloes and crossbred cows. By far, the largest number of these smaller dairies belong to traditional buffalo keepers, known as *gwalas*. Some of these households rely solely on the milk produced by buffaloes as their source of income, others may rely more on urban-based work, but keep one or two buffaloes as a source of milk for their family and as an additional source of income. Keeping buffaloes is also part of tradition. Animals may be impounded in a *baada* or *goshaala* or a *gher*, which are cattle shelters.

Dairying as an emerging Livelihood Option in Aligarh's PUI

In general, buffalo is the preferred milking animal, as consumers prefer its milk because of its high fat content. However, cows are also being domesticated by households, though in lesser number. Cows are used basically to produce bullocks for agricultural sector and its milk is also produced for self-consumption as well as for specific demands of individuals (mainly for feeding infants because this milk have medicinal value and contains less fat). But with mechanization of agricultural sector and preference to buffalo for dairying activity in PUI, there is increase in the number of local buffaloes while a decrease in number of local cows over time.

Dairying Activity is a Recent Upsurge in Aligarh's PUI

The dairying activity has emerged as an important activity in Aligarh's PUI as 107 (35%) households have reported to have adopted it as the main livelihood option. This suggests that the growing demand for dairy products in urban areas and to meet this demand, more and more households are opting for dairying activity in PUI. The popularization of this activity is also because of cash remittance of the product.

Out of 306 households reported for associated with dairy activity, only 68 pursued dairy activity for period of more than 10 years, while remaining 238 (77%) have started to perform it in the last ten years. Significantly, 57 per cent households have less than 2 cattle per households. This suggests that livestock rearing for producing dairy products in Aligarh's PUI was not the primary occupation for the rural population but it only serves as a support enterprise to agriculture. Buffaloes are reared primarily for milk, butter, ghee and other milk products as well as for animal wastes (used as manure and fuel). Buffaloes are also preferred because consumers prefer its high fat content and as a result the milk fetches a better price.

Dairying Activity is thriving in Immediate PUI

Livestock rearing is gaining importance in periurban villages with increasing number of households involved over time. A total of 306 households were associated with dairy activity in Aligarh's PUI. Almost half of it (138 households), were found to be in *immediate* PUI, followed by *intermediate* PUI (96 households) and *distant* PUI (72 households). This clearly suggests that distance from urban area is critical for dairy activity. The distance factor is critical for dairy activity because milk being a perishable commodity and with no refrigeration or preservation techniques are used, this activity thrives closer to the city.

In immediate PUI mean number of buffaloes per family was four times higher than the number in distant PUI. In the last five years only the number of buffaloes increased by 200 per cent in immediate PUI and only marginally in distant PUI. This is an indication of farmers investing in buffaloes as specialized dairy animals. This is particularly so in households near the urban centres where access to markets is better and a high demand for buffalo milk prevails. There are, however, examples of households behaving similarly from distant PUI also but these had better accessibility and well connected with Aligarh city by metalled roads.

Table 6.1: Aligarh PUI—Number of Animals reared in Sampled Households (2009-10).

Animal Husbandry	*Immediate PUI (Up to 5 km)*	*Intermediate PUI (5 – 10 km)*	*Distant PUI (10 km and above)*	*Total*
Cattle	**138** *(49.8)* (37.1)	**67** *(24.2)* (31.4)	**72** *(26)* (39.1)	**277** (47.5)
Goat / Sheep	**66** *(25.9)* (17.7)	**91** *(35.7)* (42.7)	**98** *(38.4)* (53.2)	**255** (43.7)
Poultry	**8** *(61.5)* (2.1)	**5** *(38.5)* (2.3)	—	**13** (2.2)
Pigs	**14** *(36.8)* (3.7)	**15** *(39.5)* (7)	**9** *(23.7)* (4.9)	**38** (6.5)

Note : 1. Figures in bold are absolute number of sampled respondents in the particular distance zones.
2. Figures in brackets (besides the bold figures) are percentages to the total of that particular variable.
3. Figures in brackets (below the bold figures) are percentages to the total from that particular distance zone.

Source: Based on Field Survey (2009-10).

Dairying Activity is a Joint Family Venture in Aligarh's PUI

The sample survey of Aligarh's PUI reveals that dairy activity was prominent among joint families or among households with larger family size. This is mainly because operations in dairy activity requires labour for almost all round the day and family members are best suited for the required operations. The female members contribute substantially in dairy activity.

BOX 6.3 : Faces of Dairying Activity in PUI

The dairy farming in the PUI has many dimensions:

- *Full time dairying :* This way the person opts dairying as the sole livelihood option, meaning which he is full time engaged with dairying activity. It means all the dairying operations such as production, distribution, marketing and managing the cattle (feeding, milking, cleaning, etc.) is done or supervised by the individual.
- *Only producer :* This way the person is only associated with the production side of dairying activity. It means he would be milking the cattle, the distribution and marketing will be looked after by some middleman, while other household members (generally females) will take care of management side of cattle rearing.
- *Only marketing and distribution :* This way the person is only associated with the marketing and distribution side of dairying activity. It means he would be collecting the milk or other by-products from his own household or from others also and takes it to the city. He may supply it door to door to individual consumers or to wholesaler.
- *Only in house dairying :* This way the family members (mostly women) are associated with the dairying activity. It means they would be performing all or some of the in-house dairying operations (It includes feeding, milking, cleaning, etc.)
- *Dairy workers :* These are paid labourers, working in dairies or dairy products producing households.

Big farmers on an average owned the highest number of dairy animals and the landless the least. In all other classes there is a preferential shift from cows to buffaloes retaining only a minimum number of cows for agricultural activity, manure and milk. This shift is due to three reasons, one because mechanization in farms have reduced the cattle's role in agriculture; and secondly its milk is lesser priced than buffaloes, thirdly, cows are not at all used for meat. This makes overall shift to buffaloes is accentuated in the periurban interface.

Table 6.2 : Aligarh PUI—Family Type of the Sampled Households (2009-10)

Family Type	*Immediate PUI (Up to 5 km)*	*Intermediate PUI (5 – 10 km)*	*Distant PUI (10 km and above)*	*Total*
Joint	**35** *(17.8)* (9.4)	**58** *(29.6)* (27.2)	**103** *(52.6)* (55.9)	**196** *(100)* (25.5)
Nuclear	**319** *(57.5)* (85.7)	**155** *(27.9)* (72.8)	**81** *(14.6)* (44.02)	**555** (100) (72 2)
Single	**18** *(100)* (4.8)	—	—	**18** *(100)* (2.3)
	372 *(48.3)* (100)	**213** *(23.7)* (100)	**184** *(23.9)* (100)	**769** *(100)* (100)

Note :
1. Figures in bold are absolute number of sampled respondents in the particular distance zones.
2. Figures in brackets (besides the bold figures) are percentages to the total of that particular variable.
3. Figures in brackets (below the bold figures) are percentages to the total from that particular distance zone.

Source: Based on Field Survey (2009-10).

Dairying in Aligarh's PUI : Household Consumption

Households in distant PUI households on an average consume more milk than those in immediate PUI households. This is presumably a function of availability of milk for household consumption, the immediate PUI households have pressure from urban consumers so their own consumption is lesser. However, in all the PUI households decline in own consumption has been reported, despite of the increase in buffalo numbers. The consumption of milk has declined as the market for milk sale improved. When the milk consumption is averaged overall classes, it showed a decline during the last five years. Figures clearly show inequity between the wealth categories, revealing more than three-fold difference in consumption between large farmers and the landless. Households with larger landholdings are able to consume more milk whilst landless families have to sell as much as possible to maintain their livelihoods.

Dairying in Aligarh's PUI : Milk Sales and Milk Market

Urban dwellers, are the main consumers of milk and milk products produced in periurban households. Many of the producers (122 households) market milk door to door in the urban area. This is because of good demand, higher rates, payments when required, personal rapport with customers (who sometimes help producers purchase animals by paying in advance) and the option to adjust quality of milk according to the price offered by the customer. Producers closer to the city can directly market their produce bypassing the middlemen, thus obtaining even higher revenues.

Households associated with dairy farming were found to be marketing their products from their houses (27 households, all of them were in immediate PUI). Milk was also marketed from their own shop (9 households), these are large producers and distributors of milk in the city. They also sell some quantity of milk from their own outlet. However, the involvement of middlemen as local traders and city wholesalers is high in marketing of milk and its byproducts in Aligarh's PUI. In the immediate PUI households, some farmers make effort to go to urban markets to sell a limited amount of milk does not worth it and, therefore, they operate through these traders. In the distant PUI household middlemen are active for lack of any other alternative for external marketing. In the distant PUI away from the city, the internal market is also found to be negligible and most of the production either consumed by the producer or it comes to the city.

The average milk sales per household per year in immediate PUI are almost five times higher than that of household from distant PUI (Fig. 7.8). The average income from these sales is even higher (close to six times) (Fig. 7.9). This shows the high demand of milk in urban areas and so is it is the higher returns, making this activity popular. Mean retail price of milk is higher for immediate PUI households (Rs. 24 per litre) compared to distant PUI households (Rs. 16 per litre). These mean values hide extremes. Cow's milk from distant PUI villages fetches a price as low as Rs. 12 per litre while fresh buffalo milk sold in the city can sell for Rs. 40 per litre, a 3.3 fold difference. The data clearly show that a location near the city creates more lucrative opportunities for dairying to become an important livelihood option.

The sample survey also found that the households in distant PUI, who have lesser access to the urban market prefer to convert the milk into milk products such as curd, *khoa* and *ghee* before selling them in the urban areas because the milk may get spoiled by the time they reach the city. Marketing of evening milk is also a problem from the distant PUI. Curd, *khoa* and *ghee* selling is a solution, but again these commodities are disposed of through middlemen and thus the prices they get are lesser than the prevailing market price.

Dairying in Aligarh's PUI : Use of Waste

Dung is a very important byproduct in the Indian rural economy. Almost every household has a compost pit or a heap near the house, and compost is used on the land as fertilizer or is sold if the household is landless. Dung cakes are also used as cooking fuel even in some of the houses where kerosene or LPG is used, as it is considered to provide the best temperature for cooking milk. Stalling of livestock facilitates collection of dung. On average, 50 per cent of the dung is used as manure, 30 per cent as fuel, 20 per cent is sold and some part of it is also bartered for fodder.

BOX 6.4 : Options for Milk Producers in Aligarh's PUI

The PUI, producers have a market that offers several options. Here milk can be diluted and sold to different market segments for different prices. Thus, periurban producers cater to a wide range of consumers including the poorest at prices affordable to them by adjusting the quality of milk. Cooperatives are not a preferred option in the PUI because of the easy access to urban markets and better prices. Milk collection remains a problem in the PUI and the accuracy of the quality assessment is another issue. Accessibility plays an important role in milk supply to the city. Some of the better connected villages in intermediate PUI supply more milk than poorly connected immediate PUI villages. Here bad roads add to 'frictional' distance, an indicator of the difficulty of moving goods and people irrespective of actual distance.

Status of Other Forms of Animal Farming in Aligarh's PUI

Although, vegetarianism being the predominant dietary feature of the region, still, Aligarh city population generate substantial demand for meat of goat. Similarly, Aligarh's PUI is also found to have greater demand for meat of buffalo and livestock rearing for slaughter was also reported as one of the reason for cattle rearing. Some communities, poor farmers and the landless households, raise goat and sheep for additional income.

Sheep and goat rearing in particular is also common in the PUI, these are found in good number in all the PUI villages. But this activity was more prominent among the poorer households. This is because poor and landless households do not confine them to their house and depends more on grazing on common lands, wastelands or field bunds. But it is interesting to note that their number has increased over the last 5 years, all over the PUI villages. The reason for this increase is probably due to prolificacy and easy liquidity of goats.

Sheep and goat were domesticated by 255 households (44%) in Aligarh's PUI. The sample survey showed that with distance from city, their numbers increased as distant and intermediate PUI households had more number of sheep and goats than immediate PUI households. The main reason reported for this pattern was small and congested houses and lack of open space and common land for grazing in immediate PUI.

Poultry activity is also getting popular in Aligarh's PUI, with the increase in demand mainly due to adoption of urban food habits. There were 8 poultry farms in Aligarh's PUI, 5 of them have come up only in last 3 years. Earlier these poultry farms were mainly acted as supply channel, but now they have also started to breed. They still receive supply of birds from Haryana and Delhi and keep them at their farms and supply according to the demand in the city.

Pigs are also found to be domesticated but only by some specific caste households. These animals are also found to be assets to the livelihood of these households. The price of pig was found to be two to three times higher than goats and they breed also to larger number of piglets.

BOX 6.5 : Animal Farming in PUI— At a Glance

Breeds of Cattle:

Buffalo: Murrah (local), Jaffrabadi (Gujarat), Mehasani (Gujarat).

Cow: Jersey (hybrid), Holtein Feisian (hybrid), Haryanvi, Tharparker.

Common diseases of Cattle:

Foot and mouth disease (FMD)

Haemorrhagic Septicinia (HS)

Back Quarter (BQ)

Tetanus

Trypanosomiasis (commonly known as surra)

Rabies

Common diseases of Goat:

Perdes Petitis Remnants (PPR)

Liver Parasite

Flu

Mastitis (inflammation of breast)

Enterotoxaemia (inflammation of intestine)

Diseases and prevalent medicines

Bacterial diseases – treated by Antibiotics such as Penicillin, Ampicillin, Gentomicin, Ciprofloxacine, Ceftriaxone, Ceftioful, Cefperozone, Tetracycline, Cefotoxin.

Viral diseases – controlled and treated by vaccinations such as anti-rabies vaccines for rabies, PPR vaccines for PPR, FMD vaccines for FMD.

Protozoal diseases – treated by chemical therapy such as Trypanosomiasis (surra) treated by Isometamedium, Dysentery by Metrimidazal or Timidazole, Malaria by Quinapyramine.

Anatomical defects – treated through surgery.

Deficiency diseases – treated by supplementing minerals, vitamins, proteins or carbohydrates.

Infertility – treated by nutritional supplements or hormone therapy (Oestrogen or Progesterone).

Diet and Cattle Feed

Green fodder: source of protein – barsi, chara, legumes.

Dry fodder: bhusa, cereals (jowar), dalia, chunni.

Energy feed: khal (mustard cake), groundnut cake, binola, gur.

Status of Animal Trading in Aligarh's PUI

The sample survey shows that buffaloes are the most transacted animal in Aligarh's PUI, followed by goats and cows. There was great variation in prices of these animals. An average milking buffalo can be sold at Rs. 25,000 to 40,000 price, while old buffalo or male buffalo (for slaughter) fetches around Rs. 5,000 to 10,000. Goats are lesser priced and sold according to its weight and an average 10 kg goat is sold for Rs. 1,500 to 2,000, while an average milk giving cow is sold for Rs. 5,000 to 15,000.

Animals are sold by households primarily in three ways:

- through rural periodic markets;
- through middlemen; and
- through local households.

Slaughter houses buy cattle either from middlemen or from the PUI periodic markets, and hence do not figure in this household based survey. The rural periodic market is the major outlet for sale of livestock with close to two-thirds of animals being sold here. The rural periodic market provides a wide range of customers, guarantees sale of animals and a better price. Other market options for selling the animals are considered only in case of emergency or in case a better price is offered. The second main outlet is the local household, followed by local markets. The role of middlemen was again found to be quite prominent.

Status of Animal Feeding in Aligarh's PUI

Dry fodder is the main source that sustains the livestock in all households. Immediate PUI households use a greater quantity of dry fodder (10 tons per household per year) as compared to distant PUI household (7 tons per household per year). The common fodders used are sorghum and maize stalk, paddy and wheat straw, groundnut and linseed haulm and grass hay. This is generally collected, stacked in the harvesting season and used in dry seasons. Dry fodder may come from their own lands, leased lands and others' lands. The landless in immediate PUI have to buy this and in distant PUI some of them exchange it for farmyard manure (FYM).

Green fodder is also fed to animals mostly during the wet season. The distant PUI households feed more green fodder to their animals. On an average each family feeds 20 tons of green fodder per year. Green fodder comes mostly from their own lands. The green fodder commonly fed is sorghum, maize, grasses naturally growing on waste lands and weeds from agriculture land. Cultivation of green fodder is also common in Aligarh's PUI, it is a kind of cash crop for the farmers as it always have assured market.

Concentrates are also fed in good quantities, mostly to milch animals and in some cases to working bullocks. In immediate PUI 66 per cent households feed concentrates as compared to 34 per cent in distant PUI households. The average quantity of concentrates fed in immediate PUI, intermediate PUI and distant PUI are 3,300 kg, 1,800 kg and 1200 kg per households per year, respectively. The major feed ingredients are maize, sorghum, wheat, cowpea and other pulses, rice bran, groundnut and mustard cake, other husks and jaggery. Farmers usually use materials produced by themselves or which are locally available, as they are less expensive than commercial concentrates.

Free grazing of animals is common in almost all the PUI households but intensity and type varies greatly between different PUI zones. Among the most immediate PUI, urbanized households, limited and controlled grazing and a considerable amount of fodder is "cut and carried" (dominantly sorghum, but also forage maize and hybrid napier grass) to feed stalled animals. In the other two PUI zones (the intermediate and distant) households, free and uncontrolled grazing was also one of the sources of fodder for livestock. In these zones, summer fallows are used widely for grazing of dairy herds.

Status of Animal Care in Aligarh's PUI

Health awareness was found to be poor among all the households of Aligarh's PUI. Vaccination and health care was found to be low in villages despite existence of veterinary aid centres nearby. The disease of which people have awareness is foot and mouth disease (FMD). The animals are generally vaccinated against this disease. The other diseases found are hemorrhagic septicemia (HS) and blackquarter (BQ). Sporadic cases of these diseases were reported resulting in mortality of animals. But very few households have reported having their animals vaccinated against these diseases. It is interesting to note that vaccinations against these diseases are done free of cost by the government veterinary department whereas vaccination against FMD is charged. Fewer vaccinations against these diseases is due to lack of awareness and will among the farmers. Awareness of disease and health management is better in the immediate PUI households compared to the distant PUI households. No other diseases except minor ailments like wounds, non-specific fever, bloat and impacting were reported by the sampled households.

Breeding of Animals

Breeding of animals is an important activity in dairy farming. But among sampled households awareness about breeding is found to be poor. Bull service is the major method used for breeding of animals in almost all households. This is because of lack of awareness about the success of other alternatives and non-accessibility of other breeding services. Some households, mostly immediate PUI households were also found to be using BAIF's 10 artificial insemination service.

Dairying in Aligarh's PUI: Household Management

The study of management of the animals reveals a clear division of labour among the family members. The male members mainly graze the animals, whereas the majority of other works such as milking, cleaning, feeding, sale of milk and milk products are done by female members of the family. This division of labour is more prominent in distant PUI households, where animal husbandry is not the primary livelihood. As dairy has gained more importance in the periurban economy over the last decade, the trend is changing with men being involved more in animal management. This change is most evident in immediate PUI households where dairy has become an important livelihood activity. In the immediate PUI households, dairying has become a male dominated activity, women still continue to do milking and cleaning work. Except for the wealthier households, animal husbandry is a family activity where the family members do all management and very little hired labour is involved.

7

Aligarh City's PUI : Features of Land-Use and Land Transformations

Human activities have been recognized as a major force shaping the biosphere. Understanding these actions and the social forces that drive them is crucial to understanding for managing and responding to such change. Changes in the land have often been seen as improvements by some or all land-users. Alteration is nearly inseparable from human occupation and use, and the goal is to encourage improvement and to counter forces that encourage degradation. To assess what effect a particular land transformation and its consequences would have involved difficult issues of forecasting (future resource demands and opportunities as affected by technical and socio-economic change) and evaluation (distribution and the rights of future generations). However, we now possess a better scientific knowledge of the physical extent, character and consequences of land transformation which serves as the foundation for any such assessment.

Land is not regarded simply in terms of soils and surface topography, but encompasses such features as underlying superficial deposits, climate and water resources, and also the plant and animal communities which have developed as a result of the interaction of these physical conditions. The results of human activities, reflected by changes in vegetative cover or by structures, are also regarded as features of the land. Changing one of the factors, such as land-use, has potential impacts on other factors, such as flora and fauna, soils, surface water distribution and climate. Changes in these factors can be readily explained by ecosystem dynamics and the importance of their relationships in planning and management of land resources has become increasingly evident.

BOX 7.1: Land Resource, Land-Use / Cover

Land and **Land Resources** refer to a delineable area of the earth's terrestrial surface, encompassing all attributes of the biosphere immediately above or below this surface, including those of the near-surface climate, the soil and terrain forms, the surface hydrology (including shallow lakes, rivers, marshes and swamps), the near-surface sedimentary layers and associated groundwater and geohydrological reserve, the plant and animal populations, the human settlement pattern and physical results of past and present human activity (terracing, water storage or drainage structures, roads, buildings, etc.) (FAO/UNEP, 1997).

Land-Use is characterized by the arrangements, activities and inputs by people to produce, change or maintain a certain land cover type. (Di Gregorio and Jansen, 1998). Land-use defined in this way establishes a direct link between land cover and the actions of people in their environment.

Land Cover is the observed (bio)physical cover on the earth's surface (Di Gregorio and Jansen, 1998)

BOX 7.2 : Functions of Land

The basic functions of land in supporting human and other terrestrial ecosystems can be summarized as follows:

- A store of wealth for individuals, groups, or a community.
- Production of food, fibre, fuel or other biotic materials for human use.
- Provision of biological habitats for plants, animals and micro-organisms.
- Co-determinant in the global energy balance and the global hydrological cycle, which provides both a source and a sink for greenhouse gases.
- Regulation of the storage and flow of surface water and groundwater.
- Storehouse of minerals and raw materials for human use.
- A buffer, filter or modifier for chemical pollutants.
- Provision of physical space for settlements, industry and recreation.
- Storage and protection of evidence from the historical or pre-historical record (fossils, evidence of past climates, archaeological remains, etc.)
- Enabling or hampering movement of animals, plants and people between one area and another.

A large number of different land-uses are found in the PUI than anywhere else. The city spreads out into its rural fringe like an advancing wave. But, there is more than just the advance of the built up edge. There are irregular patches of urban and urban associated land-uses. Aligarh city's PUI is characterized by ribbon like development, where city expansion is advancing along the highways and roads leading out from the city (Fazal, S., 2001). This wave like spread of irregular, scattered patches, ribbon like development and continuous subdivision at the edge of the city is associated with land conversion difficulties and generates land-use conflicts. Here we focus on land transformation in Aligarh's PUI due to expansion of Aligarh city. Since we are focusing on city expansion so the land transformation is confined only to immediate PUI only.

The present study is based on remotely sensed data (satellite images) combined with extensive field checks and surveys. The present study is based on IRS-1D with 5.8 metres resolution. The study is spread over a thirty years time span (1980 - 2010). The urban land-use and transformation mapping of Aligarh and its environs was done with the help of city guide map (prepared by Survey of India) on a 1:10,000 scale, updated in 1980, and IRS-1D geo-coded panchromatic satellite analogue imagery on a 1:12,500 scale, acquired in 2000 and 2010. The study was done in a GIS environment because the use of GIS techniques coupled with remote sensing are essential elements for an integrated evaluation map. This work was carried out using ILWIS software.

The present study is spread over 15640 hectares of land, which is much beyond the actual urban limit of Aligarh city. This extended area covers expansion of the city in all directions. From the perusal of Table 7.1 and figures 7.1, 7.2 and 7.3, it is evident that Aligarh city has witnessed large-scale changes in land-use in and around the city. The statistics shows that urban area has increased from 2,257 hectares in 1980 to 7,459 hectares in 2010 (an increase of 230 per cent). Similarly built up area has increased from 1601.5 hectares to 4679 hectares (192%). All these increase are at the expense of non-built up area, which shrunk from 13882 hectare to 10618 hectares (a decrease of about 25 per cent) during the study period. The city has witnessed major land-use changes among classes such as residential area, an increase of 2595 hectares (261% increase);

Table 7.1: Aligarh City and its Environs, Area under different Land-Uses (1980, 2000 and 2010).

Land-Use / Year	*Area (1980)*	*Area (2000)*	*Area (2010)*	*Change in Area*	*Percentage Change*
Residential	994.5 (6.35)	2736 (17.49)	3590 (22.95)	**2595.5**	**261.1**
Villages	111.5 (0.71)	135.5 (0.86)	293 (1.87)	**181.5**	**163.9**
Commercial	56.5 (0.36)	169 (1.08)	240.5 (1.53)	**184**	**328.5**
Educational Institutions	28.5 (0.18)	36.5 (0.23)	113.5 (0.72)	**85**	**303**
Government Offices	64 (0.41)	75.5 (0.48)	133 (0.85)	**69**	**107.8**
University Area	351.5 (2.24)	351.5 (2.24)	351.5 (2.24)	—	—
Aligarh Fort	17.5 (0.11)	17.5 (0.11)	17.5 (0.11)	—	—
Industrial	64 (0.41)	107.5 (0.68)	149 (0.95)	**85**	**132.8**
Recreational	42.5 (0.26)	49.5 (0.31)	101.5 (0.64)	**59**	**140.4**
Graveyards	27.5 (0.17)	36.5 (0.23)	32.5 (0.20)	**5**	**18.5**
Vacant Land	441.5 (2.81)	1374.5 (8.78)	2538.5 (16.2)	**2097**	**475.5**
Tree Plantation	172 (1.09)	67.5 (0.43)	191.5 (1.22)	**19.5**	**11**
Agricultural Land	13209 (84.40)	10407 (64.62)	7761 (49.6)	**–5448**	**–42.3**
Brick Kilns	14.5 (0.09)	15.5 (0.09)	17.5 (0.10)	**3**	**21.4**
Waterbodies/ logged	45 (0.28)	60.5 (0.38)	109.5 (0.69)	**64.5**	**142.2**
Total	**15640**	**15640**	**15640**	—	—
Total Built Up Area	1601.5	3525.5	4679	3077.5	192.2
Total Non-Built Up Area	13882	11925	10618	-3264	-24.6
Total Urban Area	2257	5019.5	7459	5202	230.4

Note: Area in hectares.

Source: Based on Aligarh City-Guide Map and IRS 1D Satellite Imageries.

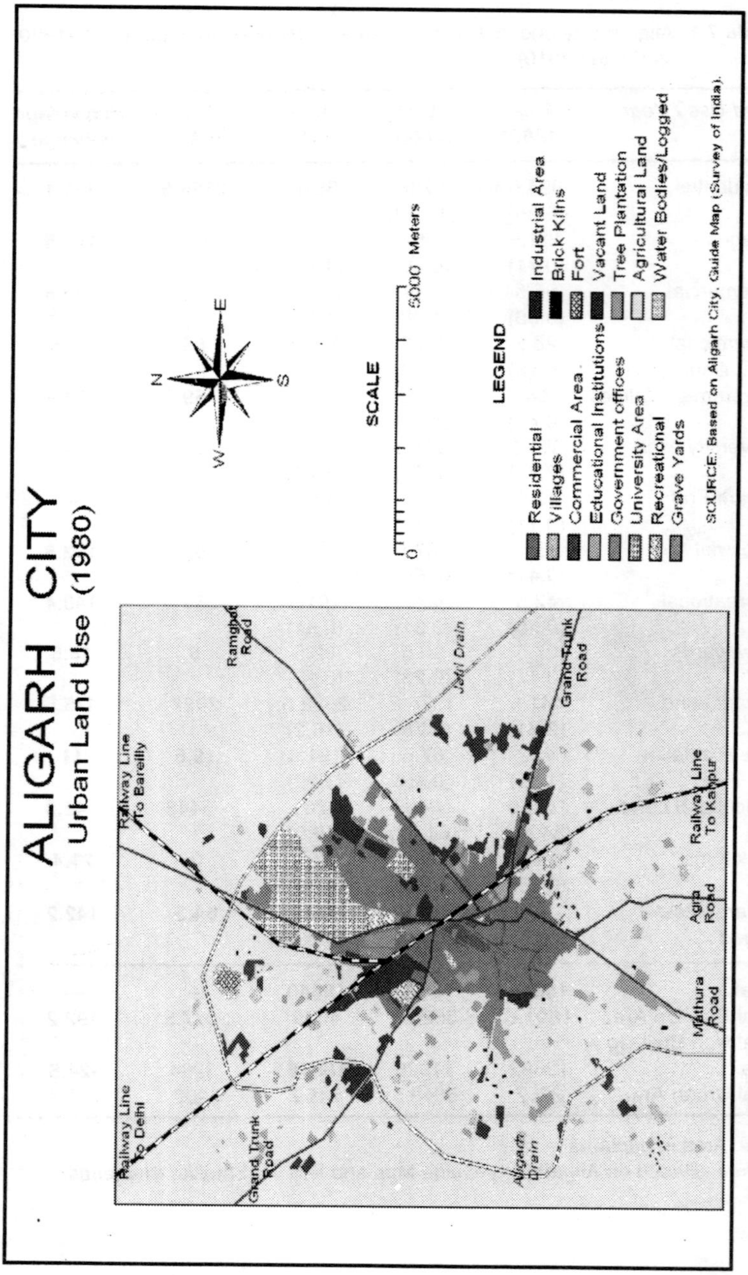

Fig. 7.1 : Aligarh City : Urban Land-Use (1980)

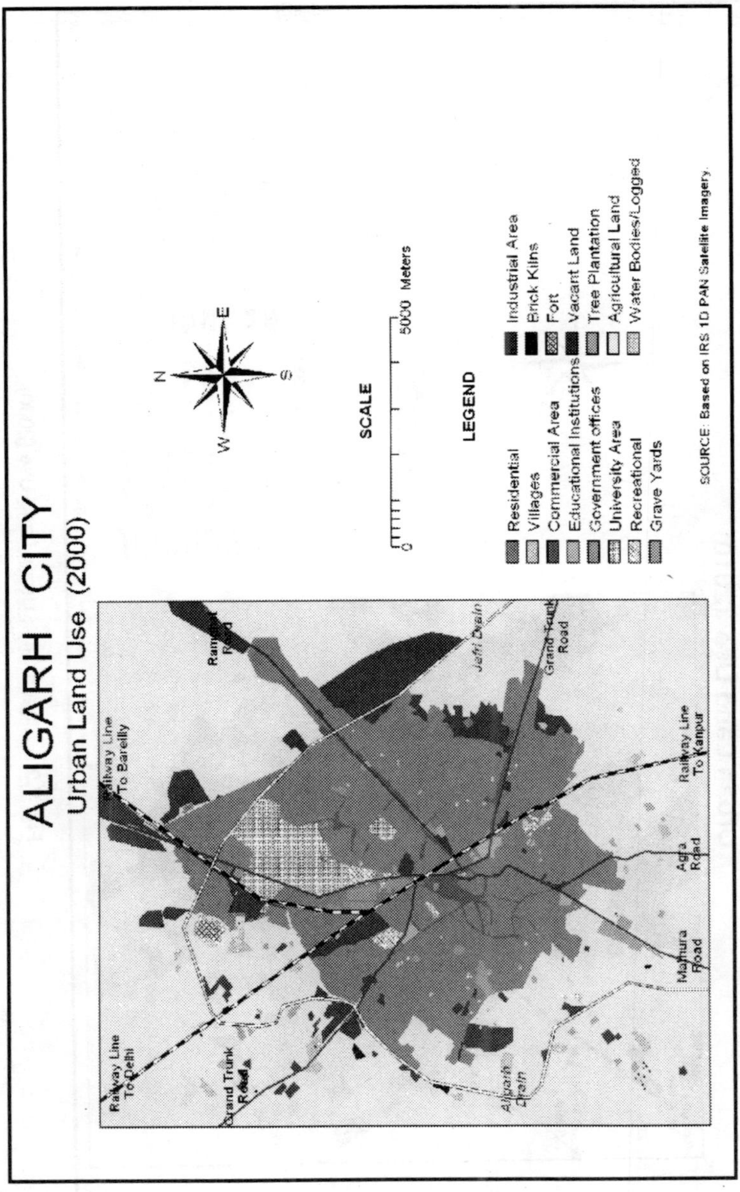

Fig. 7.2 : Aligarh City : Urban Land-Use (2000)

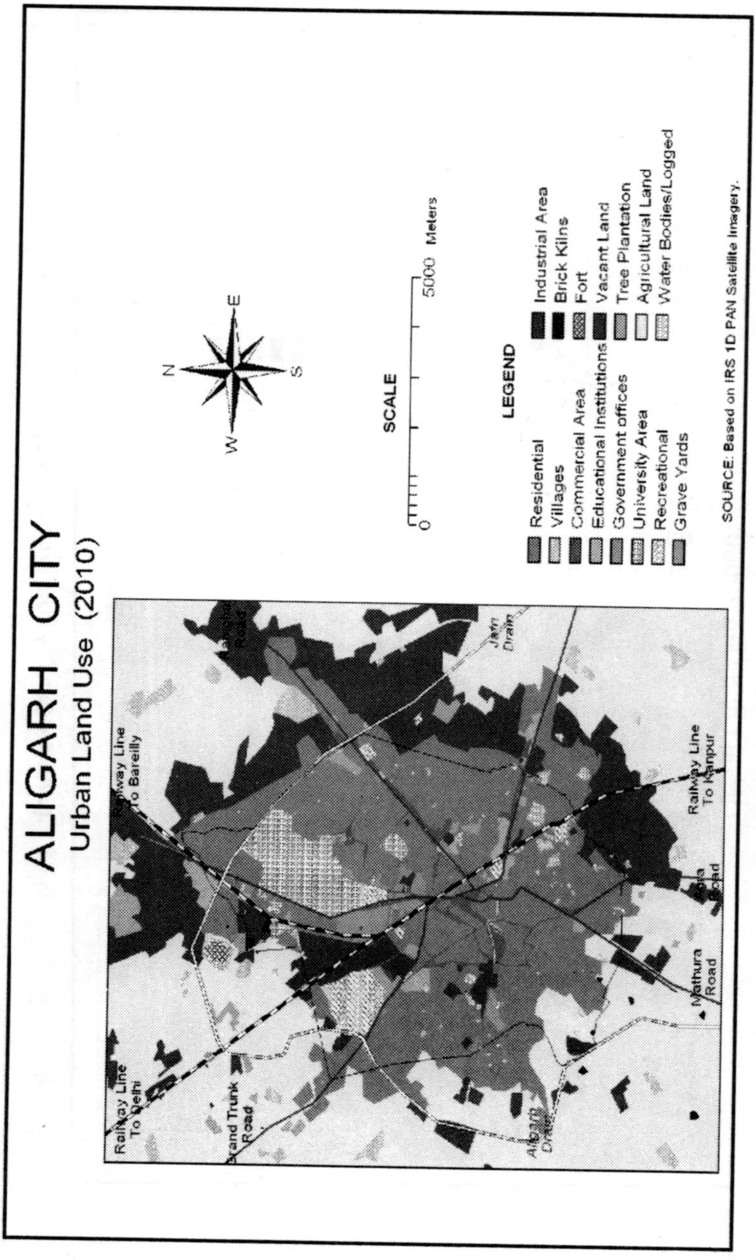

Fig. 7.3 : Aligarh City : Urban Land-Use (2000)

commercial area, an increases of 184 hectares (328% increase); vacant land, an increases of 2097 hectare (475% increase) and industrial area an increases of 85 hectares (132% increase). These changes were basically swallowed the crop land of the surrounding areas. Crop land has lost 5,448 hectares (a decrease of 42%) to the urban sprawl of Aligarh city. Among the other land-use classes not much change has been observed. Area under villages has marginally reduced as some of these villages were swallowed by urban expansion. Similarly 351.5 hectares land was occupied by the Aligarh Muslim University and 17.5 hectares by Aligarh Fort. Both of these are located in the northern part of the study area and remained unchanged. The salient characteristics, which emerge are given in Table 7.1 and Fig. 7.1, 7.2 and 7.3. Aligarh city has recorded a significant increase in built up area and this is mainly because of population growth and development in secondary and tertiary occupation structure.

Land Transformation in Aligarh City and its Environs

Land transformation is the process of identifying differences in the state of any phenomenon by observing it at different time periods. Land is in a continuous state of transformation as a result of various natural and man-made processes. The study of land transformation, therefore, requires a comprehensive understanding and monitoring of all the factors that cause the land transformation. During the study period, Aligarh city has not only expanded from its original size but there was significant interchange of land among various land-use classes. Tables 7.2, 7.3, 7.4 and figures 7.4, 7.5 and 7.6, which are prepared applying G.I.S. technique, shows the changes in various urban land-use class of the city. These changes are because of the development of city resulting in increased demand of land for residential, commercial, industrial purposes, etc. This demand of land along with site attraction, functional convenience, functional magnetism and the land value of that particular area ultimately influence the pace and direction of urban land-use change.

The residential area has increased by 2,595 hectares, capturing land mainly from agriculture (2,104 hectares), vacant land (405

Table 7.2 : Land Transformation in Aligarh City and Its Environs (1980 to 2000)

Land-Use	1 Res	2 Vil	3 Com	4 Edu	5 Govt	6 Univ	7 Fort	8 Ind	9 Vac	10 Tree	11 Agr	12 Water	13 Others	Total Area (2000)
1. Residential Area	**994.5**	33.25							144	76	1578.5			**2736**
2. Villages		111.5									57.25			**135.5**
3. Commercial Area	53.75		**56.5**						11		47.75			**169**
4. Educational Institutions	8			**28.5**										**36.5**
5. Government Offices	11.5				**64**									**75.5**
6. University						**351.5**								**351.5**
7. Aligarh Fort							**17.5**							**17.5**
8. Industrial Area								**64**		32.5	11			**107.5**
9. Vacant Land									**441.5**	47.75	1061.25			**1374.5**
10. Tree Plantation									21	**172**	30.75			**67.5**
11. Agricultural Land											**13209**			**10407**
12. Waterbodies/Logged											15.5	**45**		**60.5**
13. Others (Recreational, Graveyards and Brick Kilns)	17												**84.5**	**101.5**

Note : (i) Area in hectares.

(ii) Figures in bold letters (diagonally) are area under that particular land-use in 1980, while figures in the same column is shift in area to other classes and figures in same row are increase in area, captured from other land-use classes.

Source: Based on Aligarh City-Guide map and IRS 1D Satellite Imageries.

Table 7.3 : Land Transformation in Aligarh City and Its Environs (2000 to 2010)

Land Use	*1 Res*	*2 Vil*	*3 Com*	*4 Edu*	*5 Govt*	*6 Univ*	*7 Fort*	*8 Ind*	*9 Vac*	*10 Tree*	*11 Agr*	*12 Water*	*13 Others*	*Total Area (2010)*
1. Residential Area	**2736**	32							261.25	103.25	525.75		8.75	**3590**
2. Villages		**135.5**							88	43	58.5			**293**
3. Commercial Area	49		**169**						8.25		14.25			**240.5**
4. Educational Institutions				**36.5**					49.5	12.5	15			**113.5**
5. Government Offices	11				**75.5**				27.5	12.5	6.5			**133**
6. University						**351.5**								**351.5**
7. Aligarh Fort							**17.5**							**17.5**
8. Industrial Area								**107.5**	24.5		17			**149**
9. Vacant Land									**1374.5**	31.75	1737.5			**2538.5**
10. Tree Plantation									64.75	**67.5**	280.25			**191.5**
11. Agricultural Land									29.5		**10407**			**7761**
12. Waterbodies/Logged									31		12			**109.5**
13. Others (Recreational, Graveyards and Brick Kilns)	17								21	18	8.75		101.5	**151.5**

Note: (i) Area in hectares.

(ii) Figures in bold letters (diagonally) are area under that particular land-use in 2000, while figures in the same column is shift in area to other classes and figures in same row are increase in area, captured from other land-use classes.

Source: Based on Aligarh City-Guide Map and IRS 1D Satellite Imageries.

Table 7.4 : Land Transformation in Aligarh City and Its Environs (1980 and 2010)

Land Use	1 Res	2 Vil	3 Com	4 Edu	5 Govt	6 Univ	7 Fort	8 Ind	9 Vac	10 Tree	11 Agr	12 Water	13 Others	Total Area (2010)
1. Residential Area	**994.5**	65.25												
2. Villages		**111.5**							405.25	179.25	2104.25		8.75	**3590**
3. Commercial Area	102.75		**56.5**						88	43	115.75			**293**
4. Educational	8			**28.5**					19.25		62			**240.5**
Institutions									49.5	12.5	15			**113.5**
5. Government Offices	22.5				**64**									
6. University						**351.5**			27.5	12.5	6.5			**133**
7. Aligarh Fort							**17.5**							**351.5**
8. Industrial Area														**17.5**
9. Vacant Land								**64**	24.5	32.5	28			**149**
10. Tree Plantation									**441.5**	79.5	2798.75			**2538.5**
11. Agricultural Land									85.75	**172**	311			**191.5**
12. Water bodies/Logged									29.5		**13209**			**7761**
13. Others (Recreational,									31		27.5	**45**	6	**109.5**
Graveyards and Brick Kilns)									21	18	8.75		**84.5**	**151.5**

Note : (i) Area in hectares.
(ii) Figures in bold letters (diagonally) are area under that particular land-use in 1980, while figures in the same column is shift in area to other classes and figures in same row are increase in area, captured from other land-use classes.

Source: Based on Aligarh City-Guide Map and IRS 1D Satellite Imageries.

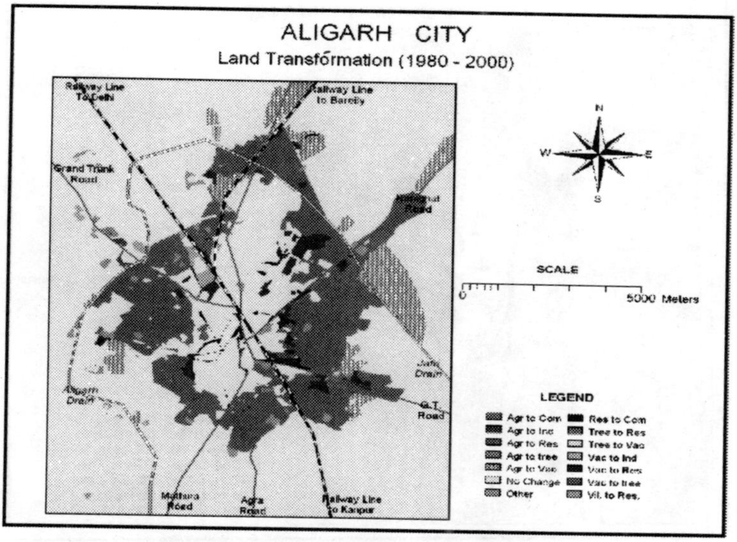

Fig. 7.4 : Land Transformation (1980-2000)

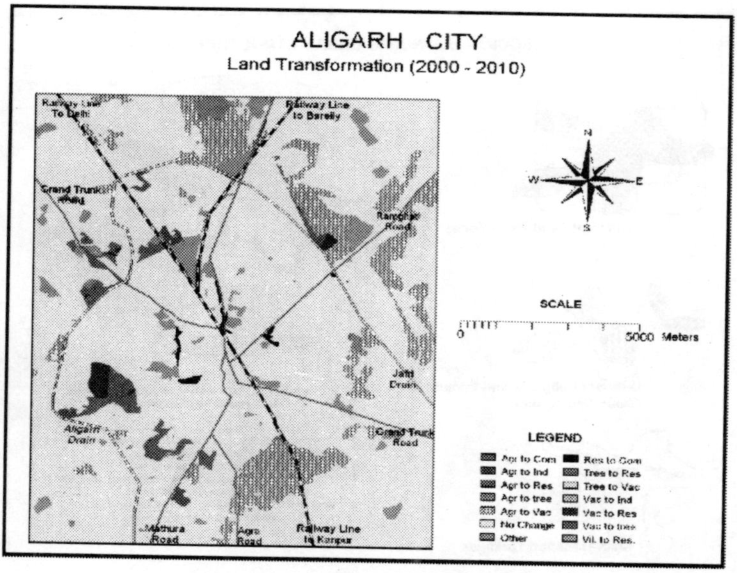

Fig. 7.5 : Land Transformation (2000-2010)

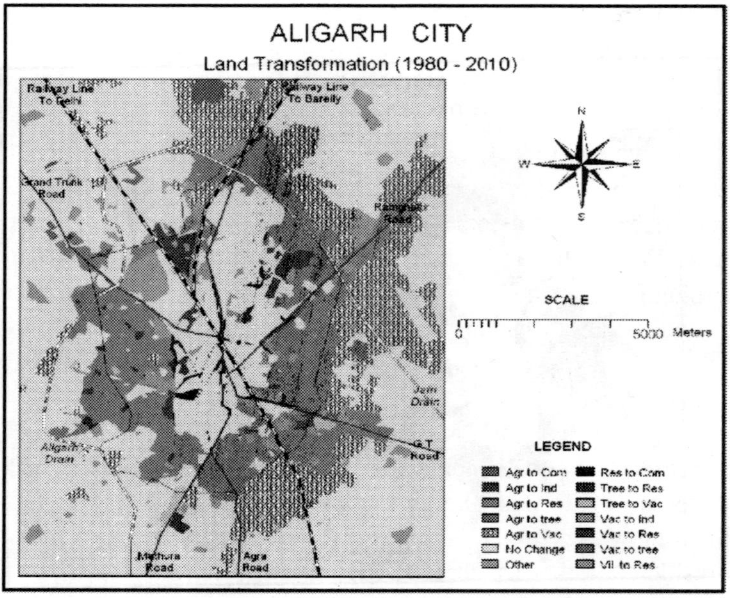

Fig. 7.6 : Land Transformation (1980-2010)

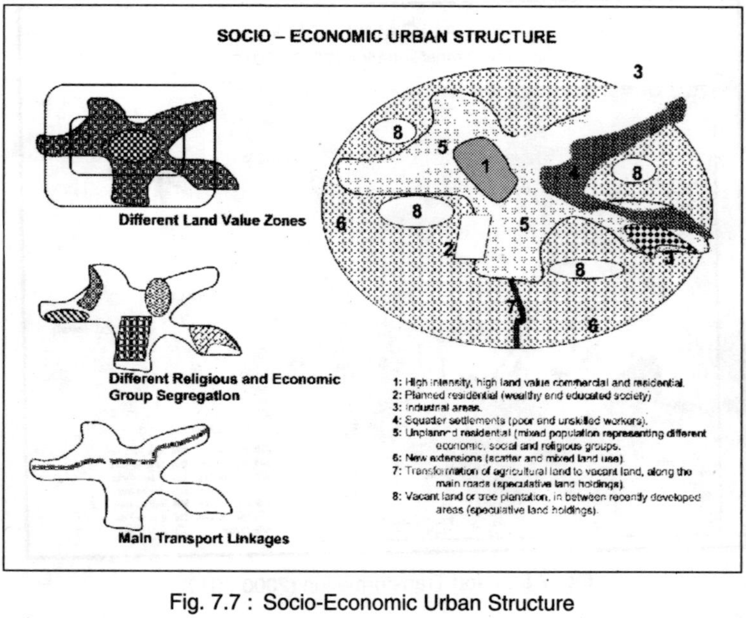

Fig. 7.7 : Socio-Economic Urban Structure

hectares), tree plantation (179 hectares) and villages (65 hectares). Residential area also lost area for commercial development (102 hectares). Commercial area has increased from 56 hectares to 240 hectares gaining land from residential area (102 hectares) and vacant land (19 hectares) in the city. Industrial area has increased from 64 hectares to 149 hectares capturing mainly the agricultural lands (28 hectares) because this development is mostly away from the city centre. Plantation area has increased marginally as significant interchange among different land-use class was observed. Tree plantation lost 175 hectares of its area for residential development, another 79 hectares converted as vacant land, 32 hectares for industrial purposes, while on the other hand, it received land from agricultural (311 hectares) and vacant land (85 hectares). The city has recorded a massive increase from 441 hectares in 1980 to 2,538 hectares in 2010 under the land-use class vacant land. It captured land from agriculture class (2,798 hectares) while lost area mainly for residential (405 hectares) development. During the study period all the city expansion is mainly on crop lands, which decreased from 13,209 hectares to 7,761 hectares resulting in heavy losses of fertile crop lands.

Loss of Crop Land due to Urban Expansion

India still is basically an agrarian country and any expansion in built-up or even non-built-up is at the expense of crop land (mostly good quality fertile land). Moreover, the study area lies in the fertile agricultural tract between *Ganga* and *Yamuna* river. This area has one of the best physical conditions for agricultural activity in the country. Therefore, any loss to agricultural land here can have far reaching implications. The present study focuses on this phenomenon where crop land is being consumed by urban expansions. Tables 7.4 and 7.5 and Figures 7.8, 7.9, 7.10 and 7.11 shows that the area under agricultural use has declined substantially. There was a tremendous increase in the urban area between 1980 and 2010 (230%) while a total of 5,448 hectares of fertile crop land were lost due to the city's expansion. Tables 7.4 and 7.5 and Figures 7.9, 7.10 and 7.11 show land transformation from three main land-use classes, namely, agriculture, vacant land and plantation. Table 7.5, which was prepared using GIS techniques, shows that, of the 5448 hectares of fertile crop land that was lost, 3,109 hectares are recoverable (land where no permanent construction has taken place, i.e., land transformation to plantation or vacant) and 2,339 hectares are not recoverable (land where permanent construction has taken place, i.e., land transformation to residential, commercial, industrial, etc.). Vacant land suffered a total loss of 633 hectares and only 115 hectares are recoverable. This indicates the rapid loss of fertile crop land, much of which is non-recoverable because some permanent construction has been undertaken. Significantly, the land where no permanent construction has taken place, i.e., that which is mainly lying vacant, can be recovered but it will not be an easy task to restore this land back to agricultural use.

Table 7.5 : Aligarh City — Loss of Agricultural Land (1980 – 2010)

Land Transformation	*Area*
Agriculture to Residential	**2104**
Agriculture to Industrial	**28**
Agriculture to Commercial	**62**
Agriculture to Vacant Land	**2798**
Agriculture to Tree Plantation	**311**
Agriculture to Others	**179**
Recoverable Loss	**3109**
Non-Recoverable Loss	**2339**
Total Loss	**5448**
Vacant Land to Residential	**405**
Vacant Land to Industrial	**25**
Vacant Land to Others	**88**
Vacant Land to Tree Plantation	**85**
Vacant Land to Agriculture	**30**
Recoverable Loss	**115**
Non-Recoverable Loss	**518**
Total Loss	**633**

Note: Area in hectares.
Source: Based on Aligarh City Guide Map and IRS 1D Satellite Imagery of Aligarh City and its Environs.

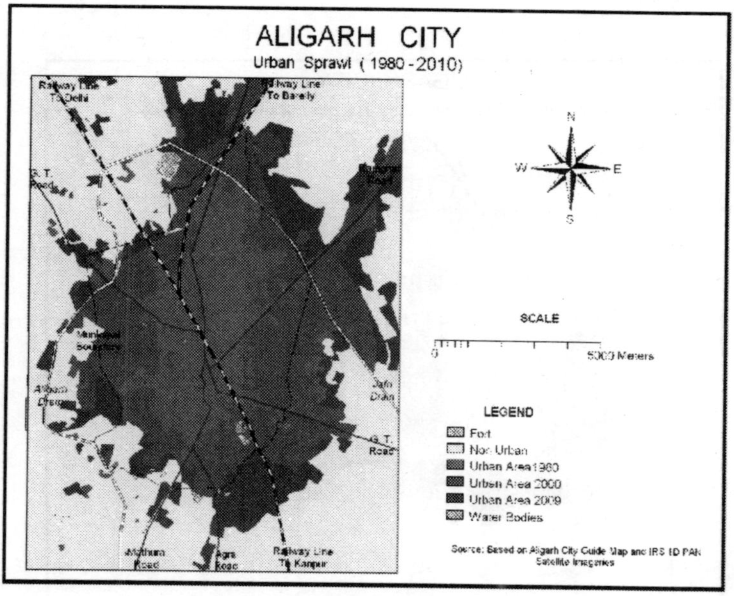

Fig. 7.8 : Urban Sprawl (1980-2010)

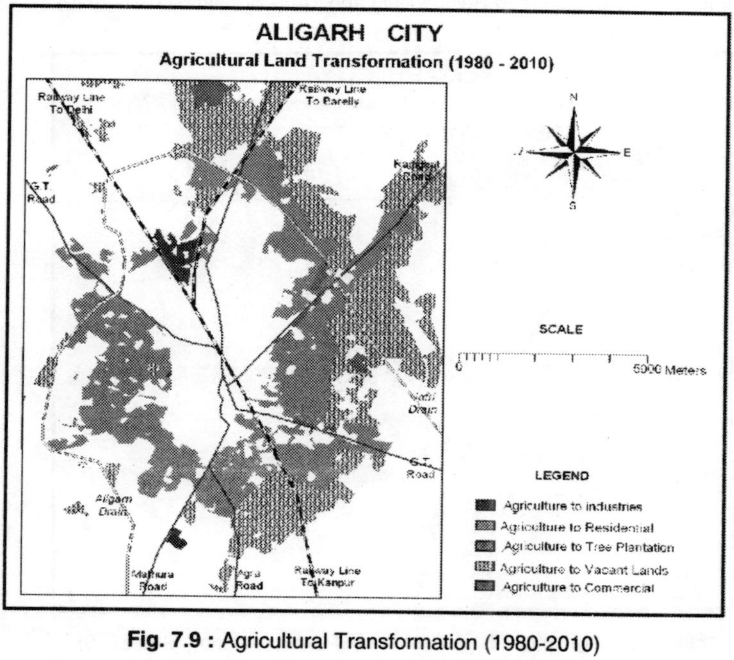

Fig. 7.9 : Agricultural Transformation (1980-2010)

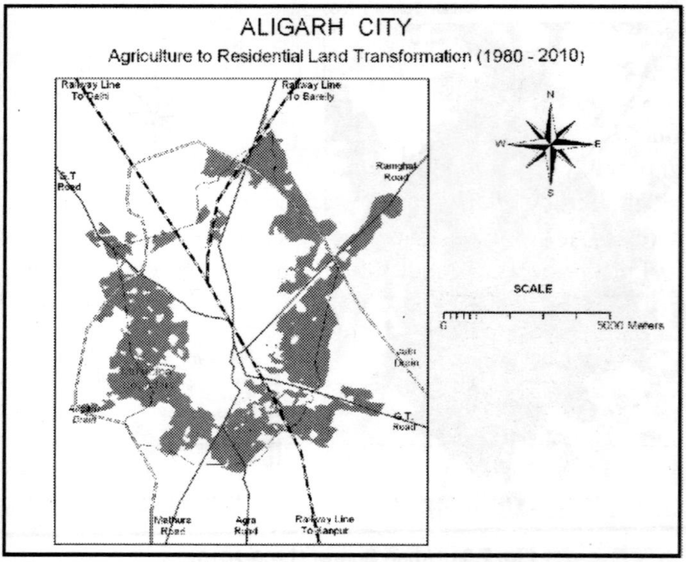

Fig. 7.10 : Agriculture to Residential Land Transformation (1980-2010)

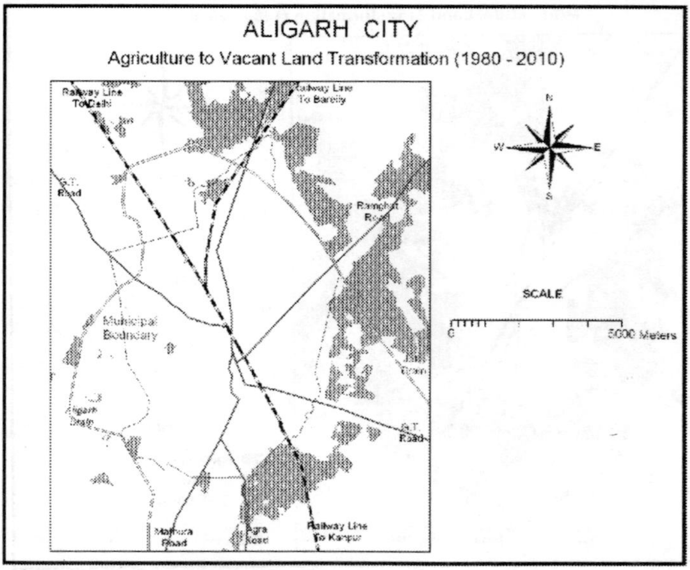

Fig. 7.11 : Agriculture to Vacant Land Transformation (1980-2010)

Tables 7.6 and 7.7 show losses of total crop land and foodgrain production. The total estimated loss of foodgrain production due to urban expansion in the study area from 1980-2010 was about 1,90,680 quintals. Aligarh is expanding by about 182 hectares annually. This implies that every year the loss of foodgrain production will increase by 6,350 quintals. If the projection that Aligarh will have around 1.2 million inhabitants by 2015 is realized and if the city continues to grow at the same rate, a further 40,000 hectares of fertile crop land will be converted to non-agricultural uses. Furthermore, around 30,000 quintals of foodgrain annually would be lost from the study area alone. These figures clearly point to the magnitude of the problem.

Table 7.6 : Loss of Cropland in Aligarh City and Its Environs (1980 – 2010)

Year	*Area under Agriculture (in hectare)*	*Loss of Cropland*	*Average Annual Loss*	*Time in Years*
1980	**13209**	**5448**	**181.6**	**30**
2010	**7761**			

Table 7.7 : Estimated Loss in Foodgrain Production in Aligarh City and Its Environs (1980 – 2010)

Year	*Foodgrain Production (in Quintals)*	*Loss in Food-grain Production (in Quintals)*	*Average Annual Loss (in Quintals)*	*Time in Years*
1980	**462315**	**190680**	**6356**	**30**
2010	**271635**			

Land Capability Evaluation

This study also made an attempt to estimate the real loss of cropland and its resultant loss of agricultural production on the basis of capability of land. The land capability evaluation was made on land which had been under agricultural use but which, due to urban influences, was brought into non-agricultural use during the study period. Land capability classification is an appraisal of the physical characteristics of land, its inherent soil qualities and the farm management practices (Shafi, M., 1969). Land capability of the land was evaluated from the following indicators: distance from the city centre, current and previous use of land practiced, soil fertility, irrigation potential, potential productivity of land and land management. The maps showing these indicators were firstly assigned a capability score which had the range value of 0 – 10 (not suitable – highly suitable for agricultural use) this way six suitability aspect maps were prepared. These maps were further combined into a composite capability map by adding the suitability scores.

BOX 7.3 : Concept of Land Capability Evaluation

LAND CAPABILITY EVALUATION	LAND CHARACTERISTICS	POTENTIAL PRODUCTION UNIT
	GOOD QUALITY LAND	
CLASS I	Highly productive when under good management	**2 P P U**
	MEDIUM QUALITY LAND	
CLASS II	Land of medium productivity even under good management	**1 P P U**
	POOR QUALITY LAND	
CLASS III	Land of low productivity due to poor physical and management characteristics	**0.5 P P U**

The real loss of agricultural land can be estimated by multiplying **P P U** factor to the agricultural land from different land capability class.

The real loss will be **Double,** if Class I land is used. While loss will be only **Half,** if Class III land is used.

On the basis of these characteristics, three – 'PPU', (potential production unit) as a standard unit for land classification was developed. A PPU is defined as the potential production from one hectare of good average farmland under good farm management practices. The application of PPU techniques for land classification helps in assessing the real loss of crop land due to urban influences and the resultant transformation to other uses. The real loss can be estimated by multiplying the PPU factor by the crop land loss of the different land capability classes (Stamp, D., 1962). The suggestion is that real loss would be double that of actual crop land loss if Class I land is used, whilst real loss would be only half this if Class III land is used.

Table 7.8: Actual Loss of Agricultural Land on the basis of *Land Capability Evaluation*

Land Capability Class	*Area (in hectares)*	*Potential Production Unit*	*Actual Loss of Agricultural Land*
Class I	2102	2	4204
Class II	2447	1	2447
Class III	899	0.5	449.5
Total	5448	..	7100.5

Table 7.8 shows how the study area has lost 1,132 hectares in the Class I land capability category, 1,347 hectares in the Class II category and 599 hectares in Class III. Using the PPU application, the estimated real loss of crop land is, therefore, 3910.6 hectares. Class I category land was mostly lost in the western part of the study area. More Class I category land in the south-eastern area has also been converted for residential and speculative land lying vacant. Of the total loss of crop land, most was in the Class II category (1,347 hectares), most of which has been converted into residential and vacant land; this was spread over the south and south-eastern part of study area along the municipal boundary. Class III category land was mostly converted for industrial, vacant and residential development in the northern part. This part is characterized by water-logging as it is low lying. This land surrounds the university, where demand for residential land is high.

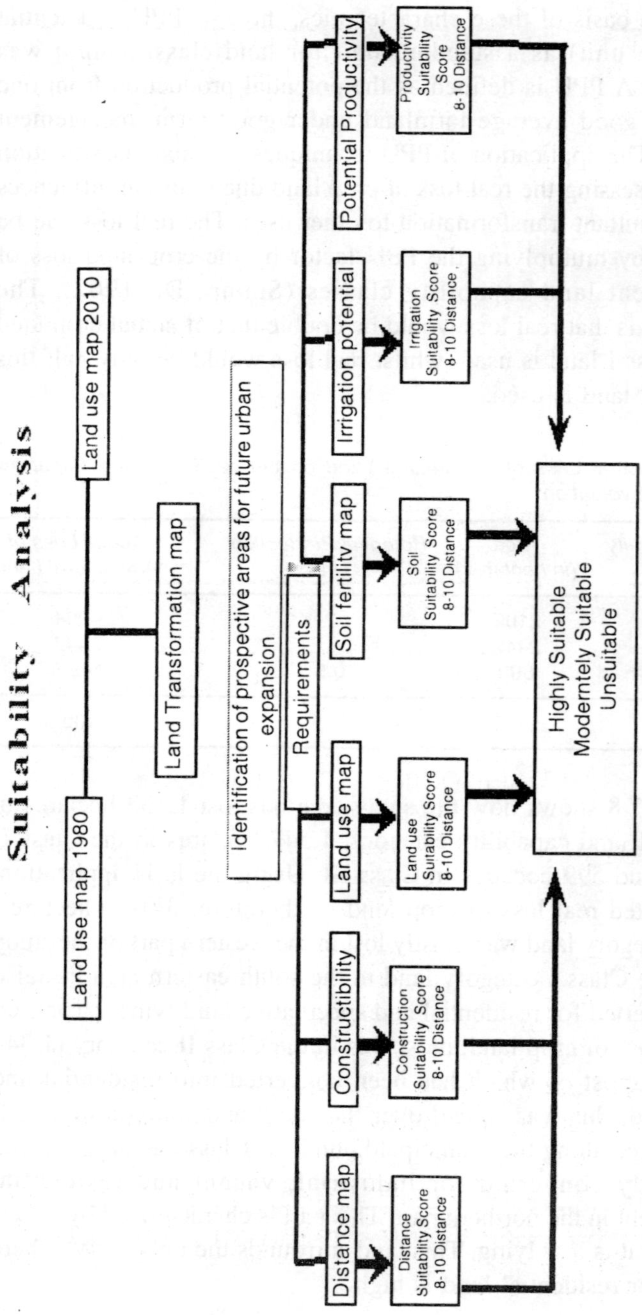

Fig. 7.12 : Suitability Analysis

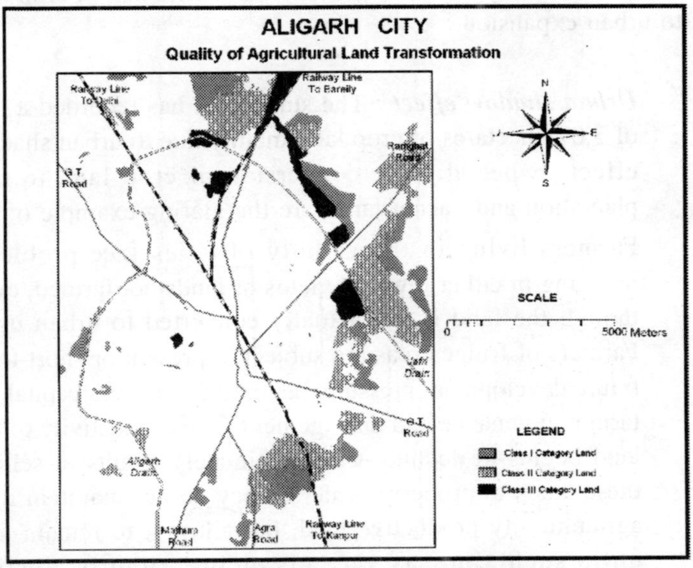

Fig. 7.13 : Quality of Agricultural Land Transformation

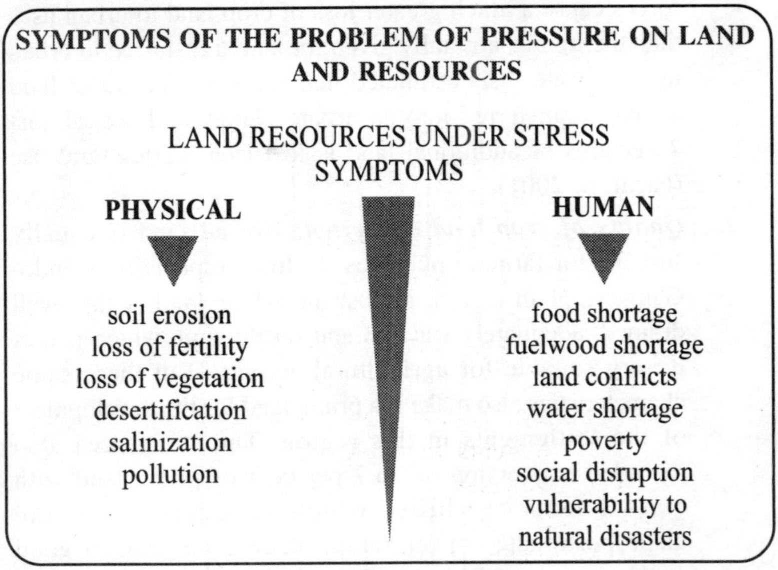

Fig. 7.14 : Symptoms of the Problem of Pressure on Land and Resources

The present study raises three main issues with loss of crop land due to urban expansion :

1. ***Urban shadow effect :*** The study area has recorded a loss of 3,078 hectares of crop land mainly due to urban shadow effect. Especially the conversion of crop land to tree plantation and vacant lands are the glaring example of it.

   Farmers living in the vicinity of cities face problems resulting in either lowered yields or lands not farmed, even though the land is not actually converted to urban uses. Farmers of fringe areas are subject to present or short-term future development pressure, begin to devote less capital for farm maintenance and management. The productivity of the land begins to decline, which ultimately results in selling these lands to property dealers. They do not maintain it as agriculturally productive land, but allow it to remain idle until such time as the advancing suburbs justify transforming it into suburban areas. The net effect of these forces cause a much greater loss of crop land to urban uses than the figures normally given for land transferred to urban uses indicate. It is estimated that for each hectare of land actually transferred into an urban related land-use, almost 2 hectares of additional land is lost from agricultural use (Fazal, S. 2001).

2. ***Quality of crop land converted:*** Not all land is equally suitable for farming purposes. In India especially in Indo-Gangetic plain region, almost the whole land is flat, well drained, adequately watered and fertile land, which makes it very suitable for agricultural activity. But these same characteristics also make it a prime land for the development of the settlements in this region. The study area also recorded conversion of 36.7 per cent of prime land with class I land capability which is indicative of the disproportionate concentration of development on good quality crop land. The significance of this is obvious. Lands in Class I yield are much higher return for the same inputs

of labour and capital. These are the lands which are of primary importance in maintaining the agricultural productivity.

3. ***Cost of crop land conversion:*** A more significant factor intensifying the problem of loss of prime crop land is associated with the cost of such land conversion. These costs are two-fold, and are related to the actual cost of replacing the lost farmland, as well as to government programmes that prompt urban expansion and encourage loss of cropland. When the prime farmland is lost, the value of the crop production is immediately foregone. The cost to replace that land is fairly substantial. The government makes effort to bring some additional land for agricultural uses by reclaiming wastelands but the question is "how much and at what cost".

Above all when agricultural land is lost due to urban expansion, in most cases most viable livelihood option of the farmer is also snatched away. This loss cannot be compensated as agriculture is a way of life for population at least in north Indian plains.

8

Aligarh City's PUI — Land Transformations : Conflicts and Role of Actors

Land transformation is a complex phenomenon. It is the outcome of inter-relationship of different social, economic, natural, cultural and even political situations. The study further tries to investigate the factors which were influencing the land transformation in the PUI.

Factors influencing Land Transformation in Aligarh's PUI

Pressures and changes in the PUI are being driven by a combination of urban and rural forces. With rapid social and economic changes, the PUI is under increasing threat, and as a consequence, appears more precious than ever before. In terms of urban development patterns and trends, the PUI is a pressure point, residual element, and container for urban structures. Urban fringe landscapes are by their nature zones of rapid transition and change, where new land uses need to be accommodated while previous ones become dysfunctional.

The study also tried to study the landowner's decision-making process. Decision about the use of land involves a multiplicity of factors: the objectives of land user, the process by which he reaches on the decision and the socio-economic factors that consciously or unconsciously influences the decision and above all the proximity of the growing urban centre too exerts pull force. The sample survey conducted on 52 households, where land transformation (agriculture to other uses) has taken place. The sampled landowners were divided into three categories on the basis of disposed land holdings by them.

Table 8.1: Aligarh PUI — Sampled Landowners Disposing Land.

Landowner category	*Size of land Disposed of*	*Number of sampled holding*	*Total land disposed of (in hectares)*	*Average land disposed of (in hectares)*
Large	(land disposed more than 2 hectares)	16	46.5	2.9
Medium	(land disposed 0.5 – 2 hectares)	25	30	1.2
Small	(land disposed less than 0.5 hectares)	11	5	0.4
Total sampled land owners	–	52	81.5	–

Source: Based on Field Survey, 2009-10.

Table 8.2: Aligarh PUI – Reasons for Disposal of Agricultural Land among Sampled Land Owners

Land owner category		*Reasons for disposal of agricultural land*							
Large (land disposed of more than 2 hectares)	Reasons	C.E.	S.S	U.P.	O.P.	I.M.	P.F.	U.L.	FR.
	Rank	1	2	3	5	6	7	8	8
	Land-owners	8	5	4	4	4	3	—	—
Medium (land disposed 0.5 – 2 hectares)	Reasons	C.E.	P.F.	I.M.	S.S.	U.P.	O.P.	U.L.	FR.
	Rank	1	2	3	4	6	7	8	9
	Land owners	8	6	6	6	5	4	1	—
Small (land disposed less than 0.5 hectares)	Reasons	I.M.	FR.	U.L.	U.P.	O.P.	C.E.	S.S.	P.F.
	Rank	1	2	3	4	6	7	8	9
	Land owners	8	5	4	2	1	1	—	—
Total	Reasons	C.E.	I.M.	U.P.	S.S.	P.F.	O.P.	U.L.	FR.
	Rank	1	2	3	4	6	7	7	8
	Land owners	17 (32.6%)	17 (32.6%)	12 (23%)	11 (21.1%)	10 (19.2%)	9 (17.3%)	5 (9.6%)	5 (9.6%)

Note: Based on field survey (2008).
Figures in brackets are percentages to total respondents. These figures are more than the total respondents as more than one reason were pointed by the respondents.

1. C.E. – Change in employment.
2. I.M. – Instant Money.
3. P.F. – Protecting Future.
4. S.S. – Social Status.
5. U.P. – Uncertainty of Profit Margins.
6. O.P. – Operational Problems.
7. U.L. – Uneconomic Landholding.
8. Fr. – Forced.

- *Large:* landowners disposed of more than 2 hectares of agricultural land.
- *Medium:* landowners disposed size of 0.5 to 2 hectares of agricultural land.
- *Small:* landowners disposed less than 0.5 hectares of agricultural land.

To know the factors, which lead to their decision of disposing of agricultural land, landowners were asked to state the reasons for their decision. Their answers were then arranged in descending order (Table 8.2). The factors which were Effecting the decision making process of the sampled landowners are discussed below:

Change in Employment

Urbanization has generated employment opportunities with increased and assured wages and landowners with better education have obtained jobs outside agricultural sector. These farmers, if their family allows are quick to dispose of their lands to get extra money. Landowners from large (34.8%) and medium (26.6%) category were found to be disposing their lands because of change in economic activity.

BOX 8.1: Law for Land Rights

Land in India is generally inherited in the family, which is divided among sons and daughters in different proportion (variation is found in different religion, caste and regional traditions). The division of land is mostly not properly documented and is rather verbal. It leads to conflict among the family members. Sometimes, these conflicts extend among families from different generations.

Another issue related to this division of land among the family members is shrinking of landholding. This lead to transformation of landholdings into uneconomic landholdings within a period of few generations. In India, where **law of inheritance** prevail, reduction in the size of operational land is adversely affecting agricultural activity.

Instant Money

Agricultural activity is being depressed actively, the cost of production is increasing and the profit margins are stagnant. The small (27.5%) and medium (20%) landowners with relatively poor economic conditions are disposing of their lands to get instant money. These farmers get some labour oriented jobs in the city and they dispose of their lands. The disposal of land is basically because their lands are not productive enough to sustain their family needs, so their entire family does work in city in different capacities while low productive lands are sold to get instant money.

Uncertainty of Profit Margins

Uncertainty of profit margins in the agricultural sector due to variation in natural – social – economic conditions also led to land transformation. The urban shadow effect has led to lower productivity, resulting in lesser priority to agricultural activity. Large (21.7%) and medium (18.4%) farmers were found to be disposing of their lands because of this reason.

Social Status

The urban forces have transformed the social-cultural mindset of the population. Owning agricultural land was once considered to possess higher social status but now social status is higher for jobs in urban area because of the higher wages. Again the large (21.7%) and medium (20%) landowners were found to be disposing of their agricultural land and disassociate themselves from rural connections. The younger population is found to be more responsive to this factor.

Protecting Future

Economic returns from the agricultural sector are lower and protecting agricultural lands from encroachment and litigations are difficult. So landowners dispose of their land when real estate prices are high and try to protect their future. The large and medium land owners who either have jobs in other sectors or feel no future in agricultural sector dispose of their lands and invest it in other sectors. Another reason which contributes in selling their lands is the tradition of joint land possession, the landowners also dispose land to avoid family dispute and get whatever money they can get which may not be possible if the dispute for division of land happens.

Operational Problems

Due to urban shadow effect landowners faces several operational problems in agricultural activity in the periurban interface. Garbage dumping, unauthorized traffic, interfering with water troughs, vandalism and higher labour costs, etc., are the common problem in farms close to urban settlements. Large landowners were worst affected by this problem due to lack of labour and management in their farms and this also led to disposing their agricultural lands.

Uneconomic Landholding

Small landowners are unable to sustain their family from the small – uneconomic landholding so they dispose their lands. The cost of production is high while the returns are lower. The small landowners work as labourers in the unorganized sector of urban centre and dispose of their unproductive and uneconomic lands.

Forced

Property dealers and land developers pressurize small landowners to dispose their lands as these people need big areas for developing colonies. Small landowners because of their poor economic and social background could not resist the pressure and forced to sell their agricultural lands.

The sample survey shows that unlike the agricultural sector, all sections of the society belonging to different categories of landowners were observing the pressure of urban forces in the periurban interface. But their responses to urban forces are different because of different economic and social background.

Large landowners (outside agricultural sector) were found to be more responsive towards the urban forces. The reason was that since they have distanced themselves from direct agricultural activity. This poses managerial and operational problems in farming activity, thus they are offering their lands in the fringe areas for urban development.

Medium landowners were found to be resisting to urban forces outside agricultural sector. Socially this section of the society is still associate themselves with farming community, but since they are also the progressive and dynamic section of the society, where they change occupation and this instigate them to dispose of their agricultural lands.

Small landowners are also responsive to urban forces for disposing of their agricultural lands. But their decision is more due to their poor and miserable economic background. They are unable to sustain themselves in agricultural sector and the lure of getting instant money goads them to sell off their agricultural lands.

The Actor's Role in PUI Land Supply

Aligarh despite a relatively small city is experiencing an extreme amount of pressure on land. Many studies have highlighted this trend as it has been found in other Indian cities, like Schenk (1997) observed unauthorised development in and around the city of Bangalore, stating that "developers in Bangalore provide for a temporary, makeshift building on their lands and invite a squatter family to come and live there for the time being and act as a guard to protect the owner's rights against other squatters". Similarly, Amitabh (1997) expresses concern about the poor service levels in the periphery of Lucknow, where there are many unauthorised colonies as well. The sale prices and rents for dwellings in colonies on these examples are much higher than in Aligarh. Nevertheless, the same mechanism and pattern of urban expansion is witnessed in Aligarh city also although the scale may vary.

Traditionally, the master plans for cities in India have been for the containment and reduction of population pressure but lately, urbanization has met with increasing approval. The proponents argue that cities create an efficient multi-opportunity environment for the rapidly growing populations in India: *"The... increase in the density of population will reduce the per-capita cost of providing various services to the people. Therefore, the growth of urban centres must be welcomed and the emphasis of policy and public investment must shift towards minimising the unfavourable aspects of urban growth and removing critical bottlenecks"* (Visaria 1997, p. 286). Due to the continuing influx into the city and the fact that government institutions do not reach the targets they set for land and housing supply, the privatisation of a large part of the sector seems inevitable.

The present study also finds that the demand for land is high which results in informal urban development fulfilling the requirements of many of the city's residents. Every piece of land is a tradable commodity, and the pursuit of short-term profits is the predominant ethic. Yet there are some problems related to the unauthorised status of the settlements. The amenities are overburdened, access routes are encroached upon and the system is corrupt and unreliable as cheating as well as extortion and intimidation to protect the influential people's interests are common. The formal planning aggressively violated, resulting in conflicts which leads to crimes and lengthy legal battles in court. Moreover, this kind of expansion (development) ultimately reflects city more as large village rather than a city (Fazal, S. 2001).

The present study points towards prevailing duality in the system of land supply, which is characterized by many current urban concerns:

- There is a chronic shortage in the supply of urban land.
- There are problems with the provision of services and infrastructure and the co-ordination of site servicing with the construction of housing.
- All the amenities and facilities do not match to the requirement putting extra load which is evident with their poor status.
- Every individual has different interests which lead to conflicts and practices of intimidation and manipulation to defend certain interests are widespread.

- There is excessive inter-mixing of spatial functions which is the result of unrestricted, uncontrolled expansions, causing adverse environmental conditions. This problem needs to be addressed, but the costs of relocation are high and the legal proceedings are lengthy.
- The chaotic development leads to pockets of very high population densities, clogging the access roads. The unauthorised construction and encroachments leads to congestion on roads which are not wide enough to sustain the traffic accompanying such high intensities of inter-urban transport.
- The poor cannot afford the high prices and rents resulting from inadequate land supply. In the absence of enough formal housing that is affordable to the economically poor section of the population, people opt to squat on public spaces, thereby creauing slums. This is also found to be one of the reasons for male specific migration to city.
- The poors are keen to save money on accommodation, therefore, they tend to opt for a low-cost hut in a slum like settlement. Local industry requires labour for both day and night shifts. Considering these people's nature of work and monetary budgets, it is rather difficult for them to commute long distances.
- The speculative landholdings also encourage people to settle temporarily. This benefits the landowners in protecting their land from illegal or forced encroachments and the migrant settler gets place to squat. However, this kind of arrangement is temporary and only till the land is developed.

Actors and their Role in Urban Land Transformation

Many researchers and planners have investigated the drivers of change in land-use and land cover. These changes are the result of broad economic, socio-cultural forces bringing in land-use and changes or transformation in land. Identifying the causative factors requires an understanding of human behaviour, their decision making process and interaction with biophysical settings and changes therein. These forces can be differentiated into two forces:

- Driving forces
- Conditioning forces.

The driving forces—that are expected to change over time, such as increase in population, land value, etc. These are fundamental forces that underpin the direct circumstances for land transformation. The driving forces are the outcome of complex interactions among social, economic, demographic forces. Driving forces operate more diffusively (i.e., from a distance) and often have bearing over stable conditioning forces.

The conditioning forces – remains relatively stable over time but may be spatially varied, such as physical setting or even cultural values. The conditioning forces involve physical actions in land transformation, impacting at local levels (such as individual holdings, local residents or society, etc.).

Both of these forces, driving and conditioning have bearing on spatial and temporal variations in land transformations at different locations. Bryant and Bailey have used the term 'actors' for the individual components of driving and conditioning forces (Bryant and Bailey, 1997). The trends and pattern of land transformation at any location are the outcome of certain 'alliances' and 'conflicts' among these individual actors. The actors in PUI are even stronger because it is characterized by intermixing of rural and urban activities and interests as well as the number of actors are greater than in any other area.

The Different Actors operating in Aligarh's PUI

The land-use and their transformation take place because of the interest of different actors. The study finds that the city is expanding, there is large scale transformations from non-built up land to built up land. There are arguments that the changes are not because of purely geographical factors like distance or land rent. But these changes are also due to changes in economic, social or cultural environment. The study finds that land-use and transformation in Aligarh's PUI are the outcome of different actors driven changes. There are number of actors active in the land transformation process and some of the dominating actors and their role are discussed below.

PUI Farmers

Land-owning farmers are the beneficiaries of agricultural land on the production side. They are the representatives of agricultural interests, although many of them may not be entirely dependent on agriculture. They have diversified their economic activities and thus have multiple interests, both as individuals and within the context of their household, which result in strategies that may or may not give priority to agriculture. The pursuit of multiple objectives influences the farmers attitude on land transactions, but this greatly dependent on the distance from the city. Whether a landowner is eager or reluctant to sell land depends mainly on his ability to find other occupations and his ability of investment for the household. Even if the farmer withdraws from agriculture as an occupation, he may keep the land for speculative purposes.

Politically, the original farming community in periurban interface is significantly influential, at least at their own local level. They belong to the area, having lived there for generations. They have access to different institutional and governmental agencies and many of them also have the financial resources to protect their interests. In private land transactions, the farmers are in a position to take a good share of the profits. The terms of trade are mainly dictated by powerful property dealers. Nonetheless, the pressure sometimes applied by large property dealers in association with locals does intimidate the local farmers. They can usually count on the backing of the dominant community in the village, which is an important force. Therefore, the predominating interests among the village population are definitely a consideration when a farmer has to decide what to do with his land.

In the context of periurban interface of Aligarh city, age and education have played significant role in land-use and land transformations. But more strikingly, these transformations within social classes have led to upliftment of backward and deprived classes in general. Non-economic factors also play significant role. Some farmers mostly older people feel a strong emotional attachment to their lands. The cultivating castes have had ownership of ancestral land for centuries. Their tie to the land has determined their life-styles, habits, and occupational preferences, whereby social status can be at least as important as economic gain. The farmers often raise the issue of emotional loss and livelihood and thus resist sale of land. But this bounding is strong away from the city and weak close to the city. Most certainly, the youngsters belonging to the original farming community become indifferent to the role of land for social status. As they are increasingly involved in the urban economy, they derive more status from typically urban activities and assets. This process clearly creates an incentive to sell off agricultural land.

There is a smaller group of farmers who do not own the land but they cultivate. Most of them are poor who earlier worked as rural labourers now they lease-in land from local landowners (who have abandoned farming activity but holding their lands). Lease contracts are usually arranged on a yearly basis. Nowadays, most leases stipulate monetary compensation (the leaseholder pays a fixed amount to the owner). In some cases, the land is cultivated on sharecropping basis also, whereby the landowner and the cultivator share the cost of the inputs and the revenues from the harvest. This form is chosen when the leaseholder is poor and cannot raise the funds to pay the amount for lease and inputs beforehand. The risks for the cultivator are lower, but so are the revenues. An increasingly common form of agricultural contract is lease by the landowners living in urban areas. These urban farmers are outsiders (living in city) with sufficient resources to lease land at various places, to hire workers, and to market the crops themselves. They specialise in high-value seasonal crops such as vegetables, fruits, flowers, etc., and are highly mobile.

Landless labourers also constitute a large group and they are also important actors. Obviously, they depend on the availability of agricultural land, but they are not farmers, they work on other people's land for wages. Most of these agricultural labourers are highly mobile seasonal migrant workers, they come back to the village during harvesting or sowing season and during lean season they are associated with non-agricultural activity in the city. This practice helps them to take advantage from both rural and urban economies. These unskilled workers have taken advantage of the city to sell their labour and in return assure of remunerations.

The landowners in the PUI (whether practicing farmers or merely owners of land) are in dilemma. The returns from land are not satisfactory in farming activity so they are willing to dispose of their lands (they may get good returns instantly as the value of land is more in non-agricultural sector). But land values are greatly varied and dependent on various factors. Thus, the landowners are holding on their lands for appropriate time and value.

PUI Residents

The PUI residents are also an important actors in PUI land market. They play a dominating role in land transformation at local level. Especially, their role has bearing on the pace and direction of land transformation.

The local population can be divided into three groups:

- The local landowning residents;
- The local landless residents (the tenants); and
- Outside settlers.

Besides this these residents also play other roles too: as farmers, residents, entrepreneurs, industrialists, as speculators, or even as political representatives and government employee. People are mainly concerned about acquiring residential space and improvements in levels of amenities and infrastructure in their locality.

Households among the original population often want to obtain additional land for residence, and there are two reasons to do so. First, families are growing and thereby splitting into separate households, for which additional housing is required. Second, the development of commercial and industrial activities in villages provides an incentive for the villagers to start businesses or other activities in part of their dwelling space. Alternatively, they rent out space to others also for that purpose; this is more likely when their residence is located along the roadside. As a result of these actions, people have to look for alternate place to live. Some original households have trouble acquiring sufficient space for housing; this is especially common among the poor section of the population. The inflated land prices make it difficult to buy additional land from the free market.

Outside settlers, the great majority of whom are migrants (AMU and other employees who draw livelihood from tertiary sector constitute a large majority of it), creates demand for space differently. They do not originally belong to the same locality, but may have spent some time there. Therefore, as individuals, they do not have much influence or powerful connections. Some find rented accommodation in the periurban interface itself, but most reside in colonies which have been built upon the former agricultural fields. They want to reside close to university (work place) as well as close to market and other social and cultural amenities and facilities. This way they cut down on their travelling expenses. There is one more important reason, because Aligarh city has history of communal disturbances so the residents settle within their own community and comfort zone. They have other priorities also, first, they prefer relatively cheap accommodation. Second, if the colony is unauthorised, they look for official assurance on legal status for the settlement. Third, they pursue for the government to invest in the public amenities for their colonies. Individually, the poor settlers are not very influential, but their power lies in their large numbers. Political parties and representatives champion their cause to gain their votes during elections. This kind of political patronage is common all over urban India.

Members of the original population sometimes complain about the dilution of their political representation. When a village becomes urbanized, the original villagers become outnumbered by migrants residing in the (newly built, mostly unauthorised) colonies. Previously, when the village was still in a rural setting, their say in elections were significant but with urbanization, this has changed and educated elites have displaced them and the interests of original people are ignored. In recent times migrants dominates in number and their interests are imposed upon original population. However, it is not always a contest between migrants and original villagers. The village population also includes land developers or landlords, many of whom are in politics as well. Often the migrants opt for a local village candidate because they expect better contacts within the governmental institutions. The villagers earn from the migrants through rent and retail. The whole population stands to gain from legalisation of an unauthorised colony through higher land prices and better infrastructural provisions. Generally, the authorisation of a colony is an issue that enjoys the support of the original population as well as the migrants. Besides, within every village there are (historical) rivalries, which are expressed in conflicting economic and political objectives. This also reflects in land, its use and transformation.

Entrepreneurs

Private entrepreneurs have an important role as actor in urban land market. They represent the demand side of the land market, as they require space for commercial and industrial activities. At more peripheral sites in the agricultural area, brick kiln owners, sand excavators, etc., are also strong actors, initiating changes on the land. They place a strong temporal claim on land as leasing of speculative land is common feature of this activity. Some of these kiln owners and operators are from the original landowning communities in the villages. The majority of them are specialized entrepreneurs who come from the city and share land resource with local community.

The pressure on the land increases closer to the better-serviced and accessible areas along the roadsides and near the villages. The greater demand leads to conversion of farmland for industrial and commercial purposes. In general, the supply of land by the government for commercial and industrial purposes is too limited. The majority of land in the market is being controlled by informal sector. Owners of industry, cold storages, storehouses, and other commercial activities on former agricultural land come almost exclusively from outside the village, although many holdings are still owned by original villagers. The latter tend to concentrate on less space consuming activities such as retail businesses and repair shops within the residential areas.

Entrepreneurs tend to work closely with local property dealers, especially in unauthorised operations. The property dealers negotiate the transaction, keep the authorities at bay, and keep an eye on the property if the transfer of title does not result in the intended new use. They also combine some speculative venture with other land uses such as plantations and orchards. In fact, most of the vacant land in the study area is kept for speculative purposes. Local farmers, developers, and even entrepreneurs engage in this practice.

Land is an attractive investment object due to the escalating land prices in the periurban interface. The owner is obviously waiting for a more profitable use to come his way or for a buyer who is prepared to pay a higher price. In many cases, speculation is mixed with other intentions. Certain land-uses are actually meant to conceal the main goal, which is speculation. For èxample, while waiting, the owner may build a farmhouse and keep a plantation or construct a marriage hall till it comes within residential limits with higher value. Adjoining land may be used for agriculture despite being sold to speculators, who let the former owner or leaseholders cultivate it until they need the land.

Property Dealers

Property dealers are involved with both the supply and the demand side of the land market. The majority of them are outsiders, although some are original villagers too. There are enormous monetary benefits connected with the development of land into residential, commercial and industrial premises. Property dealers have access to the most detailed local information on the legal status, ownership, prices and landowners who want to sell land. They occupy the space in land market to fill the gap left by the government in areas where the formal control of development is weak. They have a captive market in the large number of migrants who are looking for a place to stay or own. This seller's market is good for their business. The demand created by industrialists, speculators, and city dwellers is another important source of earnings, as the property dealers charge commission on the transaction. These property dealers also involve local goons into their deals and transactions. Since, the stakes and profit margins are so high and these goons tilt the balance for the property dealers. Quite often, the land belongs to multiple owners and even one owner declines to go with other owners, the transaction is affected. In these situations the goons act to benefit property dealers.

Some of the former and current landowners from the indigenous community are property dealers as well. They have an advantage over the outsiders due to the solidarity between the landowning group in the villages, their knowledge of the land issues, and their ease of movement in the social structures of their village. However, that as the village becomes more and more urbanized and the real estate sector expands, the community loses some of its coherence. This causes the community to lose its grip on the property business. There are reports of dubious role and complaints of property dealers in land transactions and conflicts about land and criminal acts in the land business. This job is being favoured by large number of people at different levels because it does not require much investment, it is possible for local people to enter the real estate business and do well, taking advantage of their familiarity with the residents and the local setting.

Developers

Developers are group of people with a strong financial strength and political contacts. They usually act in a group which consists of local villagers, property dealers, developer, investors and being helped by governmental and political people from behind. Many of the developers actually are politicians, making optimal use of the power and information they acquire through their office. Some of them are local villagers, but most are wealthy urban businessmen. They are in a good position to orchestrate the development of unauthorised colonies. The activities of developers in the study area are mostly illegal, they forge the land records and manipulate the development plans for their benefits. Many of the property dealers have become developers due to the knowledge of land market and its operation mechanism. However, the developers do not have good reputation of the population as they cheat the people at different stages of property development. Since the stakes are very high, often criminal or financial conspiracy also involved.

Box 8.2 : Decentralisation for Rural-Urban Development in India : Enabling Legislation for Rural-Urban Problem solving

The Government of Indian made amendments to its constitution in 1992 that lay the legislative basis for addressing some of the most difficult challenges to rural-urban environmental problem solving. Legislative factors often limit the power of different local governments to take the initiative to solve local problems and to collaborate to address mutual problems.

The Government of Indian has made several changes, which allows local governments to transcend some of the limitations in terms of decision making by specialists using mostly technical criteria, lack of access to finance on the legal leeway to raise their own finance, and political considerations for delineating municipal boundaries:

1. Municipalities were made responsible for economic development and social justice in addition to the conventional municipal functions. In place of agency led land-use planning, municipal and elected bodies would now be directly involved in matters related to rural and urban planning diffusing a share of the decision making from specialists into the hands the people and their elected representatives.
2. This requires that municipal areas shall be declared on a greater consideration of other factors, including population area and percentage of employment in non-agriculture.
3. This approach provides that every State should constitute a Governance Board for transitional areas – areas in transition from rural to urban — or the urban fringe in order to manage rural-urban interaction and problems of land-use at the fringe.
4. Local governments can achieve financial self-sufficiency through proportional access to State taxes, grants in aid to municipalities from the Consolidated Fund of the State, locally raised taxes, user charges, non-tax revenue for performance of statutory and regulatory functions, from commercial ventures, and borrowings. These mechanisms aim to ensure that local governments have the necessary financial base to address their priorities.

This legal framework allows for a greater balancing of spatial, national, regional, and local priorities, allows more information to flow from the local to regional levels, and allows national rural-urban priorities to be grounded in local reality. Under this system, Municipalities and Panchayats prepare development plans, which

(Contd...)

BOX 8.2 : *(Contd...)*

are reviewed by District Planning Committees, which consists of locally elected representatives. These Committees consolidate the plans and prepare a Draft Development Plan for the district as a whole. The draft development plan is prepared with respect to matters of common interest such as spatial planning, sharing of water and other physical and natural resources, and integrating development of infrastructure and environmental conservation. These plans are then forwarded to the State Government for approval. This potential of flow of information from people to policy makers can only become a reality if local governments take the initiative and use the doors that have been opened by these legal reforms.

Government and Public Institutions

The government enters the scene in many guises. There are several government agencies and they appear in the form of different actors, sometimes even pursuing contradictory goals. The interests and objectives of authorities do not only vary according to the roles they have as an institute, but may sometimes reflect individual or fractional interests, depending on many personal agendas. Consequently, private actors are able to influence and manipulate government administration and policies.

In India, urban development falls under the purview of State governments, which in turn delegate related responsibilities to urban local bodies as envisaged under the Constitution's 74th Amendment Act. So the State government is the highest level for politics and policy-making. For most aspects relevant to the study area, it operates through local bureaucratic channels, e.g., the Block Development Office. The government has decentralised many tasks in urban administration, creating many departments. The most important one is the Municipal Corporation and Aligarh Development Authority (ADA). Specific registration of land-use and ownership is done by the *Patwari*, who keeps records at the village level. The judiciary plays an important role in land issues. Its hand is visible in land-use policy as well as in civil cases in the event of conflict and litigation. The police perform their obvious task of preventing illegal activity in general, which includes illegal land occupations, conversions, etc. Often, the police act in partisan manner to help certain group or would not act at all, they are notorious for demanding bribe for acting in either way.

Higher level interests in the preservation of farmland are mainly a responsibility of the city development authority and the State government. The official aspects of land-use policies are formulated in the Aligarh Master Plan. This even aims to protect an agricultural belt around Aligarh just outside the city limits. Much of the administration of rural land in Aligarh formally restricts the conversion of agricultural land to non-agricultural purposes, creating an enormous gap between plans and actual practice. The effectiveness of this administration is poor and allows the illegal conversion of agricultural land. Conversion is encouraged by the shortage of housing that is a result of this situation. Besides, the administrative bodies have compulsory stipulations and financial constraints that make the execution of large-scale and ambitious land-use projects a problematic affair.

Most of the time, urban planning remains in governmental records and proposals. The actual urban development is an outcome of complicated interactions among the various government agencies and local private actors, rather than from rigid planning. Many government institutions implicitly represent conflicting interests. It is not unusual for individual ADA officials, police officers, and politicians to conspire in the creation of illegal settlements, whereby all get a share of the profits.

The governmental agencies as actor in urban land market and urban planning appears to be the most corrupt. Since it consists of many institutions and different level individuals, only few corrupt officials make the entire system look corrupt. Often, some individuals act honestly and try to clean the system, but because of high stakes, corrupt system prevails over them.

The present study finds prevailing duality in the system of land supply which is characterized by many current urban concerns as well as throws light on strengths and weakness of the actors in PUI:

- There is a chronic shortage in the supply of urban land. Every individual has different interests which lead to conflicts and practices of intimidation and manipulation to defend certain interests of specific individuals or groups. There is excessive inter-mixing of spatial functions which is the outcome of inflated land values, unrestricted, uncontrolled expansions, causing adverse environmental conditions. This problem needs to be addressed, but the costs of relocation are high and the legal proceedings are lengthy.

- The actor approach provides insight for the conduct of people and institutions involved with land transformation process in the periurban interface. The PUI is characterised by a great diversity of actors and a complex mix of conflicting and complementary interests.
- Evidences from the study area shows that 'beneficiaries' and 'victims' can be encountered in any group, depending on the local situation. The outcome is also greatly depended on the economic and political strength, the connections, and the alliances among the actors.
- The households among the original villagers who do not possess agricultural land found to have the weakest position and are the victims of this urbanisation process. They are excluded from any direct benefits of the process. Elevated land prices have further limited their ability to acquire extra residential and commercial space. These landless households only get benefit from their ancestral land that they own near the settlement. Gradually, this section of the PUI society are uprooted and pushed away from their location.
- The migrants also found to have relatively weak position, yet because of their large numbers they have reasonable presence in PUI land transformation mechanism.
- The government is both a strong and a weak actor at the same time; it depends on the individual officials and institutions. The media, court and RTI activists also contribute to strengthen the governmental institutions. On the other hand, an alliance of residents, landowners, property dealers, politicians, and developers makes them weak with their illegal acts.

- The local landowners are strong actors in the PUI land market as they possess land, further, the alliance with developers, property dealers makes them key actor; at least in economic terms. Even smaller landowners are part of a finely branched land transformation framework getting benefits from dynamic urban land market.
- The marginalized group, in this process of land transformation is the rural landless labourers (including seasonal migrants), they have difficulty in obtaining cheap accommodation when they come to live and work in city. Whether or not they are exploited in the process of starting informal settlements is a subjective judgement. They are vulnerable, since they depend on shady financial transactions and sometimes face instances of cheating and intimidation. Nevertheless, since the formal sector fails to provide access to land for the poorest, the poor are probably glad that to find a place to live in the informal settlements. This also provides opportunity to take benefits from PUI land market. Because when the land, where they squatted is developed, they take money to vacate their occupance.

9

Aligarh City's PUI —The Transformations : Issues and Challenges

Transformation means change in appearance or nature in any phenomena. Here in this chapter the focus is on transformation in the character of PUI. Here we try to investigate and analyse the transformation of the rural settlements beyond the limits of a growing city (PUI) which underwent a process of change. This change is analysed from two perspectives.

1. From the urban perspective, i.e., from the perspective of the people living in urban areas.
2. From the rural perspective, i.e., from the perspective of the people living around the urban area — the PUI.

The economic development and the process of urbanization has resulted in periurban interface development. The particularity of its geographical location enables it to have two functions: urban landscape and rural landscape. The urbanization process is quite prominent among developing countries and with its development, in areas surrounding the cities (the PUI), the boundary between rural surrounding and city is becoming less and less distinct. Traditional isolated relationship between city and rural surrounding is now replaced by a new relationship that they rely on each other and penetrate into each other. This is the emergence of the PUI.

The PUI is where urban and rural activities meet, a mosaic of rural and urban systems, which is economically and socially heterogeneous and subject to rapid change. The PUI is centre stage to the urbanization process as the transition process is rapid and effective here. The transformation process in PUI has its bearing on people, the resources and its environment. The PUI which was largely rural in character, with time have undergone transformation and become increasingly heterogeneous with complex intermixing of rural and urban character.

As in the previous chapters discussed, the formation and development in the urban fringe result from the interaction between rural surrounding and the city. The formation and development lead to the differentiation of dualistic structure of elements, functions and landscapes between rural and urban areas. Besides, the greater potential difference has brought about the interaction, communication and penetration between the two sides and enabled the evolvement of PUI. With the rural areas and urban areas penetrating into each other, a unique landscape pattern and a new way of utilizing land come into being, due to which a special environmental effect happens.

The functional force of city is the leadership mechanism of the formation of the urban fringe. The rapid development of city results also in flow of goods and capital, from urban areas to rural areas. This flow forms aerial expansion and immaterial element space spread. The spread of urban elements result from such factors as higher land price, higher tax, more serious pollution, heavier traffic and governments' policies about encouraging moving outside. The spread is influenced by the attenuation law of distance. The nearer an area is to the city, the more it will be influenced, the more urban elements it has. With the widened distance from the centre of the city, the urban elements in areas becomes less and less until they completely turn into rural elements. The space from urban elements to rural elements is the feature of PUI.

Similarly, the functional force of the rural area is the internal force of the formation of the PUI. The development of rural economy has influenced land utilization. Internal industry move outside to the boundary to make the formation of the PUI possible.

The development of the PUI is influenced not only by the radiation of the city centre and the inner-strains of its urbanization, but also by the trend of the rural surrounding to aggregate to the city. The landscape elements of the urban fringe are mainly divided into two aspects.

THE URBAN LANDSCAPE ELEMENTS

Urban landscape typically takes human's dwell environment as its centre, including building, city industries, city amenities and facilities, streets, malls, multiplexes, parks and other recreational facilities, etc. All these factors have space-time nature and are complicated. Meanwhile, influenced by the self-protection consciousness of the communities, urban landscape elements are different in different regions. Functionally, urban landscape elements are presented in high-energy and high-capacity radiation spread as well as the cultural diversity. Urban landscape is different from the city centre to the boundary, with the transmutation of the intensity and patterns of communities, population density and functions.

THE RURAL LANDSCAPE ELEMENTS

Rural landscape elements consist of two parts: natural landscape elements, including farmlands, waterbodies, orchards, etc., and human landscape elements, including villages, vernacular architecture, folk and traditional cultures, etc. Natural landscape elements are the backgrounds of the human landscape and the essential characteristics of rural settlements which are the carrier of the primary resource based predominantly farming culture. This is characterized by traditional villages with green living places which are comfortable, peaceful, and simple and combines human, nature and society into one harmonious whole.

Rural landscape in the PUI is different from urban landscape and natural landscape. It is a complex constituted by settlement landscape, economy landscape, culture landscape and environment landscape. It differs from others lies in its productive landscape and field utilization landscape as well as the unique rural culture and life.

The transformation has been witnessed largely in the following four broad areas, which were also interrelated with each other. They are:

1. Transformation in economic environment in PUI.
2. Transformation in livelihoods in PUI.

3. Transformation in infrastructural facilities in PUI.
4. Transformation in social environment in PUI.

1. The Transformation in Economic Environment in the PUI

The transformation in economic environment in the PUI is important simply because this zone is characterized by the coexistence of urban (mainly secondary and tertiary activities) and rural (mainly primary or natural resource based) activities. The PUI observe economic transformation in many ways. Some of them are discussed below:

PUI— A Place with Increased Opportunities

The households in Aligarh's PUI take advantage of the proximity to the city, the urban based economic activities (consisting of secondary and rapidly expanding tertiary sector) draw large number of workers. The urban based economic activities have employed about 33 per cent of the total sampled workers from the PUI. The proximity to the city was crucial as households from immediate PUI formed larger group of workers in these (86.4% secondary and 73% tertiary) sector. Significantly, women from this zone also had some presence and they were also found to be taking advantage of available opportunities to work in city. Majority of these workers are lesser educated and do not possess skill or expertise. That is why these workers are engaged in lower level activities mostly in unorganized sector. But they have the advantage of drawing regular and assured monthly or daily salary as well as the nature of work also requires lesser labour.

PUI— A Place which Offers a Large Market

The PUI also benefited from the larger urban market. The city with increasing population creates increased demand mainly for primary (nature based) products which they produce in rural areas. The easy access (personal contact with consumers) and monetized urban economy is of great advantage to these PUI producers. The survey reveals that the PUI supply a great variety of agricultural products (cereals, pulses, oilseeds, vegetables, fruits, flowers, etc), animal products (meat, milk, ghee, curd, butter, etc.), and other natural products (earth, brick, wood, etc.). The survey finds that an estimated 45,000 kilo litre of milk, 425 quintais of vegetables, 200 quintals of fruits, 2000 quintals of *chara* and 700 quintals of cow dung are supplied to the city. A relatively easy access to large urban market also helps the PUI producers to sell their products directly, many times bypassing the middlemen and draw higher revenues. While middlemen also play an active and dominant role (especially to household from distant PUIs) in disposing commodities in urban market. These middlemen act as channel to urban market as they purchase the commodities in village and supply to urban market. But PUI producers get much lesser profits through this kind of marketing as middlemen (mostly urban) take major chunk of profits.

PUI — A Place where Diversification of Economic Activity is the need of the hour

The PUI is influenced by urban monetized economy, larger market and greater opportunities. All this induce the PUI households to diversify their livelihood for better and improved living. The study finds that increasing number of households diversify their sources of income and draw on a portfolio of activities, such as formal waged employment, informal trading and low level services, etc. Large number of households reported that different members of the household are engaged in different types of activities and sectors of the economy.

The sample study finds that in the Aligarh's PUI, income diversification is quite common where increasing number of households is combining non-farming activity with their traditional farming activity. The sample results suggest that of the households associated with primary activity, 41 per cent depended on crop cultivation alone, while 59 per cent were supplementing with dairy activity along with crop cultivation. This diversification is necessary for enhancement in earnings required for survival in PUI. This argument is also strengthened by the fact that this trend is found to be more dominant in villages closer to the city. The survey shows

Table 9.1: Aligarh PUI — Modification in Economic Activity among Sampled Households (2009-10)

Modification in Economic Activity	*Immediate PUI (Up to 5 km)*	*Intermediate PUI (5 – 10 km)*	*Distant PUI (10 km and above)*	*Total*
Share Cropping	**10** *(16.4)* (16.4)	**26** *(42.6)* (27.6)	**25** *(41)* (40.3)	**61** (28.1)
Leasing Land	**14** *(21.8)* (22.9)	**33** *(51.6)* (35.1)	**17** *(26.5)* (27.4)	**64** (29.5)
Training & Skills	**12** *(63.1)* (19.7)	**3** *(15.8)* (3.2)	**4** *(21)* (6.4)	**19** (8.7)
Marketing & Management	**24** *(40)* (39.3)	**24** *(40)* (25.5)	**12** *(20)* (19.3)	**60** (27.6)
Others	**1** *(7.7)* (1.6)	**8** *(61.5)* (8.5)	**4** *(30.8)* (6.4)	**13** (5.9)
Total	**61** *(28.1)* (16.4)*	**94** *(43.3)* (44.1)*	**62** *(28.6)* (40.2)*	**217**

Note: 1. Figures in bold are absolute number of sampled respondents in the particular distance zones.
2. Figures in brackets (besides the bold figures) are percentages to the total of that particular variable.
3. Figures in brackets (below the bold figures) are percentages to the total from that particular distance zone.

Source: Based on Field Survey (2009-10).

that 45 per cent households in the immediate PUI are supplementing their income with adding dairying activity to their traditional farming activity. Combining farming and non-farming activities within one household play significant role in enhancing income as well as providing livelihood option which can be managed along with the farming activity.

The sample survey also finds that PUI household's women were also actively participating and contributing to household's income. Traditionally, these women contribute in farming and dairying activity but sample survey finds that women from immediate PUI are also engaged in urban based non-farm activity. The survey also points towards the declining economic significance of farming activity as it is low income generating activity, farmers are diversifying to other non-farm activities for additional income. A good number of migrants to the PUI, especially those who do not have land sell their labour to non-farm sector while their other members work in farming sector in their native rural areas. This pattern of diversification observed in the PUI is essential because it reduces dependence on one source of livelihood as well as increase the income of household which reduces vulnerability to stresses and shock of livelihood in urban economy.

PUI— A Place which Offers Higher Wages

PUI not only offers greater economic opportunities but it also provides higher and assured wages. Traditionally the wages in the rural agricultural sector are in kind rather than cash and that too is poor, irregular and incidence of exploitation and intimidation are common. The PUI with urban based activities offers these workers an opportunity to sell their labour for remittance in cash. PUI offers opportunities to all kind of workers, it includes skilled and unskilled workers in secondary sector and trained and educated employed in tertiary sector. The overall wages for all kinds of urban based activities are relatively higher and regular than in rural areas. This feature of urban based activities attracts workers from the rural areas instigating migration.

Table 9.2: Aligarh PUI — Change in Economic Activity among Sampled Households (2009-10)

Change in Economic Activity	*Immediate PUI (Up to 5 km)*	*Intermediate PUI (5 – 10 km)*	*Distant PUI (10 km and above)*	*Total*
Primary Sector	**51** (53.7) (64.5)	**29** (30.5) (87.9)	**15** (15.8) (83.3)	**95** (73)
Secondary Sector	**7** (87.5) (8.8)	—	**1** (12.5) (5.5)	**8** (6.1)
Tertiary Sector	**21** (77.7) (26.6)	**4** (14.8) (12.1)	**2** (7.4) (11.1)	**27** (20.8)
Total	**79** (60.8) (21.2)*	**33** (25.4) (15.5)*	**18** (13.8) (11.7)*	**130** (17.6)

Note: 1. Figures in bold are absolute number of sampled respondents in the particular distance zones.
2. Figures in brackets (besides the bold figures) are percentages to the total of that particular variable.
3. Figures in brackets (below the bold figures) are percentages to the total from that particular distance zone.

Source: Based on Field Survey (2009-10).

BOX 9.1 : Urban Agricultural Marketing

A major challenge for the coming years is to prepare extension services to provide relevant advice to urban farmers, since most of their knowledge is based on rural experiences and does not necessarily apply in the cities. This applies both to the methodologies used as well as to technical knowledge diffused. The available literature on marketing focuses mainly on marketing from the rural areas to the cities and exports, with an emphasis on the formal and central city markets.

The area of micro and small enterprises related to urban agriculture is a very interesting one that is worth much more attention. Business opportunities in urban agriculture abound, resulting in different kinds of enterprises that can be classified into three major categories (apart from the agricultural production enterprises):

- Processing enterprises (i.e., food preparation, packaging, milling, drying and others),
- Input delivery enterprises (i.e., agricultural supplies such as fertilizers, compost, soil media, seeds, pesticides, water, tools, feeds),
- Service delivery enterprises (i.e., special labour services such as milking, animal health assistance, book-keeping, transport and others).

Informal sector programmes often overlook such enterprises and more attention is needed for provision of training, management assistance, credit and marketing information to these micro and small entrepreneurs.

PUI — A Place of Occupational Transformation

Another striking feature observed in Aligarh's PUI is declining preference to agriculture as livelihood option. This leads to large scale occupational transformation in the PUI. This occupational transformation is influenced by popularization of education and this phenomenon is more prominent among younger generation. Moreover, this change has been clear periurban character becoming particularly strong with proximity to the city where greater choices and opportunities exist. Another reason for this transformation is decreasing land for farming activity, which means small farmers do not have choice but to opt for urban based livelihood, shedding their traditional farming activity.

PUI — A Place with Increasing Land Value

The PUI is also characterized by increasing value of land. This trend has made land as an attractive investment object in PUI. This trend has affected the PUI economy in many ways. The outcome is felt in the form of large scale as well as frequent land transformations. The agricultural land is the main sufferer which is shrinking and vacant land (the speculative land) is rapidly increasing. The use of land and its transformation in PUI is increasingly influenced by real estate developments which are instrumental in manipulating the prospects of future developments of land in PUI. The increase in land value is driven by increase in demand (the population pressure) but this increase in demand is also because of increase in land value. Land value and demand for land have bearing on each other. The increase in land value and increased demand for land in PUI has affected the agricultural system. The benefits of increases in land value have benefited more the large landowners while small landowners have been further marginalized.

Table 9.3 : Aligarh PUI –Frequency of City Visit among Sampled Households (2009-10).

Frequency of City Visit	*Immediate PUI (Up to 5 km)*	*Intermediate PUI (5 – 10 km)*	*Distant PUI (10 km and above)*	*Total*
Daily	**104** *(75.3)* (27.9)	**30** *(21.7)* (14.1)	**4** *(2.9)* (2.6)	**138** (17.9)
Weekly	**141** *(59.2)* (37.9)	**49** *(20.6)* (23)	**48** *(20.2)* (24.6)	**238** (30.9)
Fortnightly	**127** *(43.9)* (33.3)	**81** *(28)* (38.1)	**81** *(28)* (46.1)	**289** (37.6)
Rarely	–	**53** *(50.9)* (24.9)	**51** *(49)* (26.7)	**104** (13.5)

Note: 1. Figures in bold are absolute number of sampled respondents in the particular distance zones.
2. Figures is brackets and underlined are percentages to the total of that particular variable.
3. Figures in brackets (below the bold figures) are percentages to the total from that particular distance zone.

Source: Based on Field Survey (2009-10).

Table 9.4: Aligarh PUI — Purpose of City Visit among Sampled Households (2009-10).

Purpose of City Visit	*Immediate PUI (Upto 5 km)*	*Intermediate PUI (5 – 10 km)*	*Distant PUI (10 km and above)*	*Total*
Education	**67** (80.7) (18.1)	**13** (15.6) (8.1)	**3** (3.6) (2.2)	**83** (12.5)
Shopping	**164** (53.6) (44.1)	**74** (24.2) (46.2)	**68** (22.2) (51.1)	**306** (46)
Health	**52** (85.2) (13.9)	**6** (9.8) (3.7)	**3** (4.9) (2.2)	**61** (9.2)
Entertainment & Leisure	**15** (88.2) (4.1)	**2** (11.7) (1.2)	—	**17** (2.5)
Visit to their Relatives	**22** (35.5) (5.9)	**18** (29) (11.2)	**22** (35.5) (16.5)	**62** (9.3)
Others	**52** (38.2) (13.9)	**47** (34.5) (29.4)	**37** (27.2) (27.8)	**136** (20.4)
Total(Visitors to city excluding rare visitor)	**372**	**160**	**133**	**665**

Note: 1. Figures in bold are absolute number of sampled respondents in the particular distance zones.
2. Figures in brackets (besides the bold figures) are percentages to the total of that particular variable.
3. Figures in brackets (below the bold figures) are percentages to the total from that particular distance zone.

Source: Based on Field Survey (2009-10).

2. The Transformation of Social Environment in the PUI

The transformation in social environment in the PUI is important simply because this zone is characterized by the intermixing of urban way of life and rural way of living. This intermixing is in some way is constrained by cultural differences. The PUI observes social transformation in many ways. Some of them are discussed below:

PUI is a Zone of Changing Demographic Features

The PUI is witnessing rapid growth in its population as well as marked with intensification of concentration of population. There is a continuous and accelerated inflow of population in immediate PUI, both from urban core and rural hinterland. The city population is moving to PUI because this zone provides less congested accommodation that too at lesser price whereas rural people migrate to PUI to take advantage of greater economic opportunities.

Another important social feature which was observed in the PUI was improving status of women. The PUI respondents have reported of better status of women than both rural interiors and urban core. The women were found to be actively participating in economic activities, managing the household as well as taking care of household resources too. The education, political empowerment and economically activeness have made them secure. There was male specific migration in the immediate PUI resulting in somewhat skewed sex ratio, but still the overall status was satisfactory.

One important change which the PUI has witnessed in the PUI is awareness and popularization of education among the masses. Education has started to transform the PUI society. Even the poor and uneducated households have also started to push their children for pursuing education. Although, the government is injecting money and incentives but it has not made much impact. However, the social awareness has contributed significantly in improvement in education level. The respondents were found to prefer private schools only to ensure better and disciplined education. The government school education is greatly subsidized and there are provisions of other incentive like mid-day meal, school uniform, books and stationary etc. But despite of all this poor management of schools and irregular teaching have distracted the parents.

PUI is a Place of Divided Family

PUI has also witnessed transformation in family structure. The families are increasingly becoming nuclear, which includes married couple and their unmarried children. Traditionally the households followed joint family norms where all the resources were pooled and elder member of the family distribute them among all the family members. This system was suited to rural based farming activity. But with changes in occupational structure, this family norm has also been changed. The sample survey finds that increase in land values have led to higher stakes as well as disputes among family members. Thus, to avoid disputes, there is increasing number of families now divide their lands leading to fragmentation of land. This division of land also results in division of economic dependence leading to nuclear family norm. The immediate PUI have more nuclear families because of more urban based occupations and shortage of space whereas distant PUI is still dominance of agricultural activity so still joint families exists.

Table 9.5: Aligarh PUI — Use of Modern Gadgets and Appliances among Sampled Households (2009-10).

Modern Gadgets & Appliances	*Immediate PUI (Up to 5 km)*	*Intermediate PUI (5 – 10 km)*	*Distant PUI (10 km and above)*	*Total*
Luxuries	**66** *(84.6)* (17.7)	**6** *(7.7)* (2.8)	**6** *(7.7)* (3.3)	**78** (10.1)
Basic Necessities	**202** *(57.9)* (54.3)	**102** *(29.2)* (47.8)	**45** *(12.9)* (24.4)	**349** (45.4)
Negligible	**104** *(30.4)* (27.9)	**105** *(30.7)* (49.3)	**133** *(38.9)* (72.3)	**342** (44.4)

Note: 1. Figures in bold are absolute number of sampled respondents in the particular distance zones.
2. Figures in brackets (besides the bold figures) are percentages to the total of that particular variable.
3. Figures in brackets (below the bold figures) are percentages to the total from that particular distance zone.

Source: Based on Field Survey (2009-10).

Table 9.6: Aligarh PUI — Type of House Construction among Sampled Households (2009-10).

Type of House Construction	*Immediate PUI (Up to 5 km)*	*Intermediate PUI (5 – 10 km)*	*Distant PUI (10 km and above)*	*Total*
Brick–Cement with RCC Columns–Roof	**331** *(65.3)* (89.7)	**137** *(27)* (64.3)	**39** *(7.7)* (21.2)	**507** *(100)* (66)
Brick–Cement Non RCC Columns–Roof	**41** *(20.4)* (11.02)	**57** *(28.3)* (26.7)	**103** *(51.2)* (55.9)	**201** *(100)* (26.1)
Mud – Brick Thatched	—	**19** *(31.1)* (8.9)	**42** *(68.9)* (22.8)	**61** *(100)* (7.9)
Total	**372** *(48.3)* (100)	**213** *(23.7)* (100)	**184** *(23.9)* (100)	**769** *(100)* (100)

Note: 1. Figures in bold are absolute number of sampled respondents in the particular distance zones.
2. Figures in brackets (besides the bold figures) are percentages to the total of that particular variable.
3. Figures in brackets (below the bold figures) are percentages to the total from that particular distance zone.

Source: Based on Field Survey (2009-10).

Table 9.7: Aligarh PUI — General Status of Living Conditions among Sampled Households (2009-10).

Living Conditions	*Immediate PUI (Up to 5 km)*	*Intermediate PUI (5 – 10 km)*	*Distant PUI (10 km and above)*
Average per capita room occupance	**2-3**	**4-5**	**5-6**
Satisfactory sanitation	**331** (88.9)	**87** (40.8)	**22** (11.9)
Satisfactory ventilation	**115** (30.9)	**83** (39)	**68** (36.9)
Electricity connection	**372** (100)	**179** (84.04)	**142** (77.2)
Average duration of electricity supply (hours / day)	**14-16**	**8-12**	**8-12**
Fuel : LPG	**330** (88.7)	**87** (40.8)	**26** (14.1)
Kerosene/Wood	**41** (11.02)	**126** (59.1)	**158** (85.9)

Note : 1. Figures in bold are absolute number of sampled respondents in the particular distance zones.

2. Figures in brackets (below the bold figures) are percentages to the total from that particular distance zone.

Source: Based on Field Survey (2009-10).

PUI is a Place with improving Living Standards

The sample survey finds that there was a marked influence of city life on the lifestyle and living standard of PUI households. There was significant improvements in the PUI households which have become more urbanized and the quality of life have also improved considerably. Most of this improvement in PUI is because of inflow of money through sale of land or income from secondary and tertiary sector. This improvement is visible from their houses (which are mostly pucca, constructed using bricks and cement).

There have been improvements also in sanitation, ventilation, electricity connections, use of fuel, availability of modern gadgets, etc. However, all this improvements decreases with distance, as immediate PUI have better quality of life whereas distant PUI has relatively inferior quality of life.

PUI is a Place with Materialistic Mindset

PUI present a meeting point of people from different walks of life having no affinity with one another. Everyone of PUI is rational regarding economic point of view because trend of materialism is continuously growing here. In materialistic society money is considered as the key to happiness. The sense of social responsibility among the people has been reduced. Competition for space and services in monetized economy has brought change in attitude. Owning agricultural land was once considered to enjoy higher social status but now jobs in tertiary sector are preferred. Interestingly, some respondents have blamed the popularization of satellite television among the rural masses. Increasing number of rural youth and females were found to be devoting their leisure time on watching daily soaps, serials and movies. This has made effects on their social life and impacts on family relations.

PUI is a Place of Conflicts between Old Residents and Migrants

The growth of new residential colonies within the village dramatically alters the demographic and sociological profile of the villages. The old village settlement continues to exist almost intact with its original residents, while the new residential colonies house the people from the city. The social relationship between the old residents and migrants coming from the city is at best tenuous and superficial. The two communities have different perceptions of the city. However, there are some contacts between the two communities which are largely for their mutual benefits. The migrants remit their products for money which they could not get among their own social group. The supply of milk, vegetables and women are going to newly built colonies for domestic help.

PUI is a Place of New social Class

The sampled households in Aligarh PUI represent a new social class which has increasing elements of urban characteristics and decreasing rural elements. The PUI elements households showed better education levels, especially younger generation had better educational attainments. They have smaller family size but marked gender biasness. Although they showed gender biasness among kids but status of women has improved especially with educational attainments among women and higher work participation. The households where women working in tertiary activities attained higher status in the family as well as in the society. It clearly shows that economic independence is directly associated with women empowerment.

Table 9.8: Aligarh PUI – General Expenditure Pattern among Sampled Households (2009-10)

Expenditures	*Immediate PUI (Up to 5 km)*	*Intermediate PUI (5 – 10 km)*	*Distant PUI (10 km and above)*	*Total*
Food	**208** (45.5) (55.9)	**136** (29.7) (63.8)	**113** (24.7) (60.3)	**457** (59.4)
Education	**78** (65.5) (20.9)	**24** (20.2) (11.3)	**17** (14.3) (7.8)	**119** (15.5)
Health	**45** (76.2) (12.1)	**7** (11.9) (3.3)	**7** (11.9) (2.6)	**59** (7.7)
Clothing	**25** (67.6) (6.7)	**7** (18.9) (3.3)	**5** (13.5) (1.9)	**37** (4.8)
Others	**16** (16.5) (4.3)	**39** (40.2) (18.3)	**42** (43.3) (27.3)	**97** (12.6)

Note: 1. Figures in bold are absolute number of sampled respondents in the particular distance zones.
2. Figures in brackets (besides the bold figures) are percentages to the total of that particular variable.
3. Figures in brackets (below the bold figures) are percentages to the total from that particular distance zone.

Source: Based on Field Survey (2009-10).

The households have also showed association with diverse economic activity. This multi-activity household is survival response to urban monetized economy to generate higher incomes required for sustenance. This urban monetized economy has also blurred the traditional caste based social system. The PUI have a new social class, where social status is determined by household income. This income based social evolvement has also transformed the PUI society into materialistic society which have predominant urban values and way of life.

Table 9.9: Aligarh PUI – General investment pattern among sampled households (2009-10).

Investments	*Immediate PUI (Up to 5 km)*	*Intermediate PUI (5 – 10 km)*	*Distant PUI (10 km and above)*	*Total*
Land	**30** *(22.9)* (8.1)	**40** *(30.5)* (14.1)	**61** *(46.6)* (27.7)	**131** (17)
House	**182** *(67.4)* (45.9)	**55** *(20.4)* (21.1)	**33** *(12.2)* (17.9)	**270** (35.1)
Social Events	**101** *(41.5)* (27.1)	**71** *(29.2)* (33.3)	**71** *(29.2)* (38.6)	**243** (31.6)
Others	**59** *(47.2)* (15.8)	**47** *(37.6)* (22.1)	**19** *(15.2)* (8.7)	**125** (16.2)

Note: 1. Figures in bold are absolute number of sampled respondents in the particular distance zones.
2. Figures in brackets (besides the bold figures) are percentages to the total of that particular variable.
3. Figures in brackets (below the bold figures) are percentages to the total from that particular distance zone.

Source: Based on Field Survey (2009-10).

PUI is a place with changing perception

The sample survey finds that the sample households of Aligarh city have certainly benefited from urban proximity. They take advantage from the city's economic developments. The educational and health facilities of the city have greatly helped the PUI residents in the attainment of their educational and health requirements.

Overall also the city's infrastructure and facilities have helped in the development of PUI villages. However, the distance from the city was very crucial and obviously the PUI villages closer to the city drew more benefits than the distant villages in PUI. Interestingly when the respondents were enquired about the benefits from the city, the respondents from immediate and intermediate PUI were critical of the urban forces.

These respondents were concern as their economic, social and cultural activities have been greatly transformed due to urban proximity. Which in their view have changed their livelihood and lifestyle. But still these respondents do not want to shift their base, meaning which on the one hand, they want to take all the benefits of urban proximity while on the other hand they want to remain stuck with their rural lifestyle and do not wish any erosion in social and cultural values. However, this dichotomy was not evident among younger generation. The distant PUI respondents on the other hand, complain of difficulties in accessing urban benefits, they want rapid urban development and expansions so that they come closer to the city and get benefits of urban amenities and facilities.

3. The Transformation of Infrastructural Facilities in the PUI

The process of urbanization has its impact on its surrounding (the Periurban Interface) in many ways and at different scales. Urban impact on PUI is both in terms of 'site' and 'situation'. Here, 'site' is referred to the physical and cultural characteristics and attributes of the city. While, 'situation' specifies the external relations of the locale. In the context of a PUI, a change in situation usually precedes a change in the site. This is evident from the improvements in the infrastructural facilities, amenities and their access in the PUI. Better access to a location strengthens the external relations of that place leading to changes in its site. The transformation in availability and access to infrastructural facilities and amenities in the PUI has greatly improved. This is also an outcome of change in economic activities as the development of secondary and tertiary activities has helped in developing the infrastructural facilities. Moreover, there is also an improvement in general awareness for accessing and using these available facilities. The PUI observe developments in infrastructural facilities in many ways. Some of them are discussed below:

PUI is a Place with Improved Accessibility

Aligarh city and its PUI villages have improved accessibility especially in terms of roads transport. A lot of improvements have been achieved in the last decade with enhanced investments for relaying rural roads and State highways. There has been allocation of Rs.78 crore for maintenance of State highways and Rs. 30 crores for rural roads in the State budget. The PUI roads have also benefited from other development programmes (Panchayati Raj, Rural Development and Community Development) which have helped in better accessibility to the city. The improvements in roads have significantly helped the development as well as expansion of PUI.

PUI is a Place with Improved Education

One of the most important and positive impact of Aligarh city on PUI households have been the awareness to education. The proximity to the city and access to better and specialized education facilities have also helped in overall improvements among sampled households in PUI. The sampled households were found to be increasingly concern for their children's education. The urban economic environment has also contributed in enhancement of awareness to education. They consider better future of their children by educating them. Significant investments by government (Rs. 53.5 crore for school education and 23.7 crore for education for all programmes) have also improved the availability and access to basic school education. 94 per cent of total households reported of sending their children to schools. More importantly the number of dropout up to primary level was much lesser in PUI compared to average rural dropouts in the Aligarh district. The PUI households also reported of students daily commuting to Aligarh city for higher education.

PUI is a Place with Improved Health Facilities

Another positive impact of Aligarh city on its PUI villages was observed in awareness and access to health facilities. Increasing number of PUI households now approach the modern urban based health facilities. Traditionally, the rural population due to ignorance and difficulties in accessing medical facilities depended largely on untrained quacks. They also had more faith in their traditional nature based treatment for health problems. Again substantial investments by government (Rs. 30.4 crore for health and 47.9 crore for women and child care) have improved not only health facilities in the city but also in PUIs villages and rural health centres. The sampled PUI households have also reported of availing health facilities in the city. This improvement in health facilities along with improved accessibility and access has resulted in escalating number of PUI households reporting availing of health facility. Approximately 9.2 per cent of the total daily visitors to city come to city for their different medical needs.

PUI is a Place with Improved Electricity Supply

Electric connection has been made in all the sampled PUI villages. 84% of the sampled households has also electric connection in their houses. However, the electricity supply is greatly varied. The city has an average supply of 16 hours daily while rural areas have 8 to 12 hours supply. The government have allocated Rs. 83 crores for rural electrification but respondents were not satisfied with the supply of electricity. Interestingly, all PUI respondents acknowledged the city proximity as advantageous for better infrastructure and amenities but for poor supply of electricity blamed city as they feel that their share of electric supply is diverted to city.

Peri Urbanization and Environmental Issues

Environmental issues and problems have featured prominently in processes of periurbanization and the nature of PUIs almost everywhere. The Aligarh city's PUI is not independent or isolated zone, but — as defined — dynamic interfaces between urban and rural relations. PUI development and the resultant forces and pressures acting in the PUI are, therefore, not only local but also regional and even national, in terms of human mobility, commodity and financial flows and their valuation, and claims on environmental resources. The stability of the PUI landscape is relatively poor as compared to urban or rural landscapes which have a relatively better stability. The development of city and gradual expansions outward in the PUI, where land fee is lower and land-use ways are more flexible, makes PUI environmentally vulnerable.

Some important environmental concerns are discussed below:

LAND CONVERSION

In north Indian Gangetic plain, one of the most intractable environmental issues is the inevitable conversion of agricultural land to urban uses, principally housing, commercial and industrial, infrastructure and other land-extensive facilities, waste dumps, and sewage disposal, etc. The availability of larger tracts of relatively undeveloped and cheaper land in the city's PUI makes it environmentally susceptible. In other words, negative environmental externalities are imposed on the PUI.

The urban oriented land transformation results in reduced evapotranspiration, increases in runoff as natural surfaces and land cover are replaced by impervious building and road surfacing materials. Runoff creates erosion problems in the absence of adequate water drainage. Runoff also becomes contaminated by urban activities and wastes. The consequences, especially for poor PUI inhabitants of turning farm lands into bricks and concrete increase in severity as the proportion of agricultural land decreases. Conversely, urbanization represents an unparalleled opportunity to improve living conditions, quality of life, and available resources, but the outcome is contingent on local circumstances and is likely to have differential impacts both geographically and socially.

The precise process by which land leases or sales occur reflects local institutional structures, land tenure systems, and the relative power of key actors. Corruption and self-aggrandizement by influential actors are widespread, especially where high profits are available almost instantly. Displaced households may receive alternative farmland (where this is still available) or monetary compensation but that may be inadequate and all too often such households become impoverished, no longer able to live without agriculture.

Arriving outsiders comprise both rural migrants seeking more affordable land and shelter than is available in town (who are typically poorer or little wealthier than most indigenous and who may find diverse livelihood opportunities in the PUI invaluable) and urban dwellers seeking larger, cheaper plots of land beyond the built up urban area. Such people may be poor, unable to acquire any reasonable urban base or wealthier people intending to construct large, modern (often western-style) homes on larger plots. A third category comprises urban developers and speculators buying up land for later resale or on which to construct housing or industrial premises, perhaps in association with rich urban investors. All have different effects on the PUI in terms of relative numbers and the direct and indirect impacts of their investments, livelihood activities, and resultant environmental degradation.

LOSS OF AGRICULTURAL LAND

The study area has recorded a loss of 3,078 hectares of crop land in the PUI due to urban expansions. Especially the conversion of crop land to tree plantation and vacant lands are the glaring example of it. The households in the PUI are subject to present or short-term future development pressure, begin to devote less capital for farm maintenance and management. The productivity of the land begins to decline, which ultimately results in selling these lands to property dealers. They do not maintain it as agriculturally productive land, but allow it to remain idle until such time as the advancing suburbs justify transforming it into suburban areas. The net effect of these forces cause a much greater loss of crop land to urban uses than the figures normally given for land transferred to urban uses indicate. It is estimated that for each hectare of land actually transferred into an urban related land-use, almost 2 hectares of additional land is lost from agricultural use.

A more significant factor intensifying the problem of loss of prime agricultural land is associated with the cost of such land conversion. These costs are two-fold, and are related to the actual cost of replacing the lost farmland, as well as to government programmes that prompt urban expansion and encourage loss of agricultural land. When the prime farmland is lost, the value of the crop production is immediately foregone. The cost to replace that land is fairly substantial. The government makes effort to bring some additional land for agricultural uses by reclaiming waste lands but the question is "how much and at what cost".

There was an estimated 182 hectares of land which is annually transformed in the PUI since 1980. But the conversion rate of agricultural land was much more than actually recorded. The urban area which was 2257 hectares in 1980 has increased up to 7,459 hectares in 2010 recording an increase of 230 per cent in urban land. Further, this increasing trend is bound to continue and accelerate because the ADA plans to develop the city area to 11,47,000 hectares by 2021 (Aligarh Master Plan 2011).

LAND DEGRADATION IN PUI

The field survey of Aligarh's PUI finds that urbanization process has led to widespread land degradation in the PUI. The respondents complained of deterioration in productive capacity of agricultural land. This is because due to urban shadow effect farmers devote less capital for farm maintenance and management in PUI. This leads to farms being kept idle and gradually converting into vacant and abandoned wasteland, to be used for future urban development. But until development, it remains degraded, land.

There were also evidences of land degradation due to urban oriented activities. This includes degraded land due to abandoned brick kilns or soil excavation sites or unrestricted uncontrolled garbage dumping on vacant PUI lands. Similarly, the evidences of land degradation in the PUI are also because of inappropriate farming practices. These practices are the outcome of the greed for maximizing income from land in the PUI, resulting in soil erosion, salinity, alkalinity, loss of nutrients, waterlogging, etc.

The interpretation of satellite imagery of Aligarh city and its environs shows that 16.4 hectares (There were approximately 19 soil excavation sites) of land is under the borrow pits from where currently soil is being excavated. The speculative landowners lease out their lands for soil excavation (The city has a daily estimated supply of 14,000 m^3 of earth) to earn revenues from idle speculative land. There was another 31.8 hectares of land was under brick kilns (there were about 47 active and approximately 67 abandoned disused brick kilns in Aligarh PUI). The city has an estimated daily supply of 60 lakh bricks, of which 70 per cent demand is met from the PUI.

Moreover, the city also generates approximately 17,5,000 metric tonnes of solid waste daily. This solid waste consists an estimated 39 per cent organic waste, 27 per cent construction and industrial debris, 18 per cent drain silt, 13 per cent recyclable waste and 5 per cent other wastes (mixed organic and inorganic wastes). There are about 17 official and approximately 48 other dumping sites where municipality workers and private cleaners (employed by housing society) dump these garbage. All of them are in the immediate PUI along the roads where no sanitary land fill practice is followed. The garbage is damped on vacant lands to be dug by rag pickers and animals. This again is not only an environmental hazard but also an example of critical land degradation.

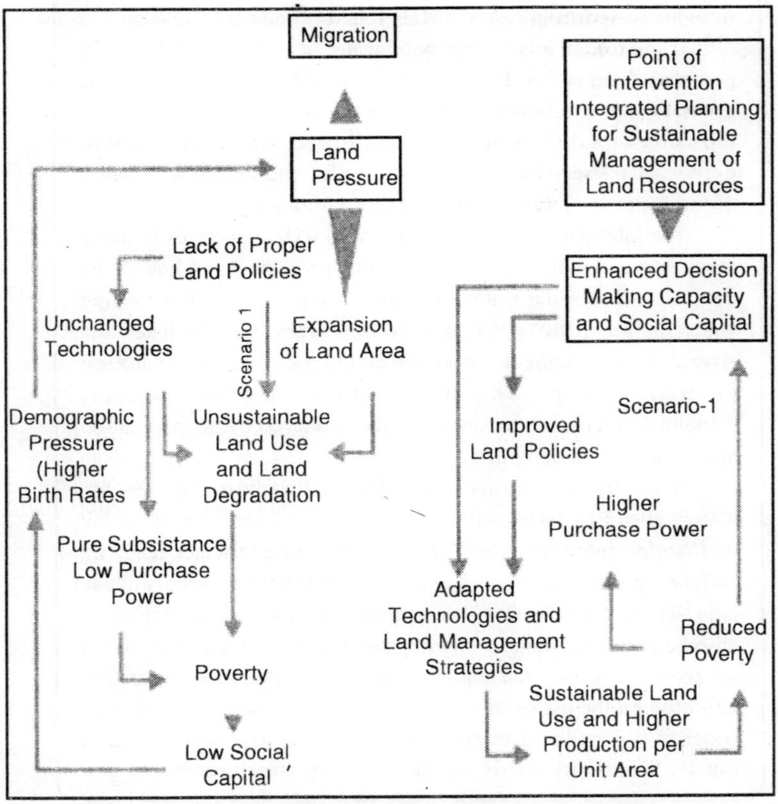

Figure 9.1: Land Resources and People's Activities

Box 9.2 : *Water Resources in Periurban Areas*

The need for water is universal, for domestic and industrial uses, for irrigation, etc. Water is an essential element, becoming increasingly scarce due to contamination and other circumstances and is not always easy to conserve.

A water system consists of the water resources, conveying and distribution systems and the sewage systems and can be a cause of contamination itself. A large urban centre including industrial areas and nearby intensive agricultural production systems may cause contamination of the aquifer by nitrates coming from cow sheds, poultry houses, city garbage, from excess nitrogen fertilizers and from products derived from the decomposing process of plant residues. Contamination may also come from chemical solubles used in industry and from heavy metals found in industrial sewage.

If the resource is underground water, it will be distributed by pumping from wells. Intensive pumping of water can lower the groundwater levels and, if the aquifer is close to the sea, the intrusion of saline water will be allowed. These factors will eventually cause salinization of the aquifer and reduce the quality of the water for drinking, industrial or farming purposes.

The intensive use of water has led to water shortages in many areas. As a result large water supply projects have had to be constructed, carrying water over great distances, and also making water more expensive. Other water resources, such as lakes and rivers, are also facing deterioration due to the common occurrence of drought years. The main problem, however, remains contamination caused by sewage water produced by the population and by industrial activities.

Normally, the sewage from cities and industry reaches the waterbodies like lakes and rivers, located in low lying areas, by discharging into them. As a result of the sewage water reaching surface aquifers and rivers and lakes, an intensive growth of algae is produced. Later, with the decomposition of the algae, oxygen is absorbed from the water, destroying microorganisms and other living agents in the water, causing it to become sterile. Such a situation will prohibit the use of this water for human consumption. Sewage water also contains detergents and salts, due to human use, and usually the salinity rate is higher than the original water.

Table 9.10 : Aligarh PUI — Status of Water Quality in Sampled Water from *Immediate* PUI (2010).

Constituents	*Indian Standard Institution ISI (1983) Standards*		*Concentration in sampled PUI Hand Pump water*
	Highest desired level mg/L	*Maximum permissible level mg/L*	
PH (Value)	6.5-8.5	6.5-9.2	8.43
Total Hardness	300	600	399
Chloride	250	1000	336
Fluoride (F)	1.0	1.5	0.9
Copper	0.05	1.5	0.85
Chromium	0.05	No relaxation	0.19
Nickel	0.020	–	0.99
Zinc	5	15	2.3
Sulphate	250	400	204
Calcium	75	200*	93
Magnesium	30	–	299

Note—The water sample was taken from a hand pump in the outskirts of Aligarh city (***immediate*** **PUI**) where nearby vegetable cultivation was being done. The water test was done in the laboratory of Z.H. Engineering College, Aligarh Muslim University.

Water Resource Degradation in PUI

The PUI is also observing in degradation of water resource as urban expansion has resulted in encroachments and obstruction on natural water channels and smaller waterbodies. These waterbodies and channels used to carry and store rain water. The choking of these water channels have adverse effect in two ways – one water storages have dried up while on other hand urban areas witness waterlogging during rainy season.

The PUI is also victim of untreated disposal of sewage (black water) and domestic waste water (grey water and sullage) in the PUI. The residents of Aligarh city utilizes approximately 95 million litres of fresh water daily of which 70 per cent water drains out in the form of sewage and sullage. The city has two drains namely Aligarh drain (*ganda nala*) and Jafri drain which runs around the municipal limit of the city. These two open drains gets discharges from 154 other big and small drains and sewers from the city. The two drains

Table 9.11: Aligarh PUI: Status of Physical, Chemical and Bacteriological Quality of the Hand Pump Water (2010).

PUI Zone	*Physical*						*Chemical*										*Bacteriological*			
	PH	*CT*	*TB*	*TS*	*TDS*	*TSS*	*Cl*	*TH*	*CH*	*MH*	*F*	*SO4*	*Cr*	*Ni*	*Cu*	*Zn*	*DO*	*BOD*	*CFU/mL*	*MPN 100ml*
Immediate PUI	8.4	1427	7	1072	1099	28	84	223	48	175	0.9	48	–	–	–	0.58	306	1.2	330	80
Intermediate PUI	7.78	721	3	491	491	11	89	238	74	167	0.4	124	–	–	–	0.35	503	–	43	4
Distant PUI	6.99	458	3	317	312	5	20	132	26	106	0.9	75	–	–	–	0.7	408	0.4	300	50

Note: **PH**-Hydrogen ion concentration, **CT**-Conductivity, **TB**-Turbidity, **TS**-Total Solids, **TDS**-Total Dissolved Solids, **TSS**-Total suspended solids, **Cl**-Chloride, **TH**-Total Hardness, **CH**-Calcium Hardness, **MH**-Magnesium Hardness, **F**-Fluoride, **SO_4**-Sulphate, **Cr**-Chromium, **Ni**-Nickel, **Cu**-Copper, **Zn**-Zinc, **DO**-Dissolved Oxygen, **BOD**-Biological Oxygen Demand, **CFU**-Coli form unit, **MPN**-Most probable number.

- Water was collected from hand pump of one sampled villages from each PUI zone randomly and tested at engineering college.
- The results are reflection of general water condition in the PUI.

gets finally join Sirsa river, 12 km in the south eastern part of the city, creating environmental hazard. The PUI also make use of this sewage water for irrigating their farms. The vegetable cultivation in immediate PUI is characterized by this sewage water.

Malpractices in PUI activities

The proximity to city and interactions with city populations has also brought some ill effects on the attitude of PUI households. The easy way of living which was the basic characteristics of rural life has changed and they are also becoming materialistic, opportunist and selfish people. There were widespread overuses of agricultural inputs such as chemical fertilizers, pesticides, insecticides along with heavy doses of irrigation water. The excessive use of these inputs leads to general degradation of land, water and air quality. Large numbers of households have complained of deteriorating status of PUI environment. The sample survey also found complaints of some malpractices where interferences and manipulation in natural processes were practiced. The milch animals and some vegetable crops are injected with 'oxytocin', for quick and extra production.

Epilogue

Aligarh is a relatively small city, compared to other cities of which literature is available but it is also a fast growing city in India, the issues examined here are certainly not limited to Aligarh city and many of the features can be traced with other cities as well. It too is surrounded by a populous rural area with productive and rich agricultural hinterland. Such conditions give rise to many conflicts between rural and urban economies, values, and people. They can also generate mutually beneficial complementarities in the rural and urban spheres. The net outcome is highly selective for different groups and different locations. The present study was spread over 21 villages where a total of 769 households were sampled for in-depth analysis.

The literature on periurban interface is in large volume but because of its dynamic nature the definition and delimitation is rather inconsistent. This is largely due to differences in site and situation which results in different kinds of urbanization process and the resultant impacts on PUI. The study considers PUI as transitory zone, where combination of rural and urban activities meet. The PUI is region of change and not a distinct boundary, where the process of change is crucial.

The development in city and the expansion of city strongly influences the peripheral rural settlements in terms of natural resources and people, both physically and in a socio-economic sense. Its influence stretches far beyond the immediately adjacent area. The implications of it were felt on the people who have lived there for generations as well on that of the migrants who came here late. This study was for assessing livelihood of people living in city surrounding (the PUI). Livelihood is a method to acquire food, income, property or inherit resources, it includes all the activities forming the means of generating a living.

A fundamental characteristic of PUI livelihood is their ability to adapt in order to survive. The feature of PUI livelihood includes change over time and adaptation to evolving circumstances and this is an ongoing process which does not remain static but varies from one season or from one year to the next. The assets can be built up, eroded or instantaneously destroyed as available activities and access to resource and opportunities may fluctuate seasonally and across the year.

The study finds that there was clear signs of modernization and transformation of economic activities in the Aligarh's PUI. The traditionally dominant agricultural activities are under increasing pressure and new possibilities are emerging for market-oriented agriculture. There were great differences in access to resources and opportunities leading to new patterns of livelihood. Significantly, options for non-agricultural occupations among the PUI households are enhanced because of their proximity to the expanding city.

The pull factor of urban infrastructure and greater employment opportunities attract migrants from the surrounding villages. There is phenomenal increase in linkages and the village economy gets tied up with the growing city. With time and improvements in the communication and transport facilities, the daily movements from the village to the city in order to supply the different commodities have increased considerably. The rural settlements in the PUI are no longer inhabited by traditional rural population only, but they also inhabit people who spend most part of the day in city.

The study has found that the livelihood in Aligarh's PUI can be categorized into two broad categories — non-cash based livelihood and cash based livelihood. The non-cash based livelihood, where households are engaged with food production and fuel or fodder collection from common land. But this form of livelihood has been almost wiped out in Aligarh's PUI. The study finds that in Aligarh's PUI, the urban elements linked with monetized economy had affected rural elements linked to natural resources resulting in their gradual depletion. Moreover, poor people who earlier depended on these natural resources from common land have lost control over it. These changes in PUI have adversely affected their non-cash based livelihood in particular.

The cash based periurban livelihoods are categorized into four broad categories. These are livelihoods based on casual employment, livelihoods based on business and trade, livelihoods based on farming activity and livelihoods based on dairy farming. Cash based casual livelihood in Aligarh's PUI has many dimensions and most of the lesser educated and lesser skilled workers belong to this category. There is increasing demand for labour oriented jobs in PUI. The employment opportunity of this kind is typically casual, short term and seasonal in nature fetching low and varying wages.

This kind of labour work can be divided into two categories: Labouring in agricultural sector, where the wages are comparatively lesser, interestingly, there is considerable shortage of labour in the agricultural sector but its remuneration does not increase to the levels of labour in non-agricultural sector of urban areas. This kind of PUI livelihood is characterized by its highly seasonal nature and this seasonal migration to them is like *"Paid holiday"*. Importantly, this sector is not gender biased, in fact women are found to have almost equal opportunity for work, but the wages are lesser than their male counterparts.

The livelihood of labouring outside agricultural sector is cash based livelihood opportunity in unorganized urban sector. The PUI offer opportunity to sell labour for remittance in cash. This livelihood option gave an opening for rural labourers to move away from primary sector and earn relatively higher wages. However, this option is typically casual, seasonal, short term and 'by day' employment. The urban proximity is an important requirement for this kind of livelihood. Moreover, this employment is highly gender biased with male dominance.

Another livelihood option in Aligarh's PUI is cash based off farm livelihood in tertiary sector which requires some skills (most of them are craft based, artisanal activities or providing lower level services), small time trading is also one of the livelihood options for this section. This option is directly linked to urban economy and thus, vibrant with proximity to the city. This option is popular with younger people with some level of education and who have distanced themselves from labour oriented agricultural activities. They prefer to work and stay in urban area and take advantages of urban infrastructure and amenities.

The livelihood as crop cultivation is the most common and widely practiced option in the Aligarh's PUI. This option in the PUI is found to have fair degree of commercialization and households were found to be producing farm products for the market to get cash returns. Significantly, distance from city has crucial bearing on nature of farming activity. The sample survey suggests that closer to the city have higher degree of commercialization and it decreases as we move away from city.

The farmers also found exploring newer options for drawing maximum returns. Especially, producers from *immediate* PUI acting in urban systems were found to be exploring most for possibilities of better marketing and management for their products. The PUI producers also showed interests in extension services offered by governmental agencies for upgrading their traditional skills. This modification was helping them in judiciously utilizing their stressed resources in PUI.

The study area lies in an agriculturally prosperous region of the country, where inputs of green revolution were adopted successfully. That is why the farms of Aligarh's PUI have reported higher level of application for agricultural inputs. The basic inputs of green revolution like irrigation, high yielding varieties of seeds, chemical fertilizers, etc., were widely used by the sampled cultivators. The cropping pattern was found to be greatly influenced by urban proximity and some crops like vegetables, peas, *arhar*, flowers, fruits and *chara*, etc., have substantial acreage, these commodities are basically grown to meet the urban demands. Whereas, farms at *distant* PUI have shown subsistence orientation in their cropping pattern, as the cropping pattern was dominated by foodgrains.

Livestock, particularly dairying, emerges as the most important natural resource based livelihood option in the PUI. The study assumes that the livestock based livelihoods are greatly influenced by urban growth. This livelihood option has inherent PUI characteristics as households afford multiple options where the men can work in the farm as well as off-farm (in some urban activity or as middlemen), similarly, women can perform the men's as well as their own tasks of raising animals. Buffalo is the preferred milking animal, as consumers prefer its milk because of its high fat content.

The distance from urban area is critical for dairy activity because milk being a perishable commodity and with no refrigeration or preservation techniques are used, this activity thrives closer to the city. Other livestock (except goats for some people) do not form a substantial part of livelihood in the PUI. Goats, though still small in number, seem to be increasing. But it is a more general than exclusive periurban phenomena.

The study for assessing the status of land resource in Aligarh's PUI finds severe *urban shadow effect* on it. There is substantial conversion of crop land to urban expansion and also for tree plantation and vacant lands in the PUI. Farmers in the PUI subject to present or short-term future development pressure, begin to devote less capital for farm maintenance and management resulting in lower productivity from the land, which ultimately results in selling these lands to property dealers. The net effect of these forces cause a much greater loss of crop land to urban uses than the figures normally given for land transferred to urban uses indicate. The study estimates that for each hectare of land actually transferred into an urban related land use, almost 2 hectares of additional land is lost from agricultural use.

The sample survey further found landowners disposing their lands in response to the urban forces differently because of diverse economic and social background. Large landowners were found to be more responsive towards the urban forces. The reason was that they have distanced themselves from direct agricultural activity. This poses managerial and operational problems in farming activity. Medium landowners were found to be resisting to urban forces and still associate themselves with farming community, but they are also the progressive and dynamic section of the society, where they change occupation and this instigate them to dispose of their agricultural lands. Small landowners are also responsive to urban forces for disposing of their agricultural land. But their decision is more due to their poor and miserable economic background.

The study finds that there is an exorbitant demand for the urban land. Every individual has different interests which lead to conflicts and practices of intimidation and manipulation to defend certain interests of specific individuals or groups. There is excessive inter-mixing of spatial functions which is the outcome of inflated land values, unrestricted, uncontrolled expansions. The PUI is characterised by a great diversity of actors and a complex mix of conflicting and complementary interests. Evidences from the study area shows that 'beneficiaries' and 'victims' can be encountered in any group, depending on the local situation. The outcome is also greatly depended on the economic and political strength, the connections, and the alliances among the actors. The households among the original villagers who do not possess agricultural land found to have the weakest position and are the victims of this urbanization process. They are excluded from any direct benefits of the process. Elevated land prices have further limited their ability to acquire extra residential and commercial space. These landless households only get benefit from their ancestral land that they own near the settlement. Gradually, this section of the PUI society are uprooted and pushed away from their location.

The study also investigated the impact of city on PUI population, this impact was found to be quite noteworthy on their economic, natural and social environment. There were strong evidences of the transformation in economic environment in the PUI. This zone is characterized by the coexistence of urban (mainly secondary and tertiary activities) and rural (mainly primary or natural resource based) activities. The study finds that PUI is a place with increased opportunities as the urban based economic activities consisting of secondary and rapidly expanding tertiary sector. The PUI also benefited from the larger urban market. The city with increasing population creates increased demand mainly for primary (nature based) products. The easy access (personal contact with consumers) and monetized urban economy is of great advantage to these PUI producers. This urban monetized economy, larger market, greater opportunities and higher-assured wages have led PUI households to diversify their livelihood for better and improved living. There have been evidences of occupational transformations and this phenomenon was more prominent among younger generation and clear periurban character particularly strong with proximity to the city where greater choices and opportunities exist.

The study also found that city impact have significantly transformed social environment in the PUI. The PUI is characterized by the intermixing of urban way of life and rural way of living. But this intermixing is in some way is constrained by cultural differences. PUI is a zone of high growth in its population marked with intensification of concentration of population. There are also signs of improving status of women who were actively participating in economic activities, managing the household as well as taking care of household resources too. The education, political empowerment and economically activeness have made them secure. Another important change which the PUI has witnessed is awareness and popularization of education among the masses. Education has started to transform the PUI society. Even the poor and uneducated households have also started to push their children for pursuing education. PUI has also witnessed transformation in family structure. The families with changes in occupational structure are increasingly becoming nuclear. The study also finds a marked influence of city life on the lifestyle and living standard of PUI households. The PUI households have become more urbanized and the quality of life has also improved considerably. The inflow of money through sale of land and incomes from secondary and tertiary sector has contributed for this improvement, but these improvements decreases with distance.

The study also finds that PUI is a place of new social class which has increasing elements of urban characteristics and decreasing rural elements. The society has better education levels, smaller family size but marked gender biasness. Although they showed gender biasness among kids but general status of women has improved. The households have showed association with diverse economic activity. This multi-activity household is survival response to urban monetized economy to generate higher incomes required for sustenance. This urban monetized economy has also blurred the traditional caste based social system. The PUI have social class, where social status is determined by household income. This income based social evolvement has also transformed the PUI society into materialistic society which have predominant urban values and way of life. The PUI residents do not have much affinity with one another and the sense of social responsibility among the people has been reduced.

The study also finds PUI a place with contradicting perception as on one hand there have been positive improvements as stated above but respondents were also concern as their economic, social and cultural activities have been greatly transformed, which in their view have changed their lifestyle and eroded their social and cultural values. However, this dichotomy was not evident among younger generation. Interestingly, the distant PUI respondents on the other hand, complain of difficulties in accessing urban benefits, they want rapid urban development and expansions so that they come closer to the city and get benefits of urban amenities and facilities.

The city impact on PUI also helped in improvements of infrastructural facilities. Urban impact on PUI is both in terms of 'site' and 'situation'. Here, 'site' is referred to the physical and cultural characteristics and attributes of the city. While, 'situation' specifies the external relations of the locale. In the context of a PUI, a change in situation usually precedes a change in the site. This is evident from the improvements in the infrastructural facilities, amenities and their access in the PUI. Better access to a location strengthens the external relations of that place leading to changes in its site. The transformation in availability and access to infrastructural facilities and amenities in the PUI has greatly improved. Moreover, there is also an improvement in general awareness for accessing and using these available facilities.

Lastly, the present study also assesses the phenomena of Periurbanization and Environmental Issues. Environmental issues and problems have featured prominently in processes of periurbanization and the nature of PUIs almost everywhere. The Aligarh city's PUI is not independent or isolated zone, but — as defined — dynamic interfaces between urban and rural relations.

The most intractable environmental issues is the inevitable conversion of agricultural land to urban uses, principally housing, commercial and industrial, infrastructure and other land-extensive facilities, waste dumps, and sewage disposal, etc., The availability of larger tracts of relatively undeveloped and cheaper land in the city's PUI makes it environmentally susceptible. In other words, negative environmental externalities are imposed on the PUI in the form of agricultural land transformation, the loss of agricultural land and widespread land degradation. The respondents complained of deterioration in productive capacity of agricultural land and land degradation due to urban oriented activities as well as because of inappropriate farming practices.

The proximity to city and interactions with city populations has also brought some ill effects on the attitude of PUI households. The easy way of living which was the basic characteristics of rural life has changed and they are also becoming materialistic, opportunist and selfish people. The sample survey also found complaints of some malpractices where interferences and manipulation in natural processes were practiced. Dairying activity being most vibrant livelihood in the PUI is the worst affected. All kinds of possible adulteration and addition to milk and its product is being done to earn easy and quick extra money. Vegetable and fruit farming and production in the PUI also faces similar problem. There is excessive use of pesticides, fertilizers, drain water (for irrigation), harmful and injurious chemicals for keeping fresh, preserving and early ripening, etc. The urban population is very concern with this health hazard. This has double impact as the city people doubt PUI producers and restrict use of their products, which affects directly the PUI producers. The result is on the one side, the urban demand for these PUI products remain unmet, while on other side PUI producer do not get appropriate returns for their products.

Suggestions

- India is urbanizing, so is the expansion of urban area is taking place. All this urban expansion is occurring on peripheral areas around the existing settlements — the *Periurban Interface* (PUI). There is an urgent need to have appropriate planning and adequate and specific policies for developmental issues for this PUI.
- The PUI is a very important zone which provides not only primary products but now also secondary commodities and tertiary services to the city, but the marketing system and channels are poor and grossly inadequate. Moreover, the marketing system is urban biased which favours the middlemen (*dalal*) who gets major share of profits from the transactions. PUI producers are victims of this faulty system

and suffer from poor payments and are also have to bear the burden of taxes and commissions. There is an urgent need to develop a balanced marketing system to safeguard the interests of PUI producers.

- The youth of PUI requires special attention, as this young human resource is in dilemma. They have distanced themselves from traditional labour oriented primary and secondary activities and their abilities do not absorb them in desired urban based tertiary sector. This way more and more young people remain idle and unemployed. They could be trained and utilized in marketing of PUI commodities.
- One of the intractable environmental issues is the inevitable conversion of agricultural land to urban uses and land degradation. The availability of larger tracts of relatively undeveloped and cheaper land in the city's PUI makes it environmentally susceptible. In other words, negative environmental externalities are imposed on the PUI. This needs to be checked immediately as in the name of development humanity cannot afford to lose indiscriminate fertile agricultural land. Because it is not only about the revenue loss due to loss of agricultural land but it is also an issue of livelihood of the people who were associated with that land.
- Livestock development should become the core of livelihood programmes in the periurban context. The study finds that land is lost for non-agricultural purposes, eroding the natural resource base of the community. Livestock emerges to be more important a livelihood than agriculture as one approaches the city. This means, more livestock have to be managed with less land. But this inverse proportion of livestock and land cannot go beyond a limit without both being affected. Fodder resources need urgent attention in preserving or promoting cropping patterns that produce sufficient fodder. The vacant land can also be utilized for producing fodder.
- Livestock, particularly dairying, emerges as the most

important natural resource based livelihood option for the PUI households. But healthcare of animals is an area of concern despite better economies and accessibility to services. The dairy producers need to be appraised about the benefits and importance of these facilities. The community can be empowered to take care of these services themselves. Training of local youth as para-vet to perform vaccinations, artificial insemination, pregnancy diagnoses and first-aid will be of immense benefit.

- The effect of urbanization is real as far as dairy farming is concerned. There are distinct dissimilarities between the immediate and distant PUI villages in composition of livestock population, livestock management, milk marketing and consumption. Development programmes need to recognize that the periurban situation differs from rural and urban ones.
- Agriculture is still an important and dominating livelihood option, but in PUI it suffers adversely due to urban forces. Agricultural activity requires special attention and protection so that it does not succumb to urban forces.
- There is a critical issue which requires immediate attention. This is about growing menace of application and adulteration of harmful chemicals into milk, vegetables and fruits. This needs to address as most of the rural producers are ignorant of its ill effects on human life. The producers should be guided and made aware of their detrimental consequences and desist them from these illegal acts.

Appendix

QUESTIONNAIRE

Evaluating Linkages and Livelihood Transformations in Periurban Interface.

VILLAGE PROFILE

1. Name of the village :
2. Block name :
3. Distance from Aligarh city :
4. Connectivity to the Aligarh city:
5. Common mode of transportation:

6. Type of roads:
7. Total population of the village:
8. Total number of household in the village—
9. Religion wise
   Hindu Muslim Others
10. Type of houses in the village (in percentage)
    Pucca Kuchcha Mixed
11. Infrastructural Facilities / Service in the village
    Post Office Telephone booth Bank
    School Hospital/Health Centres Any other
12. Status and duration of electricity supply to the village (Hours/Day)
    Agricultural purpose Domestic purpose Industrial purpose

13. Access and source of water
    Domestic Agriculture Industry
14. Major economic activity

15. Organized industries in the village

16. Ownership of the industry
    Local Outsiders Co-operative
17. Any degraded land

Brick kilns		Earth evacuation site		Any other
Active	Disused	Active	Disused	

18. Does the village has forest cover?
19. Type of forest cover
20. Does the village have common lands?
    If yes, then what type of land and for which purpose it is used?

21. Does any governmental or NGO programme has been carried out?

22. Any signs of distinct urban imprints
    Positive imprints Negative imprints

23. Other observations (if any)

RESPONDENT PROFILE

1. Name.
2. Sex
3. Age
4. Marital status
5. Religion
6. Caste
7. Educational status
8. Type of house
9. Housing condition
   No. of rooms (per person availability) Status of sanitation

   Status of ventilation

10. Any other activity carried out from the house and area devoted to it?

11. Type of economic activity associated with:
    Primary Secondary Tertiary Any other

12. Type and place of work

13. If not employed in the village – distance , frequency and mode of travel:

14. If Self-Employed, type and place of work

SOCIAL-ECONOMIC PROFILE

1. Family size
2. Total family member
3. Total number of children
4. Educational status of the family
   Male Female Age

5. Economically active members in the household
   Male Female Age

6. Status of women in the household
   Housewife Working Any other

7. Place and type of work

8. Sector-wise employment in the household
   Primary sector Secondary sector Tertiary sector Age

9. Production of primary commodities
   Crops Livestock – milk / Meat Others

10. Type of Agriculture
    Subsistence Commercial Mixed

11. Size of Landholding

12. Land-Use
    Total area
    Total cultivable area
    Total irrigated area
    Area under HYV
    Area under chemical fertilizer
    Area under Insecticides and Pesticides

13. Area under different crops and their yield :

Name	Area	Production	Yield	Rank	Comment, if any
Cereals					
Pulses					
Vegetables					
Fruits					
Cash crop					
Any Other					

14. Agricultural machinery
    Pump-set Threshers Tractor Sprayers Any other

15. Source of irrigation : Own / Hired
    Canals Tube Wells Wells Others

16. Agricultural products disposal site:
    Farm Village Mandi City Any other place

17. Buyer of the agricultural products

18. Types of goods supplied to the city
    Straw Timber Dung Cake Fuel wood Foodgrain
    Milk Fruits Vegetables Green fodder Poultry products
    Meat Earth Bricks Any other commodity

19. Value addition to the commodity?

20. Income generation from different sectors
    Primary sector Secondary sector Tertiary sector

21. Total investments
    Primary sector Secondary sector Tertiary sector

22. Have you availed any subsidy for your activities?

23. Total family income (Rs./month)

24. Total expenditure (Rs./month)
    Food Education Health Clothing
    Family expenses Leisure Other

25. Have you made any investments?
    Purchase of Land House Construction Marriage
    Any other
26. Have you borrowed money?
27. Source and reasons of borrowing
28. Any change in economic activity?
29. If yes, reasons

30. Any modification in your economic activity:
    Share cropping Leasing land Training in skills or profession
    Business / Trading Taking help from institutions/persons Other

31. Have you disposed of your land?

32. Reasons for disposal

33. Land value
    At disposal time   Current

34. Who was the buyer of your land?
35. Size of landholding sold
36. Percentage of total land you own

37. Was there any pressure to sell your land?

38. How you resisted / succumbed to pressure?

39. Do you regret your decision?

40. Livestock in the household
    Cattle   Goats / Sheep   Poultry   Pigs   Other

41. Basic purpose of animal rearing
    Milk   Meat   Agricultural purpose   Others

42. Output from animal rearing

43. Mode of disposal for animal products
    Own house   Own outlet in the city   Through local traders
    Personally carried and sell them to city traders   Wholesalers   Any other

44. How often you visit city for any work?

45. Purpose of work

46. Do you face any problem in visiting city?

47. Do you need any help from others to carry out your work in the city?

48. Do you visit city for recreation or festivals?

49. Is any member of your family migrated permanently to city?
Age Sex

50. What is the main reason of migration to the city area?
Employment Education Other reasons

51. Type of employment permanently migrated member is associated with:
Business Service Others

52. Is any member of your family migrating to city for short period of time?
Age Sex

53. Reason for migrating to city for short period of time?

54. Reason for returning back to village?

55. Do you find any change in the spending habits?

56. Modern appliances/equipments in your house:

57. Access and type of modern communication used

ENVIRONMENTAL PROFILE

1. Brick kilns in the village
   If yes: No. of Brick kilns
2. Status of Brick kilns
   Dormant Working
3. Abundance period of Brick kilns
4. Current uses of land for the abundant Brick kilns
   Vacant Reclaimed Residential Any Other
5. Do you sell earth?
6. Status of earth evacuated land
7. Do you sell wood?
8. Source and mode of wood collection

9. City garbage or solid waste dumping in your village?
10. Dumping sites
    Road side Vacant land
    Directly into the Nallah Any other place.
11. Nature of waste
    Organic/Non-organic/Mixed/Other
12. Is city waste water coming upto the village?
13. Is it used for any purpose?
    Irrigation Washing clothes Bathing Any other

14. Does it have any impact on local environment
    Crops affected Foul smell Health problem
    Any other problem

15. Vehicular traffic on roads passing through the village
    High Medium Low

16. Type and condition of vehicle
17. Are you satisfied with the facilities
18. How you rate the presence of industry in the village?
19. Are you facing any health hazard?

20. Disease profile, if any?

21. Do you feel any change in social life?
    Within family Within neighbourhood Within village
    Everywhere

22. How you rate proximity to city?
    Very advantageous Advantageous Disadvantageous
    Burden
23. Reasons

24. Have you benefited from any government policies, plans or initiatives?

25. What in your view is the major problem faced by you?
    Unemployment Destruction to natural resource
    Vulnerability to natural stress Landlessness
    Shortage of capital Social hindrance in progress
    Lack of family support Lack of skills
    Any other

26. Any other information.

Bibliography

Acharya, B.P. (1987), Policy of land acquisition and development analysis of an Indian experience. *Third World Planning Review*, 9 (2), pp. 99-116.

Adedayo Adesina; (2007) "Socio-Spatial Transformations and the Urban Fringe Landscape In Developing Countries" Presented Paper at United Nations University Institute For Environment and Human Security (UNU-UHS) Summer Academy on Social Vulnerability and Resilience Building in *Mega City*. Munich, Germany.

Adell, G., (1999), Theories and Models of the Periurban Interface: A changing conceptual landscape, *Literature Review*, Development Planning Unit, University College, London.

Aggrey Daniel Maina Thuo (2010), Community and Social Responses to land use transformations in the Nairobi rural-urban fringe, Kenya , *Field Actions Science Report*. Special Issue-1.

Agrawal, S.N. (1962), *A Demographic Study of Six Urbanising Villages*. Bombay: Asia Publishing House.

Agricultural and Forest Sciences, University of Wales and Development Planning Unit, University College, London.

Ali, S. and Singh, S.N. (1998), *Major Problems of Delhi Slums*. New Delhi: Uppal Publishing House.

Allen, Adriana and Nicholas You (eds). (2002). *Sustainable Urbanisation: Bringing the Green and Brown Agendas*, DPU, DFID and UN Habitat, London.

Amy M. Lerner, Hallie Eakin; (2010), An obsolete dichotomy? Rethinking the rural-urban interface in terms of food security and production in the global south. *The Geographical Journal* , Royal Geographical Society (with The Institute of British Geographers).

Ansari, J.H. and N. Von Einsiedel (eds.) (1998), *Urban Land Management, Improving Policies and Practices in Developing Countries of Asia*. New Delhi: Oxford & IBH.

Arya, D.S. and S.A. Abbasi (1995), *Urbanization and its Environmental Impacts*. New Delhi: Discovery Publishing House.

Atkinson, A. (1991), *Principles of Political Ecology*. London: Belhaven Press.

Baker, J. (1995), Survival and accumulation strategies at the rural-urban interface in Northwest Tanzania. *Environment and Urbanization,* 7(1): 117-132.

Banzo, M. (1998), Processus d'urbanisation de la frange périurbaine de Mexico : approche méthodologique. *L'espace géographique*, no. 2: 143-154.

Barrow, C.J. (1991), *Land Degradation, Development and Breakdown of Terrestrial Environments*, Cambridge and New York: Cambridge.

Bates, Robert H., (1981), *Markets and States in Tropical Africa*, Berkeley: University of California Press.

Bayliss-Smith, T.P. and S. Wanmali (1984), *Understanding Green Revolutions, Agrarian Change and Development Planning in South Asia*. Cambridge: Cambridge University Press.

Bentinck, J. (2000), *Unruly Urbanisation of Delhi's Fringes. Changing Patterns of Land-use and Livelihood.* Netherlands Geographical Studies No. 270, Groningen, Rijksuniversiteit Groningen.

Bentinck, J.V. (1995), Bricks or Crops? Brick Kilns and its Impact on Land Degradation in the Rural-Urban Fringe of Delhi. Groningen: unpublished MA thesis.

Bentinck, J.V.; J. Skornsek and A.C. De Vries (1999), The degradation of rural land in the rural-urban fringe of Delhi: Integration of GIS and remote sensing. In: G.P. Chapman, A.K. Dutt and R.W. Bradnock, Urban Growth and Development in Asia, Volume II: *Living in the Cities*. London: Ashgate, pp. 451-465.

Beteille, A. (1996), Caste, Class and Power, Changing Patterns of Stratification in a Tanjore Village, 2nd edition, Delhi: Oxford University Press.

Blaike, P. and H. Brookfield, (eds.) (1987), *Land Degradation and Society*. London: Methuen.

Blaike, P. (1996), New knowledge and rural development: a review of views and practices. Paper for the 28th International Geographical Congress, The Hague, August 5-10.

Boorana, S.S. (2002), 'Land Degradation and Sustainable Development' in *Human Dimensions of Sustainable Development* edited by R. B. Singh, Rawat Publications, Jaipur and New Delhi.

Bose, A. (1974), *Studies in India's Urbanization, 1901-1971*. New Delhi, Tata McGraw-Hill (First revised edition).

Bose, A. (1993), *India and the Asian Population Perspective*. Delhi: B.R. Publishing Corporation.

Bose, A. (1996), *India's Demographic Statistics: 177Key Tables with Graphics*. Delhi: B.R. Publishing Corporation.

Bradford, A.M. (2001), *Scope for Integrated Pest Management (IPM) in Sewage Irrigated Crop Production Systems in the Periurban Interface of Hubli-Dharwad, India.* Unpublished M.Sc. Thesis. University of Wales, Bangor.

Breese, G. (1974), *Urban and Regional Planning for the Delhi-New Delhi Area, Capital for Conquerors and Country*. New Jersey: Princeton.

Breman, J.; P. Kloos and A. Saith, (eds.) (1998), *The Village in Asia Revisited*. Delhi: Oxford University Press.

Brenna E. Vredeveld (2007), "Subjectivity of Land Cover Change Trajectories in Periurban Quito, Ecuador: Community characteristics, migration and participation in land use planning", *Environment*.yale.edu/hixon/files/pdf/2007_Brenna Vredeneld.pdf.

Brook, R. (2005), *Enhancing Livelihoods and Natural Resources Management in Periurban Villages*. SAFS UW Bangor. *(R8094 FTR)* April 2005.

Brook, R. and Davila J. *eds* (2000), *The Periurban Interface. A Tale of Two Cities*. Gwasg Francon, Bethesda, Wales.

Brook, R., Purushothaman *S, Hunshal* C. *eds* (2003), *Changing Frontiers. The Peri-Urban Interface, Hubli Dharwad, India.* Books for Change, Bangalore.

Brook, R. M. *et al.* eds. (2000), *The Periurban Interface: A Tale of Two Cities.* London, University of Wales and Development Planning Unit, University College London.

Brookfield, H.; A.S. Hadi and Z. Mahmud (1991), The city in the village, the *in situ* urbanization of villages, villagers and their land around Kuala Lumpur, Malaysia. Oxford: Oxford University Press.

Browder, J.; J.R. Bohland and J.L. Scarpadi, (1995), "Patterns of Development on the Metropolitan Fringe — Urban Fringe Expansion in Bangkok, Jakarta and Santiago", in *Journal of the American Planning Association*, Vol. 61, No. 3.

Bruijne G.A. de & Schenk, H. (1992), Were do the Poor live? An analysis of residential patterns of poor inhabitants in Indian cities. *The Indian Geographical Journal*, Vol. 67, No. 2, pp.1-16.

Bryant, C.R., (1995), The role of local actors in transforming the urban fringe. *Journal of Rural Studies* 11, 255–267.

Bryant, C.R.; Russwurm, L.H., McLellan, A.G., (1982), The City's Countryside: Land and its Management in the Rural-Urban Fringe. Longman, London.

Bryant, R.L. and S. Bailey (1997), Third World Political Ecology. London and New York: Routledge.

Brydon L. and S. Chant, (1989), *Women in their World, Gender issues in Rural and Urban Areas*, Aldershot: Edward Elgar.

Burns, T.R, T. Bamgartner and P. Deville (1985), Man, Decisions, Society; *The Theory of Actor System Dynamics for Social Scientists*. New York: Gordon and Breach Science Publishers.

Buxton, M., Goodman, R., (2008), Protecting Melbourne's Green Wedges—fate of a public policy. In: Amati, M. (Ed.), *Urban Green Belts in the Twenty-first Century*. Ashgate, Aldershot/ Burlington, VT, pp. 61–82.

Cadene, P., (1990), L'usage des espaces peri-urbains, une gīographie rīgionale des conflits. Etudes Rurales 118/119, 225–267.

Carney, D. (1998), *Sustainable Rural Livelihoods,* Russell Press Ltd., Nottingham. P, 4.

Carter, H (1981) *The Study of Urban Geography*, U.K.

Carter, H., Lewis, C.R., (1990), *An Urban Geography of England and Wales in the Nineteenth Century*. Edward Arnold, London.

Centre of Science and Environment (1989), The environmental problems associated with India's major cities. *Environment and Urbanization*, Vol. 1, No.1 April, pp. 7-15.

Chadha, G.K. and A.N. Sharma, (eds.) (1997), *Growth, Employment and Poverty: Change and Continuity in Rural India*. New Delhi, Vikas Publishing House.

Chakraborty, S.C. (1991), Extended metropolitan areas, a key to understanding urban processes in India. In: N. Ginsburg, B. Koppel and T.G. McGee, eds., *The extended Metropolis, Settlement Transition in Asia*. Honolulu: University of Hawaii Press, pp. 299-325.

Chambers, R. and Conway, G.R. (1992), *Sustainable Rural Livelihoods: Practical Concepts for the 21st Century*, Discussion Paper 296, Brighton, U.K. Institute of Development Studies.

Champion T. and Hugo G. (eds.) (2004), *New Forms of Urbanization: Beyond the Urban-Rural Dichotomy*. Aldershot, Ashgate.

Chandrasekaran, V.A. and M. Ramkumar (1991), Environmental Impact of Limestone Mining near Ariyalur, Tamil Nadu, India. *The Indian Geographical Journal*, Dec. 1991, pp. 120-127.

Chen T.; Liu X.; Zhu M.; Zhao K.; Wu J.; Xu J.; Huang P., (2008), "Identification of trace element sources and associated risk assessment in vegetable soils of the urban-rural transitional area of Hangzhou, China", in *Environmental Pollution*, Jan;151(1):67-78.

Chikara, S. and W. Warnar (1999), Home Truths. Delhi Speaks, *Indian Express*, 7 April, p. 5.

Cloke, P.J., (1983), *An Introduction to Rural Settlement Planning*. Methuen, London/New York.

Coleman, A., (1976) Is planning really necessary? *Geographical Journal,* 142 (3), 411–434.

Crooke, W. (1989), *A Glossary of North Indian Peasant Life*, Oxford University Press, Delhi.

D. M. Thuo; (2010), "Community and social responses to land-use transformations in the Nairobi rural-urban fringe, Kenya", Special Issue-1, 2010, Urban Agriculture. Field Actions Science Reportwww.factsreports.org © Author(s).

David Simon; (2010), "Peri-Urban Issues." *Geography and You*, Vol. 10, May-June.

Delik Hudalah, Haryo Winarso, johan Woltjer (2007), Peri-urbanization in East Asia: A new challenge for planning; *International Development Planning Review*, Liverpool University Press, pp. 503-519.

Deshingkar, Priya; Usha Kulkarni; Laxman Rao; Sreenivas Rao, Raja Reddy and B Renuka, (2002). *Poverty Traps Or Opportunity?:*

Changing Rural Livelihoods in Agriculture in Andhra Pradesh. An abstract of draft findings based on analysis in progress produced for the Rural Livelihood Futures Workshop, Delhi.

Deshingkar, P. (2006). Internal Migration, Poverty and Development in Asia. *Asia 2015: Promoting Growth, Ending* Poverty, London.

Deshingkar, P.; Kulkarni, U.; Rao, L. & Rao, S. (2003), Changing Food Systems in India: Resource-sharing and Marketing Arrangements for Vegetable Production in Andhra Pradesh. *Development Policy Review*, 21(5-6): 627-639.

Deshpande, C.D.; Arunachalan, B. and Bhat, L.S. (1980) *Impact of a Metropolitan City on the Surrounding Region: A Study of South Kolaba, Maharashtra*, New Delhi, Concept.

DFID (1999), *Literature Review on Peri-Urban Natural Resource and Management Approaches – Project Report.* London, Natural Systems Programme, Department for International Development. Unpublished Final Technical Report, by University of Nottingham and University of Liverpool.

DFID (2002), From The Livelihood Options Study Funded by DFID Rural Livelihoods Department, running until March 2003, and drawing on evidence from India, Bangladesh and Nepal http://*www.livelihoodoptions.info*

Dick, H. W. and P. J. Rimmer, (1998), "Beyond the Third World City: The New Urban Geography of South-East Asia", in *Urban Studies*, Vol. 35, No. 12.

Di Gregorio, A. and Jansen, L.J.M. (*1998). Land Cover Classification System (LCCS): Classification Concepts and User Manual.* For software version 1.0. GCP/RAF/287/ITA Africover - East Africa Project in cooperation with AGLS and SDRN. Nairobi, Rome.

Douglass Mike and John Friedmann (eds.), (1998), *Cities for Citizens: Planning and the Rise of Civil Society in a Global Age*, J. Wiley, Chichester.

Douglass, M. (1991), Planning for environmental sustainability in the extended Jakarta Metropolitan Region. In: N. Ginsburg, B. Koppel & T.G. McGee, (eds.), The extended metropolis, settlement transition in Asia. Honolulu: University of Hawaii Press. pp. 239-273.

Douglass, M. (1992), "The Political Economy of Urban Poverty and Environmental Management in Asia: Access, Empowerment and

Community Based Alternatives", in *Environment and Urbanisation*, Vol. 4, No 2.

Douglass, M. (1989), "The Environmental Sustainability of Development. Coordination, Incentives and Political Will in Land Use Planning for the Jakarta Metropolis", in *Third World Planning Review*, Vol. 11, No.2.

Douglass, Mike, (1998), "A Regional Network Strategy for Reciprocal Rural-Urban Linkages. An Agenda for Policy Research with Reference to Indonesia", in *Third World Planning Review*, Vol. 20, No.1.

Douglass, Mike, (1998), *Rural-Urban Linkages and Poverty Alleviation: Toward A Policy Framework*, International Workshop on Rural-Urban Linkages, Curitiba, Brazil.

Dreze, J. & A. Sen (1996), *India: Economic Development and Social Opportunity*. Delhi: Oxford University Press.

Druijven, P. (1990), Basket weavers and producers of Mezcal in Mexico: The importance of rural industry in household livelihood strategy. Industrialization seminar paper no. 90/4, Institute of Social Studies, The Hague.

Druijven, P.C.J. (1996), The urban fringe of Delhi: The socio-economic impact of the interpenetration of city and countryside. Paper for the 28th International Geographical Congress, The Hague, Aug. 5-10.

Druijven, P.C.J.; T. Dietz and D. Foeken (1992), Coping mechanisms and livelihood strategies; a summary of concepts. In: H. Reitsma, T. Dietz and L. de Haan, (eds.), Coping with semiaridity: how the rural poor survive in dry-season environments. *Netherlands Geographical Studies 146*, Royal Dutch Geographical Society / University of Amsterdam, pp. 37-43.

Dupont (2004), Urban Development and Population Distribution in Delhi: Implications for categorizing population. In: Champion, T. & Hugo, G. (eds.) *New Forms of Urbanization: Beyond the Urban-Rural Dichotomy.* Aldershot, Ashgate, pp. 171-90.

Dupont, V. (1997), Les 'rurbains' de Delhi, espace, populations, societes, 2-3, pp. 225-240, Paris: ORSTOM.

Dupont, V. (2000), The 'Rurbans' of Delhi. In: Guilmoto, C.Z. and Vaguet, A. (eds.) *Essays on Population and Space in India.* Pondicherry, Institut Français de Pondichéry, pp. 133-51.

Duncan, Otis Dudley, and Albert J. Reiss, Jr. (1958) "Suburbs and

Urban Fringe", pp. 45-66 in William M.Dobiner (ed), *The Suburban Community*. New York: Putnam's.

El Bashir Ibrahim, H. (1997), Coping with famine and poverty: The dynamics of non-agricultural rural employment in Darfur, Sudan. In D.F. Bryceson and V. Jamal (eds), *Farewell to Farms: De-agrarianisation and Employment in Africa*. Ashgate, Aldershot.

Ellis, F. (1998), Household strategies and rural livelihood diversification. *Journal of Development Studies*, Vol 35, No.1, pp.1-38.

Ellis, F. (1999), *Rural Livelihood Diversity in Developing Countries: Evidence and Policy Implications*. Natural Resource Perspectives Number 40. Overseas Development Institute, London.

Ellis, F. (1982), Agricultural Price Policy in Tanzania. World Development, 10(4), 263–283.

Ellis, F. (1983), Agricultural Marketing and Peasant State Transfers in Tanzania. *Journal of Peasant Studies*, 10(4), 214–242.

Ellis, F. (2000), *Rural Livelihoods and Diversity in Developing Countries*. Oxford: Oxford University Press.

Ellis, F., and Bahiigwa, G. (2003), Livelihoods and Rural Poverty Reduction in Uganda. *World Development*, 31(6).

Emmanuel Adu. Ampong, Frank Cudjoe, Rita Amonyiwa Edusah, Martine Hoogsteen, Lily Oteng, Frederieke Vlek, Eva van de Water Zeno Wijtten; (2008), "Socio-economic transitions; changing livelihoods in the periurban interface. Case study of Ahenemah Kokoben and Tikorom in The Peri-Urban Interface of Kumasi. Draft Report (July 25, 2008), Tropenbos International, Ghana, Amsterdam University, College of Agriculture and Natural Resource, KNUST

ESCAP (1990), *Case Studies on Metropolitan Fringe Development with Focus on Informal Land Sub-divisions*. Report No. ST/ESCAP/593, New York, (ESCAP/UNCHS) United Nations.

Evans, H. E. (1990), *Rural-Urban Linkages and Structural Transformation*. Report INU 71, Infrastructure and Urban Development Department, The World Bank, Washington DC.

Fall, A.S. (1998), Migrants' long-distance relationships and social networks in Dakar. *Environment and Urbanization* 10(1): 135-146.

FAO/UNEP, (1997) Negotiating a Sustainable Future for

Land. *Structural and Institutional Guidelines for Land Resources Management in the 21st Century.* FAO/UNEP, Rome.

Fazal, S. (2000), *Urban Expansion and Loss of Agricultural Land. A GIS Based Study of Saharanpur City, India.* Environment and Urbanization, Vol.12, No.2, IIED, London, pp. 133- 149.

Fazal, S. (2001), *Application of Remote Sensing and GIS Techniques in Urban Sprawl and Land Use Mapping : A Case Study of A Growing Urban Centre in India.* Asian Profile, Vol. 29, No.1, Canada. pp. 45- 62.

Fazal, S. (2001), *The Need for Preserving Our Farm Lands : A Case Study from a Predominantly Agrarian Economy.* Landscape and Urban Planning, Vol. 55, No.1, Elsevier Science Publication, United Kingdom. pp. 1 -13.

Fazal, S. (2008), *Farmers Adaptation to Urban Forces: Dynamics in the Urban Fringe of a Growing Urban Centre in India in Edited Volume by Christopher R. Bryant, Edward Makhanya and Thora Martina Herrmann,* The Sustainability of Rural Systems in Developing Countries. *Laboratoire de Développement durable et dynamique territoriale, Universitī de Montrīal, Canada., pp. 71 - 84.*

Fazal, S. (2010), *Ills of Urbanization in Developing Economy.* Lambert Academic Publishing *Germany.*

Fazal, S. (1994), *Factors Deciding Farmer's Choice of Crops.* Asian Profile, Canada, Vol. 22, No. 5, pp. 413-426.

Fazal, S. (2011), Developments at the Rurban Fringe: Impact on Agriculture and Rural Land. *Indian Journal of Regional Sciences,* Kolkata. Vol. XXXXIII, No. 2, pp. 96 - 109.

Fazal, S. (2009), Urban fringe modelling for future residential demands: A case study. *The Geographer,* Vol. 56, No. 1. Aligarh., pp. 51 -63.

Fazal, S. (2002), Suburban Land Conversion and its Impact on Agricultural Land: A GIS Based Study from a Predominantly Agrarian Economy, India. *Annals of the National Association of Geographers, India*, Vol. XXII, No. 1, June 2002. pp. 14 – 30.

Fellmann, J.; A. Getis and J. Getis (1997), Human Geography, landscapes of human activities. Madison: Brown and Benchmark.

Firman, T. (1997), Land Conversion and Urban Development in the Northern Region of West Java, Indonesia. *Urban Studies*, Vol. 34, No. 7, pp. 1027-46.

Firman, T. (1996), Urban Development in Bandung Metropolitan

Region: A Transformation to a Desa-Kota Region. *Third World Planning Review,* 18(1): 1-22.

Friedmann, John and Mike Douglass, (1975), *Agropolitan Development: Towards a New Strategy for Regional Planning in Asia*, University of California, Los Angeles.

Gant, R. Robinson, G and Fazal, S., (2011), Land-use change in the 'edgelands': Policies and Pressures in London's rural–urban fringe. *Land Use Policy*, Elsevier Science Publication, Vol. 28, No.1 United Kingdom., pp. 266-279.

Garreau, J., (1991), *Edge City: Life on the New Frontier*. Doubleday, New York.

Geddes, R., (ed.) (1997), *Cities in Our Future: Growth and Form: Environmental Health and Social Equity*. Washington D.C: Island Press.

Giddens, A. (1990), *The Consequences of Modernity*. Cambridge: Polity Press.

Ginsberg, N., Koppel, B. and McGee, T. G., eds (1991) *The Extended Metropolis — Settlement Transition in Asia*. Honolulu, University of Hawaii Press.

Goutam *et al.,* (2002), 'Pattern of Land Utilization in Sagar Division of Madhya Pradesh' in *Human Dimensions of Sustainable Development* edited by R. B. Singh, Rawat Publications, Jaipur and New Delhi.

Gugler, J. (ed.) (1996), *The Urban Transformation of the Developing World.* Oxford, Oxford University Press.

Haggett, P. (1983), *Geography: A Modern Synthesis.* New York/ London: Harper & Row.

Hall, P., (1996), "Revisiting the Nonplace Urban Realm: Have we Come Full Circle?", in *International Planning Studies*, pp. 7-15.

Hamid, G.M. (1992), Livelihood patterns of displaced households in Greater Khartoum. *Disasters*, Vol. 16, nr. 3.

Haque, T. and D. Jha (1997), Agricultural growth, employment and poverty in India: A critical review. In: G.K. Chadha & A.N. Sharma, (eds.), Growth, Employment and Poverty: Change and Continuity in Rural India. New Delhi Vikas Publishing House, pp. 110-122.

Hardoy, J. E. and Satterthwaite, D. (eds) (1986), Small and Intermediate Urban Centres: Their role in national and regional development in the Third World. Hodder and Stoughton, London in association with IIED.

Hardoy, J.E., D. Mitlin and D. Satterthwaite, (1992), *Environmental Problems in Third World Cities*. London: Earthscan.

Harriss-White, B. (1995) Maps and landscapes of grain markets in South Asia. J. Harriss, J. Hunter and C. M. Lewis (eds). *The New Institutional Economics and Third World Development*. Routledge, London.

Harvey, D., (1995), "Cities or Urbanisation?", in *City* No. 1-2, pp. 38-61.

Harvey, J. (1989), *The Condition of Postmodernity*. Oxford: Blackwell.

Haumont, Nicole and A. Marie, Alain (eds.), (1987), Politiques et pratiques urbaines dans les pays en voie de développement, L'Harmattan, Paris.

Helle Overgaard Larsen, Lise Herslund, Bir Bahadur Khanal Chhetri, Lila Puri, Sanjeeb, Bhattarai, Narayan Gautam. (2010) "The role of forest products with increasing urbanisation, *http://sbhattarai.com.np/wp-content/uploads/2010/09/Larsen_etal_2010_IOF_conference_proceeding_paper.pdf*

Hill, R. (1986), Land use change on the urban fringe. In: *Nature and Resources*, 22 (1-2), pp. 24-33.

Hill, R.D. (1995), The impact of urbanisation on rural-urban linkages in Thailand and Malaysia. *Asian Geographer*, Vol. 14. no 1. pp. 28-44.

Hodder (2000), *Development Geography*. Routledge, London.

Hubert De Bon, Laurent Parrot and Paule Moustier (2010), "Sustainable urban agriculture in developing countries : A review"; Agronomy Sustainable Development; Volume 30, Number 1, January-March.

Iaquinta, D. & Drescher W.A. (2001), More than Spatial Fringe: An Application of the Peri–Urban Typology to Planning and Management of Natural Resources. Unpublished paper presented at DPU International Conference on *Rural-Urban Encounters: Managing the Environment of Peri-Urban Interface*, Development Planning Unit, University College, London, November 2001.

IFAD (1994), "Women's Roles in Livestock Production" in *Women Livestock Managers in the Third World: A Focus on Technical Issues Related to Gender Roles in Livestock Production*, IFAD, by M. Niamir-Fuller. ***http://www.ifad.org/gender/thematic/*** *livestock/live_2.htm*

IFPRI (1990), *The Growing Place of Livestock Products in World Food Products in the 21st Century,* International Food Policy Research Institute, Washington.

Ingram, Gregory K., (1998), "Patterns of Metropolitan Development: What Have We Learned?", in *Urban Studies*, Vol. 35, No 7.

Jacquemin, A. (1999), *Urban Development and New Towns in the Third World – Lessons from the New Bombay Experience*. Aldershot: Ashgate.

Janakarajan, S. (2009), 'Urbanization and periurbanization: aggressive competition and unresolved conflicts - The case of Chennai city in India', *South Asian Water Studies*, 1 (1): 51-76.

Jones, Gavin W. and Pravin Visaria, (1997), *Urbanization in Large Developing Countries: China, Indonesia, Brazil, and India*, Clarendon Press, Oxford.

Kabra, K.N. (1980), *Developing an Urban Fringe, Blueprint for Voluntary Action*. New Delhi: Indian Institute of Public Administration.

Kamete, A.-Y. (1998), Interlocking livelihoods: farm and small town in Zimbabwe. *Environment and Urbanization,* 10(1): 23-34.

Kaerekar, M. (1995), Gender dimensions in labour migration: an overview. In: L. Schenk-Sandbergen, *Women and Seasonal Labour Migration*, IDPAD 16, New Delhi: Sage, pp. 23-78.

Kataria, V., S.K. Aggarwal and J.V. Bentinck (1997), Environmental and health implications of industrialization in an urban village at Delhi's fringe. Paper for the International Seminar on the Promotion of Environmentally Sound and Healthy Cities.

Kelly, P. (1998), The politics of urban-rural relationships: land conversion in the Philippines. *Environment and Urbanization,* 10(1): 35-54.

Kirby, A. (2002), Do cities have a purpose. *Cities,* Vol. 19, No. 6, pp. 371-2

Koppel, B. (1987), Does integrated rural development really work? Lessons from the Bicol river basin. *World Development*, 15: 205-220.

Kriiger, F. (1998), Taking advantage of rural assets as a coping strategy for the urban poor. *Environment and Urbanization,* 10(1): 119-134.

Krishan, G. (1993), The slowing down of Indian urbanisation, *Geography*, pp. 80-84.

Kumar, B., (ed.) (1998), *Urbanization and Land-Use Conflict at Urban Fringes*, A.P.H. Publishing Corportation, New Delhi.

Kumar, M.S. (2001), Devouring Agglomerations and their Outgrowths in India: Beyond Rural-Urban Divide. Unpublished paper presented at DPU international conference on *Rural-Urban Encounters: Managing the Environment of Periurban Interface*, London, Development Planning Unit, University College London, November, 2001.

Kumar, N. (1999), The provision of infrastructure services in Rohtak and Bhiwani Districts, Haryana, India, 1981-98: *A Geographical Analysis*. University of Durham: thesis.

Kundu, A. (1997), Urban Land Markets and Land Price Changes: A Study in the Third World Context. Aldershot: Ashgate.

Kundu, A. (1989), The dynamics of city hinterland relationships: the Indian case. In: P. Vennetier, ed., La péri-urbanisation dans les pays tropicaux, Centre d'Études de Géographie Tropicale, Valence., pp. 306-325.

Kundu, A (2003), "Urbanisation and Urban Governance: Search for a Perspective beyond Neo-Liberalism", *Economic and Political Weekly,* Vol. 38, No. 29.

Kundu, A (2006), "Globalisation and the Emerging Urban Structure: Regional Inequality and Population Mobility", *India: Social Development Report,* (New Delhi: Oxford University Press).

Kundu, A (2009), "Urbanisation and Migration: An Analysis of Trend, Pattern and Policies in Asia", *Human Development Research Paper 2009/16*, United Nations Development Programme.

Kundu, A. and D. Kundu (2009), "Globalisation and Exclusionary Urban Growth in Asian Countries" in R. Kanbur and B. Guha Khasnobis (ed.), *Development in an Urban World* (Helsinki: UNU-WIDER Series).

Kundu, A., Pradhan, B.K. and Subramanian, A. (2002), Dichotomy or Continuum: Analysis of Impact of Urban Centres on their Periphery. *Economic and Political Weekly*, Vol. 37, No. 14, pp. 5039-46.

Kundu, A.; Schenk H. and Dash Bal, P. (2002), *Changing role of state in urban governance. Provision of basic amenities to poor in the context of unplanned growth in metropolitan peripheries of Delhi and Hanoi*. Delhi, Institute for Human Development.

Kundu, A.; Schenk, H. and Dash, B.P. (2001), *Changing Role of State in Urban Governance – Provision of Basic Amenities to Poor in the Context of Unplanned Growth in Metropolitan Peripheries of Delhi and Hanoi*. Delhi, Institute for Human Development.

Kurtz, R. A. and J. B. Eicher, (1958), "Fringe and Suburb: A Confusion of Concept", in Social Forces, No. 37.

Lamba A.L. and S.S. Solanki (1987), *Impact of Urbanization and Industrialisation on Rural Society*, New Delhi, Wily Eastern.

Lambin, E. F. and Geist, H. J., (editors) (2003), "Causes and Trajectories of Land Use/ Cover Change" in Land-Use and Land-Cover Change: Local Processes and global Impacts, p. 41. Springer.

Leeming, L. & Soussan, J. (1979) Structures at the Fringe of the City. *International Social Sciences Journal*, Vol. XXX1, No. 2: pp. 273-281.

Lepper, M.J.C. De; H.J. Scholten and R.M. Stern, (eds.) (1995), *The Added Value of Geographical Information Systems in Public and Environmental Health*, Dordrecht: Kluwer Academic Publishers.

Lewis, O. (1958), *Village Life in Northern India, Studies in a Delhi Village*. Urbana: University of Illinois Press.

Lin, G.C.-S. (1994), Changing theoretical perspectives on urbanisation in Asian developing countries, *Third World Planning Review*, 16 (1).

Lintelo, D.T.; Marshall .F. and Bhupal D.S. (2001), *Delhi Peri-Urban Agriculture* [Internet]. Available from: <http:fao.org/ DOCERP>.

Lipton, Michael, (1977), *Why Poor People Stay Poor: Urban Bias in World Development*, Maurice T. Smith, London.

Lucas, P. and Van Oort, G.M.R.A., (1993), Dynamiek in een stadsrandzone: werken en wonen in de stadsrandzone van de agglomeratie Utrecht, Dynamics in a rural-urban fringe: working and living on the edge of the city of Utrecht. Faculteit Ruimtelijke Wetenschappen, Rijksuniversiteit Utrecht, Utrecht. Nederlandse Geografische Studies no. 154.

Lynch Kenneth, (2005), *Rural-Urban Interaction in the Developing World Rural-Urban Interaction in the Developing World*, Routledge Perspectives on Development (4). Routledge.

Manzanal, M. and Vapnarsky, C. (1986), The development of the Upper Valley of Rio Negro and its periphery within the Comahue Region, Argentina. In J. E. Hardoy and D. Satterthwaite (eds) *op. cit.*

Maria Saleth. (1997), Occupational diversification among rural groups, a case study of rural transformation in Tamil Nadu, *Economic and Political Weekly*, pp. 1908-1916, July 26, Mumbai.

Mbiba, B. (1995), *Urban Agriculture in Zimbabwe*. Avebury, Aldershot. Gatekeeper Series No. SA76 16.

McGee T.G. and Robinson, I.M. (1995), *The Mega-Urban Regions of South Asia*. Vancouver, UBC.

McGee, T., (1971), *The Urbanization Process in the Third World: Explorations in Search of a Theory*, Bell, London.

McGee, T., (1991), "The Emergence of Desakota Regions in Asia: Expanding a Hypothesis", in N. Ginsburg, B. Koppel and T. McGee (eds.), *The Extended Metropolis: Settlement Transition in Asia*, University of Hawaii Press, Honolulu.

McGee, T.G. (1998), Globalisation and Rural-Urban Relations in Developing World. In: Fu-Chen Lo and Yue-Man Yueng eds. *Globalization and the World of Large Cities*. Tokyo, United Nations, pp. 471-496.

McGee, Terry, (1997), "Globalisation, Urbanisation and the Emergence of Sub-Global Regions", in Watters R.F. and T. McGee (eds.) *Asia Pacific: New Geographies of the Pacific Rim*, Hurst and Company, London.

McGranahan, G. and C. Tacoli (2006), "Rural-urban migration in China: Policy options for economic growth, environmental sustainability and equity", International Institute for Environment and Development, London. May 2006 – IIED, *Human Settlements Working Paper*, ISBN 978-1-84369-617-9.

McGranahan, G., Singsore, J. and Kjellen, M. (1996) Sustainability, poverty and urban environmental transitions. In C. Pugh (ed.). Sustainability, the Environment and Urbanization. Earthscan, London.

McGregor D., Simon D., Thompson D., (eds.) (2006), *The Peri-Urban Interface: Approaches to Sustainable Natural and Human Resource Use*. London/Stirling, VA: Earthscan. pp. 336.

Mendez, R.P. (1993), Alternative livelihood systems in the drylands: The need for a new paradigm. Geo Journal 31.1, pp. 67-75.

Michael Mattingly; (2009), Goodbye to Natural Resource Based Livelihoods? Crossing the Rural/Urban Divide. Issue of Local Environment (Vol. 4, No. 9).

Miglani, D. (1993), *Politics and Rural Power Structure*. New Delhi: Deep & Deep Publishing House.

Mohan, R. (1996), Urbanization in India: Patterns and Emerging Policy Issues. In: J. Gugler, (ed.), *The Urban Transformation of the Developing World*. Oxford: Oxford University Press, pp. 94-131.

Monika Vij. (2008), "Fringe and Fusion: A Study in Urban Dynamics". http://www.a-a-r- s.org/acrs/proceeding/ACRS2008/Papers/TS%2023.5.pdf

Morris, A. (1997), Market behaviour and market systems in State of Mexico. In: P. van Lindert and O. Verkoren (eds). *Small Towns and Beyond: Rural Transformation and Small Urban Centres in Latin America*. Thela Publishers, Amsterdam.

Mulay and Ray (1973), *Towards Modernization: A Study of Peasantry in Rural Delhi*, National Pub. House; overseas distributors: Books from India, London (Delhi).

Murdoch, M. (1998), *The Spaces of Actor-Netwok Theory*. Geoforum Vol. 29, No. 4, pp.357-374.

Mutizwa-Mangiza (1999), *Strengthening Rural-Urban Linkages*, Habitat Debate. 5 (1), 1-6.

Mycoo, M. (2006), Sustainable livelihoods in the periurban interface: Anse La Raye, St.Lucia in D.McGregor, D.Simon and D.Thompson, eds. *The Periurban Interface: Approaches to Sustainable Natural and Human Resource use*. Earthscan VA, USA., pp. 134-148.

Nagpaul, H. (1996), *Modernization and Urbanization in India; Problems and Issues*. Jaipur: Rawat Publishing House.

Nangia, S. (1976), *Delhi Metropolitan Region – A Study in Settlement Geography*. Delhi, K.B. Publishers.

Narain, V. (2009), 'Growing City, Shrinking Hinterland: Land Acquisition, Transition and Conflict in Periurban Gurgaon, India,' *Environment and Urbanization*, 27 (2), 501-512.

Narain, V. and S. Nischal. 2007. The periurban interface in Shahpur Khurd and Karnera, India. *Environment and Urbanization* 19 (1), 261-273.

Nath, V. (1993), Planning for Delhi. *Geo Journal* 29.2, pp. 171-180.

Nicodemus Mandere *Mandere*, Barry Ness and Stefan Anderberg; (2010), "Peri-urban development, livelihood change and household income: A case study of periurban Nyahururu, Kenya"; *Journal of Agricultural Extension and Rural Development*. Vol.2 (5). pp.73, June, 2010; http:// academic-journals.org/JAERD. ISSN- 2141 -2154 ©2010 Academic Journals.

Nottingham and Liverpool Universities, (1998), "Literature Review on Peri-Urban Natural Resource Conceptualization and Management Approaches", Initial Draft, Peri-Urban Production Systems Research, Natural Resources Systems Programme, DFID, London.

NRSP (2000), Unpublished call for project proposals, HTS Development Ltd., Hemel Hempstead.

Nunan F. (2000) 'Waste Recycling through Urban Farming in Hubli-Dharwad' in *Growing Cities, Growing Food: Urban Agriculture on the Policy Agenda*, edited by Nico Bekkar, Marielle Dubbeling, Sabine Grūndel, Ulrich Sabel-Koschella and Henkde Zeeuw. Deutche Fūr Ernāhrung and Landwirtschaft, Feldafing, Germany.

Oatley, Nick, (1997), "Lexicons of Suburban and Ex-urban Development", Research Project, City Words Programme, UNESCO-CNRS.

ODI (2002), *Rural Urban Linkages, Key Sheets for Sustainable Livelihood,* 10, Overseas Development Institute, London.

Nunan, F., K. Bird and J. Bishop (2000), *Valuing Peri-Urban Natural Resources: A Guide for Natural Resource Managers*. School of Public Policy, University of Birmingham. A Report produced for DFID, Natural Resources Systems Programme.

Omuta, G.E.D. (1985), Land use and environmental dereliction in the urban fringe: The case of Benin City, Bendel State, Nigeria. *Socio-economic Planning Science*, Vol. 19, No. 5, pp. 303-311.

Oscar Musadan Nyanayaro, (2008), "Access to Relatively Space and Quality of Life for Peri-Urban Communities of Suatter Towns of South Africa. Public Transport insight from the Limpopo Province" www.up.ac.za/dspace/bitstream/2263/6257/1/ Musandu.pdf

Pahl, R (1965), *Urbs in Rure* (London: London School of Economics, Geographical paper 2).

Pantip Jongkroy (2009), Urbanization and changing settlement patterns in periurban Bangkok. Department of Agriculture, Social Science, No. 30/3 (September-December 2552), pages 303-312.

Papola, T.S. (1997), Extent and implications of rural-urban migration in India. In: G.W. Jones, G.W. and P. Visaria (eds.), *Urbanization in Large Developing Countries*, China, Indonesia, Brazil, and India, Clarendon Press, Oxford. pp. 315-320.

Paul W. Kurtz (1958), Has Mr. Flew abandoned "The logic of ordinary use"? *Philosophical Studies,* Volume 9, Numbers 5-6, pp. 73-78.

Pearce, D.W. (ed.) (1981), *Dictionary of Modern Economics*. London: Macmillan.

Pond, B. and M. Yeates (1994), Rural/Urban Land Conversion II: Identifying Land in Transition to Urban Use. *Urban Geography*, 15, 1, pp. 25-44.

Potter, R. B. *et al.* (1995), Urban-Rural Interaction: Physical form and Political Process in the Third World. *Cities*, Vol. 12, No. 1, pp. 67-73.

Potter, Robert and Tim Unwin (eds.), (1989), *The Geography of Urban-Rural Interaction in Developing Countries: Essays for Alan B. Mountjoy*, Routledge, London.

Potter, Robert and Tim Unwin, (1995) "Urban-rural Interaction: Physical Form and Political Process in the Third World", in *Cities*, Vol. 12, No. 1.

Potts, D., (1995), Shall we go home? Increasing urban poverty in African cities and migration processes. *The Geographic Journal,* 161: 245-264.

Potts, D. and Mutambirwa, C. (1998), 'Basics Are Now A Luxury': perceptions of the impact of structural adjustment on rural and urban areas in Zimbabwe. *Environment and Urbanization* 10 (1): 55-76.

Preston, D. (1994), Rapid Household Appraisal : A Method for Facilitating the Analysis of Household Livelihood Strategies. *Applied Geography*, 14, pp. 203-213.

Prins, W.J.M. (1994), Urban growth and housing delivery past and present: a comparative analysis of nineteenth-century London and contemporary Delhi. Ph. D. thesis, University of Leiden.

Pryor, R.J., (1968), Defining the rural–urban fringe. *Social Forces* 47, 202–215.

Pugh C. (ed.) (2000), *Sustainable Cities in Developing Countries*. London, Earthscan.

Pugh, C. (1990), *Housing and Urbanisation : A Study of India.* New Delhi: Sage Publishing House.

Pugh, C. (1996), 'Urban bias', the political economy of development and urban policies for developing countries. *Urban Studies*, 33 (7).

Puntip Jongkroy.(2009), Urbanization and Changing Settlement Patterns in Peri-urban Bangkok. *Kasetsart Journal.* (Social Science) Vol.30, pp. 303 – 312.http://kasetsartjournal.ku.ac.th/kuj_files/2009/A0912220931290625.pdf.

Rahman A.; Agarwal S P.; M. Netzband; and Fazal S. (2011), Monitoring Urban Sprawl Using Remote Sensing and GIS Techniques of a Fast Growing Urban Centre, India. IEEE-Journal of Selected Topics in Applied Earth Observations and Remote Sensing. Urban Remote Sensing (Special Issue). Vol. 4, No. 1, pp. 56-64 March, DIO: 10.1109/JSTARS.2010.2084072.

Rakodi, C (1999), *Poverty and Wellbeing in the Peri-Urban Interface of Developing Countries.* DFID NRSP Report, Project PD70.

Rakodi, C., (1998), "Review of the Poverty Relevance of the Peri-urban Interface Production System Research", Report for the DFID Natural Resources Systems Research Programme, 2nd Draft.

Ramachandran, R. (1989), *Urbanisation and Urban Systems in India.* Delhi, Oxford University Press (Reprint 2001).

Rao, M.S.A. (1970), *Urbanization and Social Change*, New Delhi: Orient Longman.

Rao, M.S.A. (1991), A rural community on the Delhi Metropolitan Fringe. In: M.S.A. Rao, C. Bhat and L.M. Kadekar, (eds.), *A Reader in Urban Sociology.* New Delhi: Orient Longman, pp. 389-409.

Rees, W. (1992), Ecological footprints and appropriate carrying capacity: what urban economics leaves out. *Environment and Urbanization,* 4(2): 121-130.

Richards, J.F. (1990), "Land transformation" in Turner, B L *et al.* (editors), *The Earth as Transformed by Human Action,* Cambridge University Press, Cambridge, UK.

Ribot, J.C. (1998), Theorizing access: forest profits along Senegal's charcoal commodity chains. *Development and Change,* 29: 307-341.

Robinson, G.M., (1991), The city beyond the city. In: Robinson, G.M. (Ed.), A Social Geography of Canada. Dundurn Press, Toronto/ Oxford, pp. 302–329.

Robinson, G.M., (1994), Conflict and Change in the Countryside: Rural Society, Economy and Planning, revised ed. John Wiley & Sons, Chichester/New York.

Robinson, I. (1995), Emerging Spatial Patterns in ASEAN Mega-Urban Regions: Alternative Strategies. In: McGee, T. & Robinson, I. (eds.) *The Mega Urban Regions of Southeast Asia*. Vancouver, UBC Press, pp.78-108.

Rodriguez, O. (1995), *Land Use Conflicts and Planning Strategies in Urban Fringes : A case study of Western Caracas*, Venezuela. ITC publication 27.

Rodriguez, D.A.; Khattak, A.J.; Evenson, K.R.; (2006), Can new urbanism encourage physical activity? Comparing a new urbanist neighbourhood with conventional suburbs. *Journal of the American Planning Association;* 72 (1), 43–54.

Rohilla, S.K. (2004), Role of Groundwater in Urban Development- Case study of Delhi and its periurban areas. Unpublished paper presented at Association of American Geographers Centennial Conference, Philadelphia (March 2004).

Rondinelli, D. and Ruddle, K. (1978), *Urbanization and Rural Development: A Spatial Policy for Equitable Growth*. Praeger, New York.

Rondinelli, Dennis A., (1983), *Secondary Cities in Developing Countries: Policies for Diffusing Urbanisation*, Sage Publications, Beverly Hills.

Rondinelli, Dennis A., (1984), *Applied Methods of Regional Analysis: The Spatial Dimensions of Development Policy*, Westview Press, Boulder, Colorado.

Rondinelli, Dennis and Hugh Evans, (1983), "Integrated Regional Development Planning: Linking Urban Centres and Rural Areas in Bolivia", in *World Development*, Vol. 11, No 1.

Rondinelli, Dennis, (1991), "Asian Urban Development Policies in the 1990s: From Growth Control to Urban Diffusion", in *World Development*, Vol. 19, No 7.

Rostow, W.W. (1960), *The Stages of Economic Growth: A Non-Communist Manifesto*, Cambridge University Press, Cambridge.

Saini, N.S. (1989), *Rural Development at Metropolitan Fringe: resource conservation Approach.* Anmol Publications, New Delhi.

Sara C. Nelson; "Farming on the Fringes: Changes in Agriculture, Land Use and Livelihoods in Peri-Urban Dar es Salaam, Tanzania"; Macalester College, (2007), Honors Projects. Paper 10; *http://digitalcommons.macalester.edu/geography_honors/10*

Scarlett Epstein, T.; A.P. Suryanarayna and T. Thimmegowda (1998), *Village Voices, Forty Years of Rural Transformation in South India.* New Delhi: Sage Publications.

Schenk, H. (1997), The rurban fringe: A central area between region and city: The case of Bangalore, India. In: M. Chatterji and Y. Kaizhang, *Regional Science in Developing Countries*, New York: MacMillan, pp. 212-223.

Schenk, Hans and Dewit, Michael (2001), The Fringe Habitat of Bangalore. In: Schenk, Hans ed. *Living in India's Slums : A Case Study of Bangalore.* New Delhi, Manohar Publication House, pp. 113-135.

Schenk, Hans (2004), Towards Apartheid? Policies of segregation and deprivation in Delhi. In: Gupta, K.R. (ed.) *Urban Development Debate in the New Millennium.* New Delhi, Atlantic, pp. 96-115.

Schenk-Sandbergen, L. (1995), *Women and Seasonal Labour Migration*, IDPAD 16, New Delhi: Sage Publications.

Schmink, M. (1984), Household economic strategies: review and research agenda. In: *Latin American Research Review*, Vol. 19, No. 3, pp. 87-101.

Schteingart, Martha (ed.), (1989) *Changement Social et Mutations Urbaines en Amérique Latine*, Bordeaux, CNRS - ORSTOM.

Schteingart, Martha, (1989), "The environmental problems associated with urban development in Mexico City" in *Environment and Urbanization*, Vol. 1, No.1, April, England.

Scoones, (1998), 'Sustainable Rural Livelihoods: A Framework for analysis', *IDS Working Paper,* No. 72. IDS Brighton.

Seppala, P. (1996), The politics of economic diversification: reconceptualizing the rural informal sector in Southeast Tanzania. *Development and Change,* (27): 557-578.

Shafi, M (1969), "Land use planning, land classification and land capability; methods and techniques", *The Geographer,* Vol. XVI, Aligarh.

Shaw, A. (2005) Peri-urban interface of Indian cities. Growth, governance and local initiatives. *Economic and Political Weekly,* Vol. 40, No. 2, pp. 129-136.

Shindhe, K.C. (2010), The National Highway bypass around Hubli-Dharwad and its impact on periurban livelihoods. In D.McGregor, D. Simon and D. Thompson, (eds.) The periurban interface: approaches to sustainable natural and human resource use. *Earthscan*, VA, USA, pp. 181-195.

Shiva, Vandana (1996), *A Policy of Ecocide of Indigenous Cattle Breeds and a Policy of Genocide for India's Small Farmers*, January,

Simelane, S.H. (1995), Labour migration and rural transformation in post-colonial Swaziland. *Journal of Contemporary African Studies* 13(2): 207-226.

Simon, D (2008), Urban Environments: Issues on the Peri-Urban Fringe. Ann. Rev. Environ. Resour. 33: 167-185. URL: *http://arjournals.annualreviews.org/doi/pdf/*

Simon D.; McGregor D.; Nsiah-Gyabaah K. (2004), The changing urban-rural interface of African cities: definitional issues and an application to Kumasi, Ghana in *Environment and Urbanisation*, Vol.16, No. 2 Oct. 2004. pp. 235-247.

Singh, Krishna B. (2002), 'Land Use Systems and Changes in India' in *Human Dimensions of Sustainable Development* edited by R. B. Singh, Rawat Publications, Jaipur and New Delhi.

Singh, R.B. and P.C.J. Druijven (1994), Environmental degradation and its socio-economic implications in the rural-urban fringe of Delhi. Project outline IDPAD. 4.1.1, Delhi/Groningen.

Solanki, S.S. (1987), Environmental Hazards – A Case of Delhi Villages. In: A.L. Lamba and S.S. Solanki, *Impact of Urbanization and Industrialisation on Rural Society*, New Delhi, Wiley Eastern, pp. 154-158.

Sorensen, A. (1999), Land readjustment, urban planning and urban sprawl in the Tokyo metropolitan area, *Urban Studies,* 36 (13) (1999), pp. 2333–2360.

Spalding, H.; J.R. Wood (1998), Greed, need or creed? Farmland ethics in the rural-urban fringe. *Land Use Policy*, Vol. 15, No. 2, pp. 105-118.

Squires, *2002* In: G.D. Squires, Editor, *Urban Sprawl: Causes,*

Consequences, and Policy Responses, The Urban Institute Press, Washington, DC (2002).

Srinivas, M.N. (1996), *Social Change in Modern India*. Bombay: Allied Publications.

Stamp, L.D., (1950), *The Land of Britain: Its Use and Misuse*. Longman Green and Geographical Publications Ltd., London.

Steinberg, J. (1993), Le Périurbain: définition, délimitation, et spécificités. *Mītropolisation et périurbanisation*. Cahiers du CREPIF, no. 42, pp. 9-18.

Stephenson, D. (2001), Problems of Developing Countries. In: Maksimovic, C. and Guibert, A.T. (eds.) *Frontiers in Urban Water Management –Deadlock or Hope*. London, IWA.

Stohr, W.B. and Taylor. D.R.F. (eds.) (1981), Development from Above or Below? *The Dialectics of Regional Planning in Developing Countries*, Chichester: John Wiley and Sons.

Styers Diane Marie; Chappelka, A.H.; Marzen, L.J.; Somers G.L., (2010), "Scale matters: Indicators of ecological health along the urban–rural interface near Columbus, Georgia", Ecological Indicators, journal homepage: www.elsevier.com/locate/ecolind 10, 224–233.

Subhas, M. S. (1997), *Baseline Study and Introductory Workshop for Hubli–Dharwad City-region*, Karnataka, India, Draft Final Technical Report, Vols. 1 & 2, School of Public Policy, University of Birmingham

Sundaram, K.V. and V.L.S. Prakasa Rao (1984), Metropolitan expansion in India: Spatial dynamics and rural transformation. In: T.P. Bayliss-Smith, and S. Wanmali (1984), *Understanding Green Revolutions, Agrarian Change and Development Planning in South Asia*. Cambridge: Cambridge University Press, pp. 80-100.

Swindell, K. (1988), Agrarian change and periurban fringes in tropical Africa. In: D. Rimmer, (ed.), *Rural Transformation in Tropical Africa*. Ohio University Press, pp. 98-115.

Tacoli, Cecilia, (1998), "Rural-urban Interactions: a Guide to the Literature", in *Environment and Urbanization*, Vol. 10, No 1.

Tacoli, Cecilia, (1998), "Rural-urban Linkages and Sustainable Rural Livelihoods", in Carney, Diana (ed.) *Sustainable Rural Livelihoods*, DFID, London.

Teeffelen, P., L. L. Van Grunsven and O. Verkoren, (eds). (1991), *Possibilities and Constraints of GIS Applications in Developing Countries*. Netherlands Geographical Studies 152, Utrecht.

Thakur, B. (1991), *Land Utilization and Urbanization : The Rural-Urban Fringe*, New Delhi: Deep & Deep. Publishing House.

Thomas, D., (1974), "The Urban Fringe: Approaches and Attitudes", in Johnson (ed.), *Suburban Growth, Geographical Process at the Edge of the Western City*, Aberdeen University Press, Aberdeen.

Thornton, A. (2008), Beyond the Metropolis: Small Town Case Studies of Urban and Peri-urban Agriculture in South Africa. *Urban Forum* 19(3). URL: *http://www.springerlink.com/content/y2050p8753125276/*

Tiffen, M., M. Mortimore and F. Gichuki (1994), More people, less erosion: environmental recovery in Kenya, Chichester: Wiley.

Tim Hall and Phil Hubbard (1996), "The entrepreneurial city: new urban politics, new urban geographies?" *Progress in Human Geography* Vol. 20, No. 2, pp. 153-174.

Tyagi, V.K. (1982), *Urban Growth and Urban Villages (A Case study of Delhi)*. New Delhi: Kalyani Publishing House.

UN Habitat's Best Practices Database: *http://www.bestpractices.org*

UN. (2001). *World Population Prospects*: *The 2000 Revision*. Population Division, Department of Economic and Social Affairs, United Nations, New York.

UNDP (1994), *Human Development Report*, Oxford, Oxford University Press for UNDP.

UNDP (1996), *Urban Agriculture: Food, Jobs and Sustainable Cities*, United Nations Development Programe, Publication Series for Habitat II, Volume One, New York.

UNDP/UNCHS (Habitat) (1995), Rural-urban linkages: policy guidelines for rural development. Paper prepared for the Twenty-Third Meeting of the ACC Sub-Committee on Rural Development, UNESCO Headquarters, 31 May-2 June 1995.

UNFPA (1996), *The State of World Population 1996: Changing Places: Population, Development and the Urban Future*, Marshall, Alex (ed.), United Nations Population Fund, New York.

UNITED NATIONS (1995), The challenge of urbanization: the world's largest cities. New York: Department for Economic and Social Information and Policy Analysis, Population Division.

United Nations Centre for Human Settlements (UNCHS) (1996), *An Urbanizing World: Global report on Human Settlements,* 1996. Oxford University Press, Oxford.

Universities of Birmingham, Nottingham and Wales at Bangor, (1998) *Baseline Study and IntroductoryWorkshop for Hubli-Dharwad City-Region, Karnataka, India,* Final Technical Report, DFID Project R6825,Volume 1, pp. 128.

Unwin, Tim, (1989), "Urban-rural Interaction in Developing Countries: A Theoretical Perspective", in Potter and Unwin (eds.) *The Geography of Urban-Rural Interaction in Developing Countries: Essays for Alan B. Mountjoy*, Routledge, London.

US Census Bureau, (2000). *World Population Growth Rate*, 1950 – 2050. US Census Bureau International Database.

Vennetier, P. (1989), 'Evolution des Espaces Péri-urbains a Brazzaville (Congo) et Cotonou (Bénin)', in P. Vennetier (ed.), La Peri-urbanisation dans les Pays Tropicaux, Bordeaux: Universitaire de Bordeaux, Centre d'Etudes de Geographie Tropicale.

Verburg, P.H.; D.E. Groot, W.T. and Veldkamp, A., (2003), "Methodology for multi-scale land-use change modelling: Concepts and challenges." In: Dolman A.J., Verhagen, A. and Rovers 78 C.A. (editors), Global environmental change and land use. Kluwer Academic Pub, Dordrecht, the Netherlands.

Visaria, P. (1997), Urbanization in India: An Overview, in Jones, G. and Visaria, P. (eds.) *Urbanization in Large Developing Countries*, Clarendon Press, Oxford, pp. 266-288.

Visaria, P. and R. Basant (1994), (eds.), *Non-agricultural employment in India.* New Delhi: Sage Publications.

Vries, A.C. De, J.V. Bentinck and J. Skornsek (1999), Land Use Mapping of Delhi's Rural-Urban Fringe Using Remote Sensing. In: G.P. Chapman, A.K. Dutt and R.W. Bradnock, *Urban Growth and Development in Asia*, Volume II: Living in the Cities. London: Ashgate, pp. 466-473.

Wadhwa, K. (1983), Urban fringe land markets, an economic analysis. New Delhi: Concept Publishing Company, Pvt. Ltd.

Weherwein, E.G. (1942), The rural urban fringe. *Economic Geography*, Vol. 18, pp. 217-228.

Wildavsky, A. (1995), *But is it true? A Citizen's Guide to Environmental Health and Safety Issues.* Cambridge: Harvard University Press.

Wissink, G. A., (1962), American Cities in Perspective: With Special Reference to the Development of their Fringe Areas, Assen, USA.

Wolf, E., (1972), "Ownership and Political Ecology," *Anthropological Quarterly*, Vol. 45(3), pp. 201-205.

World Bank (2000), *Rural-urban linkages and interactions: Synthesis of issues, conclusions and priority opportunities emerging from workshop*, World Bank. NY.

World Health Organisation (1993), *The Urban Health Cirsis. Strategies for Health For all in the case of Rapid Urbanisation.* Geneva.

Yadav, C.S. (1987), *Rural-Urban Fringe*. New Delhi: Concept Publishing House.

Yadav, K.N.S. *(1989), Rural-Urban Migration in India. Determinants, Patterns and Consequences*. Delhi: Independent Publishing Company.

Yeh, A.G.O. and X. LI, (1996), Urban Growth Management in the Pearl River Delta: An Integrated Remote Sensing and GIS Approach. *ITC Journal,* 1, pp. 77-86.

Yeung, Y. (ed.) (1993), Pacific Asia in the 21st Century, Geographical and Developmental Perspectives. Chinese University Press, Hong Kong.

Zoomers, A. E. B. and Kleinpenning, J. (1996), Livelihood and Urban-Rural Relations in Central Paraguay. Tijdschrift voor Economische en Sociale Geografie 87(2): 161-74.

Index